FOR
LAUGHING
OUT LOUD

ED MCMAHON

with David Fisher

FOR LAUGHING OUT LOUD

My Life and Good Times

with an introduction by Johnny Carson

WARNER BOOKS

A Time Warner Company

Warner Books, Inc., 1271 Avenue of the Americas, New York, NY 10020
Visit our Web site at http://warnerbooks.com

A Time Warner Company

Printed in the United States of America
First Printing: October 1998
10 9 8 7 6 5 4 3 2 1

Library of Congress Cataloging-in-Publication Data

McMahon, Ed.
    For laughing out loud : my life and good times / Ed McMahon with
David Fisher and with an introduction by Johnny Carson.
        p.   cm.
    Includes index.
    ISBN 0-446-52370-4
    1. McMahon, Ed.   2. Television personalities—United States—
Biography.   I. Fisher, David.   II. Title.
PN 1992.4.M45A3   1998
791'.092—dc21   98-7766
[b]   CIP

Book design and composition by L&G McRee

To Pam,
For all you've done for me
I love you

Acknowledgments

Well, let's start at the beginning with thanks to Mom and Dad. Eleanor taught me courtesy and kindness to others and Edward Sr. showed me the way—the value of hard work and how to strive to succeed.

Then there's the progeny that stayed the course with me. "The kids." Claudia, my late son Michael, Linda, Jeffrey, Lex and Katherine Mary, Peter—Linda's husband, Martha—Jeff's wife, and of course the grandkids, Alex, Sarah, Matt, and the newest, Maggie McMahon. And to those that are on their way . . . welcome aboard!

And the friends—Charlie Cullen, my best friend of all, who through the highs and lows was always there. The Skipjacks, the only club I ever really wanted to belong to. And my cousin Arthur Brennen, who supplied some valuable pictures that I had lost in a fire.

And in random order: Gary Mann, Bill Rosenthal, Bob Newhart, Jeff Sotzing, Susan DuBow, Barbara Berkowitz, Neil Papiano, Peter Xiques, Kenny Stein, Shelly Schultz, Jack Whittaker, Bob and Marti Gillin, Jack Drury, Bob Muir, Bob Reilly, Caroline and Tom Galloway, Jayne Meadows and Steve Allen, Bob Allen, Al Masini, Norm Crosby,

ACKNOWLEDGMENTS

Ken Browning, Bee Barksdale, Phyllis Diller, Rudy Duenzel, Arnie Greenberg, Leo Keimenson, Robert Calandria, John Lahey, Don Davidson, Denise Kovac, Bob Lachky, Jay Leno, Doc Severinsen, Tommy Newsom, Shelly Cohen, Margaret Norton, Roseanne Kahn, Terry Laughlin, Irving Harris, Bob Duffner, Mark Begley, Josie and Ken Castleberry, George Engel, Fred Hayman, Bob Lutz, Dennis Washington, Terry Giroux, Arnie Morgen, Patrick Terrail, Bob Ross, Michael Roarty, Roger Bulkley, Red Buttons, Jimmy Orthwein, Dick Whitehead, Jerry Clinton, Fred Shotwell, Art Williams, Gussie Busch, Milton Berle, Father Herbert Ward, Charlie Barrett, Michael McCreary, Harry Gold, T. J. Escott, Harry Blake, Jon Jon Parks, Carroll and Manny Draluck, Toots Shore, Deborah Hurn, Dr. Soram Khalsa, Dr. Phil Levine, and Dr. Larry Heifetz, who handled our son Michael so beautifully, Dick Howard, Chris Boyhan, Desirée Bermani, Susan Caughman, Rob McMahon, Chris Barba, Frank Weimann, Jimmy Franco, Dick Martin, John Facienda, Harry K. Smith, Phil Sheriden, Gil Weiss, Pastor and Betty Price, Jay David, Father Gilbert T. Hartke, Jimmy Breslin, Allan Browne, Alan Levy, and Rick Wolff, of Warner Books, who agreed at our very first meeting to do this book and who was a very valuable editor.

And most especially—Fred de Cordova, Perry Leff, Paul Tobin, Mort Rosen, Don Rickles, Bob Delaney (from the old Michael's Pub days), and some wonderful assistants: Suzette McKiernan, Pinky Coleman, Corrine Madden, and Madeline Kelly. A lady who was invaluable in the making of this book, Toni (Cefalone) Holliday, who started as a nanny with Katherine Mary and became one of the greatest executive assistants any guy would be lucky to have, and Joan Curtis, who put the words to paper. The man who made "You are correct, sir" famous—Phil Hartman, and his wife, Brynn. Lester Blank, Tony Amendola, Lillian and Harry Crane, and of course, Dick Clark—and Johnny! I tell an old

ACKNOWLEDGMENTS

joke when I'm emceeing about always liking to be close to success, like selling Alpo and Budweiser and having them become the largest sellers in the world. And then taking that skinny kid from Nebraska . . . the laughter starts when I say "skinny kid." The folks always get the joke! But what really happened is that he took "Big Ed" with him to the top, enough to warrant writing this book. Thank you, J. C.!

And thirty years working on my favorite charity, the Muscular Dystrophy Association, with the one and only Jerry Lewis. And Sammy Davis Jr., who taught me that the audience comes first, always!

And then there is David Fisher. The man who wrote the line in his proposal that convinced me that he should be the one to write this book with me. The line "I went off to the Korean War and left thirteen television shows that I was doing in Philadelphia and people were shooting at me and they never saw any of my shows." (That was a clincher.)

And Dan Kelly, along with the master, Frank Sinatra, who taught me generosity and class!

And to anyone else I've failed to mention, my apologies. If you're not in the book, you're in my heart!

Ed McMahon
June 1998

Introduction

I like Ed McMahon—a lot. It would be impossible for me to work so closely with someone for over thirty years and not like him. During our time on *The Tonight Show* we developed, I believe, a unique relationship—similar to that which married couples often experience—an unspoken method of communication. If we engaged in a mock argument about the relative merits of the swit (an exceptional bird) and the shark, we had no ordained blueprint, but we both sensed the possibilities in the subject that could be mined for laughs—so by a look, a pause, body language, or tone of voice we could tell each other the direction to go. When it was really working well, it was euphoria. When it wasn't, there was always the next night.

Ed is a remarkable fellow, as you'll discover from reading this book. He would have been successful in whatever he had chosen to do. I'm glad he chose to spend part of his career with me.

JOHNNY CARSON

P.S. Ed—I still believe the swit has tougher survival instincts than the shark. Then again, I could be wrong.

1

I will never forget the very first time I met a young man named Johnny Carson. The producer of my good friend Dick Clark's famed *American Bandstand* had heard Johnny was looking for an announcer for his new afternoon quiz show, *Who Do You Trust?*, and had recommended me. Johnny's office was in the Little Theatre, on West Forty-fourth Street, directly across from the Shubert Theatre. As I entered his office, Johnny was standing at a large window, watching as four huge cranes raised the Shubert's new marquee. I watched this from the other window as he interviewed me. "It's nice to meet you, Ed," he said.

I laughed.

"Thanks for coming up from Philadelphia," he said.

I laughed just a little louder.

"Tell me a little about what you're doing down there," he said, with that little boy twinkle in his blue eyes.

I laughed even louder, and longer.

"So, Ed," he asked in that friendly voice, "have you spent much time in New York?"

I laughed so loud and so hard tears formed in my eyes.

"Okay," he said, nodding, "you got the job."

Well, maybe that's not exactly the way it happened. But just in case Johnny Carson decides to come out of retirement, I'm not taking any chances.

• • •

Recently my beautiful young daughter, Katherine Mary, came to me with her electronic pet, her Tamagotchi. "It's broken, Daddy," she said, handing it to me. "Can you fix it for me, please?"

I didn't have the slightest idea how to fix it. "I'm sorry, darling," I said. "That's not what I do. I do 'Good evening, ladies and gentlemen, there they are, weren't they wonderful, let's hear it for them.' I do, 'How's your Aunt Ida, did Uncle Joe get out of jail yet?' I'm the guy who says, 'Heeeeere's Johnny' and 'Hi-yoooo!' and 'You are correct, sir,' and 'How cold was it?' and '*Everything* you ever wanted to know about mosquitoes is in that thin little book?' and 'I hold in my hand the final envelope, which has been hermetically sealed . . . ,' and 'Once again let us welcome the seer from the East . . .' I'm the guy who says, 'You may have already won ten million dollars,' and 'Budweiser, the only beer that's beechwood-aged,' and 'You cannot be turned down . . . ,' and 'I've lost twenty-nine pounds by following the Jenny Craig diet . . .'"

Katherine Mary sighed deeply, then sat down.

"See, sweetheart, I'm the guy who says, 'Our spokesmodel champion has owned the stage for two weeks, but her challenger intends to . . . ,' and 'Jerry, our new total is forty-one million, seven hundred thousand dollars,' and 'Dick, this next practical joke is based on the fact that celebrities usually get . . . ,' and 'The next giant balloon coming down Broadway on this magnificent Thanksgiving Day is our old friend . . .'"

Katherine Mary yawned.

"I'm the former marine combat pilot who served as the grand marshal of the Indianapolis 500 and the king of Bacchus at Mardi Gras, and played the secret Santa Claus at the White House. I'm the former host of *Snap Judgment* who used the great W. C. Fields line '"Twas a woman that drove me to drink, and I never had the decency to write and thank her' in my nightclub act. I'm the guy who used to work in bingo parlors announcing, 'Under the B, it's fifteen,' and the guy who promised on an infomercial, 'With this incredible cooking device you can make french fries, fried shrimp, crispy onion rings without any fat or grease in your oven or microwave.' I'm the guy who works for wonderful charities like St. Jude's Ranch for Children in Boulder City, Nevada, the Muscular Dystrophy Association, and the United Negro College Fund. And I'm the guy who's made movies, recorded albums, and written books. The guy who worked with Johnny Carson for thirty-four years and Jerry Lewis for thirty years and Doc Severinsen and Frank Sinatra and John Wayne and Dick Clark and Don Rickles and Bob Newhart and Sammy Davis and Rosie O'Donnell and Coolio and Sinbad and the magnificent Tom Arnold. I'm the guy who pitched the incredible Morris metric slicer on the boardwalk in Atlantic City by telling people, 'With the blade in the lower position, just look how thin you can slice a tomato. You could read a newspaper through that tomato slice. I know a lady in Bayonne, New Jersey, who had one tomato last her all summer long . . .'"

Katherine Mary stood up. "Oh, that's okay, Daddy," she said. "I'll ask Mommy."

My given name is Edward Leo Peter McMahon. And I am one of the very fortunate people who grew up to do exactly what I spent my whole childhood dreaming of doing, even if no one is quite sure exactly what it is that I do. One night, for example, I was having dinner with the

3

brilliant producer of *The Tonight Show,* Freddy de Cordova, at Chasen's Restaurant. We would do that periodically. We each had one of Pepe's flaming martinis, we discussed the show, what had happened recently, what was going to happen, then we each had a second flaming martini, and finally Freddy looked at me and said warmly, "Ed, I want to tell you something. I've been producing this show for twenty years and I still don't know exactly what it is that you do, but whatever it is, you're the very best at it."

My lovely daughter Linda often complained that the most difficult question to answer on an application was "Father's Occupation?" I think that what I do might best be described as a host or master of ceremonies, or maybe a second banana or a sidekick or a straight man. Certainly I'm a well-known television personality, an entertainer, a spokesperson, a pitchman, and a salesman. I'm definitely a broadcaster, but I'm also an actor and a comedian. I'm a performer.

That's what I do. But I'm still trying to figure out what my good friend the great Dick Clark does.

Many people have told me that the thing I do best is make it look as if I'm not doing anything. My talent is making it seem that I have no talent. That just about anybody could get up there on the stage and do what I do. But believe me, that's not an easy thing to do. It took me years of hard work to be able to convince an audience that I wasn't working. So when it looked as if I wasn't doing anything, I was actually doing it very well.

Even more difficult than making it look as if I was doing nothing was knowing when to say nothing. The most difficult thing for me to learn when I began working with Johnny Carson, for example, was when to say nothing. There were many nights when I was sitting next to Mr. Carson and I wanted to say a line but didn't. Believe me, at times saying nothing was tough. But I got very good at nothing.

I take after my father. Edward Leo Peter McMahon. It was never very easy for me to figure out what it was he did either. It's probably simplest, and kindest, to describe him as . . . a promoter. He was an entrepreneur, a traveling salesman; he raised funds for charities and hospitals and clubs by selling punchboards and running bingo games; he operated carnival games and owned a boardwalk bingo parlor. For a brief time when he was starting out he even ran away and joined a minstrel show as the interlocutor, the man who stood between the end men—Mr. Tambo, who played the tambourine, and Mr. Bones, who rattled the bones—hosted the show, and told the jokes like, "Did you hear what Mr. Mason said to Mr. Dixon? We've got to draw the line somewhere!" It was a very early version of a talk show.

Sometimes my father did extremely well, and we were rich. I mean very rich. How rich were we?

Thank you for asking, but I'll do the straight lines.

I'll tell you how rich we were. We were so rich that for a brief time we lived in a large suite in the luxurious Top of the Mark Hotel in San Francisco. I would wake up in the morning and call down to room service for breakfast. I thought every kid in America lived that way. Later we briefly lived in London Terrace in New York City, an apartment complex so fashionable that the doormen were formally dressed as London bobbies. We were so rich that once, during the depression, my mother bought me a thirty-two-dollar leather cap—that hat cost more than most people paid monthly for rent. We were so rich that my father drove a Hupmobile, a beautiful sedan with a picnic compartment built into the backseat. And for a time in the 1930s he and a business partner even leased a six-passenger airplane, complete with two pilots and a stewardess. Can you imagine how many punchboards he had to sell to lease an airplane?

But more often he did not do very well. I vaguely remember there being some problem with oil leases in California, and we lived in a cold-water flat in Bayonne, New Jersey, or a dingy walk-up on East Fifty-fifth Street in New York. But even when we were struggling he always acted as if he were the most successful man in the whole world. As the great radio newsman Gabriel Heatter used to say, "He could look at a brick and see a house."

My father traveled on business and the advice of counsel. He never cheated people or did anything illegal, but he had a way of making things seem better than they actually were. He was a great salesman. In his carnival booths, for example, he would always put the least expensive prize or the lamp with a scratch on it in the most prominent position on the top shelf. It looked as though it was supposed to be overlooked, which of course immediately made it the most desirable. When a winner asked for it he would try to talk them out of it. When they demanded it he would make a big show of climbing to the top and hauling it down—thus ensuring that the customer would never complain about the scratch on the base or the fact that it was falling apart.

My father used to tell a story about a friend, a close friend, who would buy a broken-down thoroughbred race-horse for a few bucks and sell fifty-cent chances on him at county fairs. A lot of people would take a chance sight unseen on winning a throughbred racehorse. He could often sell two hundred dollars' worth of tickets on a ten-dollar horse. If the winner was less than satisfied when he finally saw his prize "racehorse," and admittedly that was often the case, this friend would simply give him back his fifty cents.

The three things I inherited from my father were his size—he was a big, broad man as I am—his work ethic, and his ability to tell a story. Oh, Eddie McMahon could tell a story. That was the Irish in him. On occasion my father and several friends would go away for a weekend on a fishing trip. This was about as much a fishing trip as the great El

Moldo was a psychic. He knew nothing about fishing. I never saw him take a fishing rod or reel with him, or a tackle box. Worms had nothing to fear from my father. The guys never came home with a fish. But inevitably something funny would have happened during the weekend—something that they could talk about—and each of them would start to tell his version of the story. But then they would pause and agree, "Let Eddie tell it." Because Eddie McMahon could tell a grand story. He was a charmer, and he was known for his ability to improve upon the truth.

It was my father who told me about my great-great-great-grandfather, Patrick Maurice Mac-Mahon, the president of France. General Patrick Mac-Mahon was an Irishman, but according to my father, Napoleon III loved him and was instrumental in his becoming the president of France in 1873. And according to my father, in his honor his favorite sauce was named Macmahonaise, which was eventually shortened to mayonnaise. People have sent me cookbooks that seem to confirm this derivation of mayonnaise. It's possible we really were related to the Irish president of France. But like many of my father's stories, it doesn't matter if every part is true. It's a story that belongs in the most prominent position on the top shelf.

I always felt this incredible need to prove myself to my father. That's probably what gave me my drive. One night, for example, he was running a Monday night bingo game at a Moose hall. It was a big room; hundreds of people would play for money and prizes. Bingo cards were ten cents each, three for a quarter. I guess I was about twelve years old. I hounded my father to let me put on an apron and sell cards. My mother worked on him too, and finally he agreed. He gave me a stack of cards and two dollars in nickels and dimes so I could make change. I was very excited, but as I turned to start selling, I overheard him tell someone, "There's two dollars we'll never see again." I mean, can you imagine that? Hearing that insult just set me on fire. I had to prove him wrong. So instead of selling three cards for a quarter, I sold each card for a dime. I sold every card that I had. If the cards I had should have been worth ten dollars, I handed the cashier twelve bucks. I remember my father congratulating me, putting his arm around me. That part isn't so clear; the insult, I'll never forget.

My mother taught me ethics and manners. Her name was Eleanor Russell and she was a dark-haired beauty. She was Pennsylvania Dutch, a German-English mix. I called her "Muth," short for "mother." I probably got my love of performing from her. She had been raised in her grand-mother's theatrical boardinghouse. I know my mother acted in a few local productions, but she surrendered whatever dreams she once had to the charms of my father.

My mother insisted that I use proper manners. She was the only person who called me Edward; even today when I hear someone use that name I straighten my shoulders. She would always warn me, "Edward, you must do this or you'll displease me." "You'll displease me" was the biggest threat she would make, and most of the time it was enough. Occasionally she would punish me, but I knew her heart wasn't really in it. I was her only child at a time when big families were quite normal. But she had almost died giving birth to me. I weighed nine pounds ten ounces, and she was told by doctors it would be best not to have any more children.

I was closer to my mother than to my father; I felt very protective of her, and I pretty much knew how to get what-ever it was I wanted from her. As a parent, I think I've always been a lot like her. Once, for example, when Kather-ine Mary was about nine, she came running into my office and said excitedly, "Daddy, I have to ask you . . . ," and then she stopped and frowned. "Oh, I can't start with you," she said with all the wisdom of a nine-year-old, "because if you turn me down, there's nowhere else to go."

My mother and father did not have a happy marriage. They lived on the road, following the carnivals and bingo games and fund-raising jobs. Eventually they separated. At times my father lived with us, and then one day he would be gone again. They never divorced, I don't know why, maybe because they were Catholic and at that time Catholics did not get divorced. But they were always civil with each other. I was born in Detroit, Michigan, in 1923, when my parents stopped there on the way to a fund-raising job for the Shriners or the Rotary Club or the Kiwanis or the Elks Club or the Moose in Peoria, Illinois. My mother stayed in Detroit six weeks, not even long enough for me to get to know the kid in the next crib very well. We must have liked each other, though, because he cried when I left.

I refer to Detroit as my hometown, pretty much by default. We never stayed anywhere for more than a few months. As my idol, W. C. Fields, would have said, "My dear, we changed towns more often than a nervous pick-pocket." By the time I was five years old I'd probably been through forty states. We lived in New York, San Francisco, Philadelphia, Muskogee, Peoria, Bayonne, East Hartford— wherever there was money to be made. It was a terrible way to grow up. I had a lousy childhood. I attended several schools before I started high school—and then I went to three different high schools. When we lived at London Ter- race I walked down the block to P.S. 23. When we couldn't afford that apartment anymore and were forced to move across the Hudson River to Bayonne, New Jersey, I wanted so desperately to continue at P.S. 23 that I commuted by Greyhound bus every day.

I had no friends. None. We never stayed in one place long enough for me to get to know anyone. Most of the time we didn't stay long enough for the kids to even know my name, so they referred to me by the town I'd come from. I wasn't Ed McMahon, I was, "Hey, Lowell," or "Peoria." I was also painfully shy, and just to make things a little worse, I had bad acne. I'll tell you how bad it was for me: little Donnie Rickles probably had more friends than I did.

I think it's pretty easy to figure out that the reason I wanted to be an entertainer gets right down to my desire to be accepted, to be needed and loved. That need was instilled in me very early in life. And when you combine that need with the exhilarating feeling you get when someone laughs at something you say, you're hooked. That feeling of pleasing people is addicting. The first time you do it is amazing, so you try to figure out how to do it a second time. And if somehow you can figure out how to do it a tenth time, well, then you're in show business.

The happiest moments of my childhood were the summers I spent with my grandparents at their home in Lowell, Massachusetts. Joseph F. and Katherine Fitzgerald McMahon had emigrated to Lowell from Ireland during the potato famine. My grandfather became a master plumber and founded the J. F. McMahon Plumbing Company. He could walk into a building and determine at a glance exactly how many BTUs of steam would be needed to provide adequate heat and how much it would cost. All my uncles worked for him. For a few summers I worked with my Uncle Artie as a plumber's helper, the worst job I've ever had. I used to have to crawl underneath the Elks Club in Lowell to unclog the soil pipes, the pipes that drained the bathrooms. That turned out to be a very important job for me, because whatever I did after that, no matter how tough it was, it wasn't as bad as unclogging the soil pipes. Compared to that, listening to the unusual tones of Tiny Tim singing "Tiptoe through the Tulips with Me" was a great pleasure.

My grandmother was my best friend. The proudest day of my life was the day I came home from flight school and pinned my Marine Corps pilot wings on her. I knew that my success was the greatest gift I could give to her. She died three months later. She was buried in a plain black dress bearing a single decoration, my gold wings.

Katie was a member of the Fitzgerald clan of Boston. Her cousin, Rose Fitzgerald, married into the Kennedy family. At that time Joseph Kennedy was one of the richest and most powerful men in Massachusetts. He was a politician and a bootlegger, and of those two professions I think we respected him more as a bootlegger. I grew up knowing that the Kennedy children were my cousins. I don't think the Kennedy brothers knew Ed McMahon was their cousin. Joe Kennedy Jr., the oldest son, was a naval aviator who was killed flying an extremely dangerous mission. I knew he was a pilot and I desperately wanted to be one too. But I don't remember if my passion for flying originated with him. My own kids grew up knowing they were related to the Kennedys. In fact, my beautiful daughter Claudia often told people that the only reason she and John Kennedy Jr. weren't married was because they were cousins.

My grandfather designed and built a six-bedroom house in Lowell, the only place in my entire childhood that I ever considered home. The six upstairs bedrooms opened to a central hall, but there was only one bathroom. My grandfather was a master plumber, but there was only one large bathroom. Downstairs was Katie's kitchen, the most important room in the house. I never needed an alarm clock because at five each morning I would be awakened by the most wonderful aromas of the bread and fruit pies she was baking in the wood-burning stove. I learned work ethics from my father and good manners from my mother. But from Katie I learned how to eat. Breakfast consisted of two pork chops, home fried potatoes with gravy, whatever fried cabbage was left over from the night before, apple pie with a wedge of cheese, and a small loaf of bread baked especially for me. That usually kept us full at least until lunch.

Because Joe and Katie had survived the potato famine, potatoes were served at every meal. We had baked potatoes, mashed potatoes, home fries, cottage fries, potatoes O'Brien. And I always had to finish every last bite on my plate. "Finish your plate," Katie would tell me. "There are people starving in . . ." My grandmother had people starving in countries that hadn't been named yet. Iran was still Persia, but she already had people starving in Iran.

To me, the most impressive room in the entire house was a tiny bathroom right off the kitchen. It wasn't even a full bathroom, it was just a john with a pull chain, but to me it represented real status. I'd never known anyone who had a bathroom in their kitchen. The house also had a dining room that sat twenty people, although it was used only on Thanksgiving and Christmas. I remember the lovely French doors with mullioned windows that led into the parlor were always closed; the parlor was used only for weddings and wakes. But it was in that parlor that I dedicated myself to broadcasting.

I don't remember how old I was the first time my grandfather put his heavy crystal set headphones over my ears and I heard an announcer speaking clearly from station KDKA in Pittsburgh, Pennsylvania. But I know that changed my life. It was absolutely astonishing to me that someone could be speaking hundreds of miles away and his voice would travel through the air right into our house at 452 Chelmsford Street. Sometimes it's pretty hard for me to believe that in my lifetime I've gone from listening to that single voice on a crystal set to appearing live and in full color in homes around the world standing next to a skinny guy from Nebraska who is dressed as an old woman and keeps hitting me in the crotch with a cane. Now that's progress.

My grandfather had the very best, if not the first, crystal radio in Lowell. But rather than putting up a very tall antenna on the roof to catch the signal, he wrapped aerial wire around the house. Fifty years later auto manufacturers began doing the same thing. If you didn't live through the birth of radio it isn't possible to appreciate its impact. Radio changed the way we lived. For the first time we were able to learn what was happening anywhere in the world almost immediately; we were able to hear the actual voices of the president of the United States and the most famous performers, people like Al Jolson and Rudy Vallee, and we were able to be entertained in our own homes.

Cigar box crystal set radios very quickly evolved into beautiful pieces of furniture. They were built into elegantly carved wooden cabinets. The radio became the focal point of the room. At night I would lie on my stomach on the floor and look at the radio and imagine what I was hearing. Sound effects were used to replace pictures. A whole new form of entertainment had to be created to fill the needs of radio. *Amos 'n' Andy,* with white actors playing black characters, became the very first situation comedy. It was so popular that when it was being broadcast live, entertainments like vaudeville and moving pictures would stop and a radio would be wheeled onstage so the audience could listen to the show. Otherwise no one would leave their homes when these shows were on the air. That's how powerful radio was.

Comedians like Jack Benny began using the people who worked on their shows as comic foils: Benny's cast of characters included his bandleader, Phil Harris, who was supposedly a big drinker and party guy; Dennis Day, the boy singer who was always impeccably dressed; his large-sized announcer, Don Wilson, who laughed too loud at the boss's jokes and ate too much; and Rochester, Benny's chauffeur and valet, who was constantly insulting him. Apparently while I was lying on the floor of the house with my chin propped in my hands in Lowell, Massachusetts, listening to *The Jack Benny Show,* Johnny Carson was lying on the floor of his house with his chin propped in his hands in Lincoln, Nebraska, doing exactly the same thing, because years later he created his own broadcasting family. I was the character who drank too much and ate too much and laughed loudly at the boss's jokes; when Skitch Henderson led the orchestra he was our well-dressed dandy; Doc Severinsen wore the wallpaper; and bland Tommy Newsom was the man who did so much for the color brown. Johnny Carson learned from Benny that it didn't matter who got the laughs on his show. One night Rochester might have had the best lines, but Benny knew that in the office the next morning people would be talking about *The Jack Benny Show*. And one night on *The Tonight Show* Doc might have gotten the biggest laugh or Tommy Newsom might have gotten a big . . . well, maybe not Tommy. But the next morning everybody would be saying, "Wasn't Carson funny last night?"

I loved radio, I just loved it. The first person in my life I ever asked for an autograph was Joe Penner, a radio comedian who became famous for asking, "Wanna buy a duck?" Of course, that phrase doesn't have the same beautiful grace and rhythm as "You may have already won ten million dollars," but it was the first national catchphrase. Everybody knew it and said it.

But the biggest stars of early radio were the bandleaders. Frank Sinatra was the boy singer with Harry James, but Harry James was the star. Peggy Lee was the girl singer with Benny Goodman. Doris Day was the girl singer with Les Brown and his Band of Renown. Tommy Dorsey, Fred Waring, Guy Lombardo—the leaders of the great big bands were the stars. Glenn Miller was on three nights a week for fifteen minutes. Whatever I was doing I would stop and run home to hear his show. To me, listening to Glenn Miller on the Zenith was like being with a beautiful girl in the backseat of a car. Not that I had ever been with a girl in the backseat of a car, I just had a great imagination.

For a time I tried to be a musician, just like these men I admired so much. The only thing that held me back was a complete lack of musical talent. I played the cornet. A cornet is a trumpet that never grew up. The truth is that I spent more time cleaning my instrument than playing it.

Now there's a straight line for you.

My father was in the American Legion, so I signed up to be in the Sons of the American Legion Drum and Bugle Corps. I marched in one parade, but I was just so awful that they drummed me out of the Drum and Bugle Corps. I was summarily dismissed. Marched out to the parade grounds at dawn and stripped of my epaulets! Not a pretty sight.

I still wanted to lead a band, though, so I tried to become the drum major for the Lowell High School marching band. The drum major is the person who strides proudly at the head of the band, kicking his legs high into the air, thrusting his baton up and down to set the rhythm for the entire band. I practiced by myself in my grandmother's backyard, marching back and forth with no one behind me, singing loudly. I wasn't very good at it, though. Even when I was marching all by myself I was out of step. I never led the band.

The people I most identified with on radio were the announcers. The only thing they had to do was speak clearly. And I could do that. The announcers introduced the songs, did the commercials, and bantered with the host. Men like Don Wilson, Harry von Zell, Bill Goodwin, and Norman Brokenshire were almost as well known as the orchestra leaders and the performers. "And now, ladies and gentlemen," they'd say smoothly, "from high atop the Taft Hotel in the heart of beautiful Manhattan, we are pleased to bring you the romantic renditions of Enoch Light and his Light Brigade. . . . And as we dance to the melodies that have haunted us so . . ."

When I was about ten years old I decided to be an announcer. While other kids played baseball or football or cowboys and Indians, I played Broadcaster. I practiced doing commercials. I guess even then I knew where the big money was in show business. I would go into Katie's parlor with my dog, Prince Valiant, close the French doors so no one could hear me, and practice. I'd create my own shows. I'd hold a flashlight under my chin as if it were a microphone, cue up records on my grandfather's classic RCA Victor phonograph, and announce, "The Ed McMahon Show." I even had my own theme music, Benny Goodman's "Let's Dance." I'd pretend I was broadcasting from one of the grand ballrooms high atop one of the great cities. That sounded a lot more impressive than "I'm here in the parlor of my grandma's house in Lowell, Massachusetts, with my dog . . ."

I was miserable in school, I had no friends—but in my grandmother's parlor I was a star. Being in radio was my dream, my fantasy. Radio was my escape. "Good evening, ladies and gentlemen," I'd say in the deepest tones I could manage with my ten-year-old voice. "This is Ed McMahon. And here's a little number that Bing Crosby does with that great voice of his. And it goes something like this . . ."

Actually, it went *exactly* like that. I mean, it was a record, it wasn't going to suddenly change. But "it goes something like this" was a cliché that disc jockeys used. And saying it made me feel very professional. Then I'd cue up one of my grandmother's 78 rpm records—cueing up without scratching the record was a skill—and play the song. After two songs I'd pause for "a commercial message," which was an ad I would read directly out of *Time* magazine. "Look at this," I'd tell my imaginary listeners and Prince Valiant. "Can this guy make you healthy? We'll find out in a minute, right after this beautiful number from Mr. Benny Goodman." Several years later, when I heard my recorded voice, I finally appreciated how valiant that dog really was.

I tried to pattern myself after my idol, Paul Douglas, who later would become a movie star and somehow wind up at the end of every picture with Eve Arden, but at the time he was Fred Waring's announcer and second banana. On the show they had a rivalry; they were always arguing about football games or movies and Paul Douglas never backed down to his boss. What I liked so much about Paul Douglas was his casual attitude. Most announcers were more like Graham McNamee or Milton Cross, who very . . . Carefully. Pronounced. Every. Single. Word. With. Perfect. Grammar. McNamee would read a Texaco commercial as if he were announcing the election of a pope. Not Paul Douglas. He was a casual kind of guy, the kind of guy you'd want to pal around with at the place on the corner. When he told America, "Yah gonna like the taste of Chesterfield," people believed him.

Many years later I was costarring in the movie *The Incident* with Jan Sterling, who had been married to Paul Douglas. "You remind me of my husband," she said. "You could play every one of his roles." Well, that made me feel pretty good about myself, at least until she added, "Yes, Paul always used to say, 'One reason I'm successful is that when a woman looks at me, if she's being really honest with herself, I look like the guy she knows she's going to end up with.'"

I desperately wanted to be in broadcasting. If I couldn't be a performer, a bandleader, or an actor, I was going to be a broadcaster. I didn't even know what that word, "broadcaster," meant exactly, but I knew it meant being in radio so I wanted to be a broadcaster. And I'll tell you something, if I hadn't made it as an announcer, I would have been a producer or director or sold commercial time or been an executive. Somehow I would have been in the radio industry.

I certainly was not the only person perfecting my future craft. In Nebraska, nine-year-old Johnny Carson had sent away for a magic kit that was guaranteed to make him both a magician and the life of the party. He'd spend hours every day standing in front of a mirror perfecting card tricks. Out in the small town of Arlington, Oregon, Doc Severinsen was practicing his trumpet for hours and tie-dyeing his cowboy shirts.

By the time Johnny was fourteen he was performing his magic act at the Rotary Club and local parties as the Great Carsoni. Doc was Oregon's champion junior trumpeter by the time he was twelve, and auditioned for Tommy Dorsey's band when he was fourteen. It was tougher for me; my biggest talent was speaking into a flashlight. There just wasn't a lot of work for a teenage announcer. I didn't even know what my voice sounded like to other people. There were no such things as tape recorders and no one in my family knew anything about show business. The only feedback I ever got was from my mother, who would remind me, "Children should be seen and not heard," which was not very good advice for someone planning on a career in radio. All I knew was that my dog seemed to like me. Of course, he also liked fire hydrants. Really all I had was determination, and that I had in abundance. And hope: I used to lie in bed at night and pray that I would have a good voice.

I landed my first broadcasting job when I was fifteen years old. A small circus carnival was pitching its tents and sideshow on Lowell Common. In those days sound trucks, trucks with signs plastered on the sides and loudspeakers on the roof, were used to advertise events. As the sound truck drove slowly down the street, someone inside the truck would loudly promote everything from politicians to circus clowns.

That's another straight line for you, just fill in your own punchline.

I convinced the owner of the sound truck to hire me to be the mike man. It wasn't exactly show business—I was cramped in the back of the truck where no one could see me—but it was a microphone and people could listen to me. To be honest, they had to listen to me. The biggest advantage of a sound truck is that the audience can't change the channel or turn down the volume. I wrote my own patter. "Eight of the biggest days and nights of your life!" I boomed proudly as we drove through Lowell. "And the admission? Why, it's ab-so-lute-ly free." And then I reminded them of the biggest attraction, the sideshow, which featured girls "dancing as you have never seen them dance before!"

The truck drove right down Main Street, right past a storefront my father had rented as the headquarters for whatever charity he was raising funds for. I wanted to surprise him. My mother made my father stand outside on the sidewalk as the truck drove by. I couldn't see him, but when he heard my voice, I felt him smiling.

My father wasn't there for many of the important moments of my childhood. I understood why; he was working. He was on the road somewhere, selling something, promoting something, doing whatever it was he had to do to earn a living. It hurt, but I understood it. And I understood it even more when I had children of my own and missed major events in their lives because I was working. And that probably hurt a little more.

My father was a hard worker. Every member of the McMahon family was a hard worker. And so I'm a hard worker. One of my greatest talents is that I show up on time wearing a clean shirt. I'm there, wherever it is I have to be, whenever I have to be there, and I'm prepared to work. If I have a script, I know my lines. I've always been that way, whether it meant producing and hosting the broadcast of a presidential inauguration gala or selling toy gyroscopes for a dollar in a department store on Christmas Eve. Some of the jobs I've had were incredible; it is a great pleasure to be able to banter with Carson, do commercials with Frank Sinatra, give away millions of dollars with Dick Clark, or introduce new talent like Rosie O'Donnell, Sinbad, or Drew Carey. But many of the jobs I've done haven't been that exciting. I've cleaned out soil pipes, sold pots and pans door-to-door, dug ditches, run a laundry delivery service, and even hawked the famous Morris metric slicer on Atlantic City's boardwalk. Like my father, I did whatever job I had to do to earn a living, and I did it to the best of my ability and I did it with enthusiasm.

Johnny Carson would often kid me about all the different jobs I had, many of them at the same time. On the first *Bloopers and Practical Jokes* I cohosted with Dick Clark, Johnny walked onstage and explained to the audience, "From the first day on *The Tonight Show,* twenty-two years ago, Ed has treated *The Tonight Show* like . . . a part-time job. The man comes in, gets his mail, splits. . . . He's got three other jobs tonight after this. He's doing Celebrity Mud Wrestling, Bowling for Towels, and, a week ago, I opened my front door and there was Ed in a dress, claiming he was the Avon lady."

I laughed. And protested, "You know I gave up mud wrestling."

"Sure," Johnny responded, "but only because it conflicted with the paper route in the morning."

I remember a story my good friend John Wayne once told me about the worst movie he ever made, a 1930s comedy for Fox titled *Girls Demand Excitement.* The key scene in the movie was a boys-against-girls basketball game to determine if the girls would be permitted to stay in college. Duke had played football at USC, so he was really embarrassed to be seen playing basketball against a girls' team in this movie. He was walking on the Fox lot muttering to himself when Will Rogers stopped him. "What's the matter, kid?" he asked.

"Oh," Duke told him, "they got me in this movie playing basketball against girls. And they want—"

Rogers interrupted him. "You workin'?"

"Yeah."

Rogers nodded. "Keep workin'," he said, and he walked away.

. . .

And that's exactly what I've done my whole life. When I was about ten years old I wanted a bicycle. But we were going through one of my father's cold-water-flat periods and he couldn't afford to buy one for me. I found out that if I sold enough subscriptions to the *Saturday Evening Post* I could earn a bicycle. I sold three subscriptions my first afternoon. It turned out I was a born salesman. I was very sincere and polite. So I learned very early in my life that I could turn a few afternoons into a bicycle if I worked hard enough. Ironically, fifty years later, after decades with Johnny Carson, after appearing in movies and in the theater, after hosting countless television programs, I was right back where I started, selling magazine subscriptions door-to-door. This time, though, I was doing it by mail and I was going to just about every door in the country. But in all that time I had learned something extremely important about selling. Sincerity and politeness were still vitally important . . . but I could sell a lot more subscriptions if I also promised to give away ten million dollars.

. . .

In 1963 *Time* magazine reported that I often worked as many as four jobs at once and rarely worked less than seven days a week. Obviously that wasn't quite accurate; I can't remember the last time that I had only four jobs. I had learned very early in life that the answer to the question "How much money is enough?" was always going to be "Just a little more than I have." Hard work has never scared me. It's the thought of being without work that terrifies me. I started working when I was about ten years old and I've learned something from every job I had. So eventually I'm really going to figure it out. For example, my lemonade stand taught me that you cannot sell a product for nine cents that cost ten cents to produce and expect to make up the difference in volume. My shoeshine stand taught me the importance of location: businessmen waiting for the ferry were a lot more likely to have their shoes shined than women on the way to a big sale.

When I sold the *Bayonne Times* I learned about advertising. That was a highly profitable situation; I bought my papers for a penny and sold them for two cents, earning a 100 percent profit on each transaction. It was very competitive, though; there were a lot of people hawking newspapers. To sell my papers I had to convince potential customers that there was something in the *Bayonne Times* that would make a difference in their lives. Let us say, for example, that a grocery store had cut the price of chopped beef. While I was selling papers in a wealthy neighborhood, I would shout, "Read all about it! Big drop in the market today." If I was selling in a less prosperous neighborhood, I might scream, "Read all about it. Slasher at work in local grocery store." That's what is known as effective advertising.

The first time I faced a tough audience was in a bingo parlor. I've worked on the Broadway stage, I've worked nightclubs; I estimate that in my career I've stood in front of at least twenty thousand different audiences. Twenty thousand. Please believe me, there is no tougher audience than serious bingo players waiting for their number to be called. Often there were hundreds of people in the audience, and they were there to win money and prizes, *not* to be entertained. And I was the entertainer. Somehow, I became responsible for the numbers I called. In all the years I did *The Tonight Show*, for example, no one ever said to me, "Gee, Robin Williams wasn't that funny tonight. What's wrong with you?" But bingo players often blamed the caller when they lost.

Most of the bingo games I worked traveled with carnivals or small circuses. We carried the entire setup in the back of a large truck, including the tent and tent poles, the stools, the planks and legs that became long "tables," sound equipment needed to call the games, cards and prizes of all sizes and shapes, and yards and yards of black velour that added that *je ne sais quoi* to the operation. And believe me, these bingo games needed as much *quoi* as could be added. We would set up in the midway for a few days, then pack up and drive to the next town, never staying anywhere for more than a week.

I had to work my way up to bingo caller. On occasion I had worked in a concession when a carnival my father was promoting came to the town in which we were living. My first job in a carnival was making change in the Hoop-La booth; that was a game in which prizes sat on wood blocks and if a customer successfully tossed a hoop completely over a block, he won whatever prize it held. Now, ladies and gentlemen, I am not saying it was impossible to fit that hoop over the block on which the pricey camera was placed—I am not saying that—I'm just pointing out that it was much easier to get it over the block on which the rather inexpensive plastic toy was displayed.

When I was sixteen years old my father got me a summer job at Salisbury Beach, Massachusetts, with Mulcahey and Dean, who operated several different carnival games, working in a Sport of Kings booth. That was a game in which customers raced their horses along a track by rolling balls into holes. I started as a counterman, making change, but eventually started calling the races. "Annnnnd they'rrrre off . . ." was one of my best lines, followed by, "at the clubhouse turn, numm-ba two, Fire Chief, is in the lead, but here comes numm-ba six, Wish Upon A Star . . ." After I'd called races for about a week, just like in the movies, the very, very low-budget movies, Gene Dean heard my spiel and said those magic words I had longed to hear, "Your kid's got a voice, Eddie. Let's give him a shot as a bingo announcer."

It wasn't exactly *A Star Is Born*. I went on the road with a bingo game as a laborer. Our first stop was a carnival midway in Mexico, Maine. I helped pitch our tent, set up the sound and electrical systems, and did whatever was necessary to help the game run smoothly. Being sixteen years old and traveling with a carnival is the kind of adventure that prepares you for almost anything imaginable in later life. Except maybe things like working with Jerry Lewis, of course.

From my first day I loved being "with it," the expression used to identify people working in the carnival. I loved the excitement and the color and the people who worked on the midway and in the sideshows. I was "with it," I was in show business. And I very quickly began to learn the code of ethics. The carnival had a girlie show called "Have You Seen Stella?" Now, the amount of Stella available to be seen varied from town to town, depending on the willingness of local law enforcement to accept gratuities. But whatever Stella was revealing in Mexico, Maine, was more than I'd ever seen, and during my very first break I got in line to see her show. One of the best men I worked with was an Indian known as Blackie. Blackie had once been a circus aerialist, a wire walker, but after ruining his back with a fall he became a carny. Blackie saw me standing on line and pulled me out. "You can't go in there, kid," he said. "You're 'with it' now. If Stella saw you in there and then met you over at the chuck wagon, she might get embarrassed." Show people, everybody from star performers to laborers, no matter what type of act or work they did, he explained, had to be treated respectfully. It was a good rule, and I remembered it many strange nights on *The Tonight Show*.

I got my big break when our bingo caller got drunk. He was slurring his numbers. The players didn't like that and started throwing the hard kernels of corn used as markers at him. After a few games the manager of the game said something like, "Okay, McMahon, you think you've got what it takes to be a bingo announcer? Take the mike." He handed me the microphone.

My primary qualification for the job was that I was sober. I took the mike. I loved the feel of the cool metal in my hand. Except for a few times in school, this was the first time I'd ever stood in front of an audience. I cleared my throat and looked out at a vast sea of hair, punctuated occasionally by a bright patch of bald head—every player was staring down at their cards, waiting for a number to be called. I took a deep breath, reached into the fishbowl, and pulled my first number. "Unnnda the O," I said happily, "sixty-four. Sixty-four under the O."

I read the numbers just as I thought my idol, Paul Douglas, might have. Let me tell you something, Paul Douglas would have been a terrible bingo announcer. I was awful. I had no rhythm, no patter, I didn't know how to build excitement or suspense. Players began throwing corn kernels at me; I suspect this kind of behavior might be the derivation of the word "corny." I was corny. But I kept working, and ducking, and somehow I got a little confidence and I got better. By the end of that summer I had been sent to work as relief man for a legendary bingo caller, Whitey McTaag, on a twenty-counterman show. That was the bingo big time. With practice I had become smooth. I'd learned about timing and how to create suspense. When several players were one number away from bingo, I'd pick a number and stare at it, then announce, "Here it is. Who has it, who's going to be our big winner? The number . . . under the I . . . itttt'ssss . . . twenty-two! Twenty-two under the I."

The next summer Gene Dean gave me the mike for my own show. And for an extra fifteen dollars a week I drove a big rig, an eighteen-wheel semi, from carnival to circus to fairgrounds. I was on my own, earning pretty decent money. For the first time in my life, I really was "with it."

Somehow I always found a way to earn the money I needed. When I was at Boston College I chauffeured students back and forth to classes, worked as a laborer on a construction site, and serviced the vending machines at the mills in Lexington and Concord and the Bethlehem Steel Yard. I did whatever I had to do to pay tuition and buy the necessities.

If I couldn't find a job that fit my schedule, I created one. After earning my wings as a marine fighter pilot in World War II, I came home with a wife, the former Alyce Ferrell of Lacoochee, Florida, a baby daughter, Claudia, big plans, and no money. This is when I really became a salesman. Selling appealed to me because I could make my own schedule, my success or failure depended totally on my own ability, and I got to deal directly with people. I was good at it and so I loved it, although that sentence might just as easily be written the other way around. I started with one of the most difficult of all selling jobs, hawking fountain pens on the boardwalk in Atlantic City.

I didn't actually sell the pens; I gave the pens away. I sold fountain pen *points*. How could I make money selling pens by giving them away? The same way the fine people at American Family Publishers make money by giving away ten million dollars to sell twenty-dollar magazine subscriptions. All I needed were a box of pens and points, a block to stand on, a big voice, and great patter. Great patter. There was a lot of competition for the same audience on the boardwalk, and the most entertaining pitchmen usually attracted the biggest crowds. "Ladies and gentlemen," I began in a booming voice, "please step right over here if you'd like your very own free fountain pen. That's right, step right up. Your eyes are not going to believe what your ears are hearing . . ."

As the crowd gathered, I'd begin by demonstrating how a fountain pen worked. This was not a big secret; this was just before ballpoint pens became widely available and everyone used fountain pens with interchangeable points. "I am now about to shock you," I continued, "by announcing that I am not selling this beautiful pen for two dollars. Not for one dollar. Not even for fifty cents. No, ladies and gentlemen, I am giving this pen away . . . absolutely free to every man, woman, and child who buys one of these absolutely necessary gold-finish fountain pen points without which it is impossible to use any fountain pen . . .

"Wait. Wait one second. What did I hear you say, sir? Did I hear you right? You think you have to buy this point to get the free pen? Oh no, not true my friends, not true at all. Do you think I would dare stand before you and make this offer if that were true? But show me a man who does not want one of these fine, durable, gold-finish writing pen points at the miniscule price I am allowed by special permission of the company to offer to you today, and I'll show you a man who doesn't recognize an incredible offer when he sees one, a man with no business sense whatsoever, and believe me, just by looking at you I can tell there are no such shortsighted people in this gathering . . .

"Now friends, who will be the first person to step right up and buy one of these extraordinary gold-finish pen points for only fifty cents . . . that's right, you heard me, only fifty cents, one-half of one dollar, four bits, and receive this guaranteed fountain pen absolutely free!"

It was a show and I was the act. I made people smile, I made them laugh, I made them like me. Once I had their attention I demonstrated my product and tried to convince them that they had to have it right then and there. My incredible offer wouldn't be repeated later or tomorrow. You had to put your money down now! There was no school that taught this technique. I learned it by standing in the back of the crowd watching boardwalk legends like Oshi Morris and Lester Morris kibitz with the crowd. I watched, I listened, I learned. And after only a few weeks, that's right, just a few short weeks, ladies and gentlemen, selling this remarkable gold-finish . . . Well, I got so good at giving away fountain pens that I began selling empty boxes.

I've often made the claim that I could sell any product so long as I could hold it up or point to it. I believe that. If you can sell empty boxes, you can sell anything.

The hardest part of the job was gathering a crowd. As people strolled along, I'd catch their attention then try to pull them in with humor: "Excuse me, sir, that's right, you, sir. Come right up to the counter. That's right, just move your feet, your body will follow. I've asked you to come over because you look like a very intelligent man, a man smart enough to appreciate a great bargain. Just nod your head if you understand me . . ."

But the most effective way to draw a crowd was to engage their curiosity. To make an impossible offer, an offer they knew couldn't be true. Then they would stop to listen to my patter to find out what I was really selling. No one really believed I was selling empty boxes. "That's right, friends," I promised, "these boxes are guaranteed to contain absolutely nothing. But I'm only going to be able to sell six empty boxes to six lucky people. Look at this beautiful box," I would continue. "Why, this is a box that could hold an expensive Waterman pen. It could even hold a watch or some other fine gift. But, wait, what's that, madam? You're wondering who would possibly pay a buck for an empty box? Thank you for asking that question, I've wondered myself if there still are people bold enough to do so. Certainly not your staid, conservative, solid, unimaginative man with no romance in his soul. But those of you who know that there's often more to something than meets the eye, those of you who wonder why a man would stand before you and dare try to sell you an empty box for one dollar, you will say to yourself, 'There must be more to this offer.'

"Now, for those six lucky people who purchase these empty boxes, I must remind you, when you open your box, if you're surprised, if you yell out, 'This box is not empty!' that will be perfectly okay, it will not upset my selling because I am selling only those six boxes. For the rest of you, after I've sold these six empty boxes, please, please do not embarrass me or yourself by asking me to sell you the seventh box because I am not permitted to do so in this demonstration . . ."

As I continued this patter the crowd would grow. Everyone wanted to know what was inside those boxes. Eventually six people would each lay a dollar bill on top of my six boxes. Then I would ask those people to open their boxes. "And if it's empty, just as I said, yell out loudly, 'It's empty!' Okay, open the boxes."

Now, you don't really believe I would sell empty boxes to people for a dollar, do you? A dollar was a lot of money to pay for an empty box in 1946. You want to know what was really in the box? To find out all you have to do is send one dollar, one thin dollar bill, one tenth of a sawbuck to . . . Of course not, but see how effective my pitch was? In fact, the boxes were opened to reveal . . . nothing. As I had promised, they were empty. But I had my crowd gathered and I wasn't about to let them get away. So immediately I began my spiel for perhaps the single finest product ever sold on the magnificent boardwalk in beautiful Atlantic City—I only wish this book was accompanied by a sound track so you might hear the pronouncement of trumpets—the legendary, the one and only, famous Morris metric slicer.

"Now, ladies and gentlemen, I told you those boxes were empty and, indeed, they were empty. Now what does that prove? It proves I'm an honest man. That I was telling you the truth. So now you must believe me when I tell you that I am privileged to be able to offer to you the greatest item I have ever been authorized to sell, the handy Morris metric slicer.

"To start with, I want you to forget the two dollars these incredible gadgets were made to sell for. Okay, I like you people, so I'm cutting the price in half. One dollar. Just look at the way it slices cucumbers. Is that great or is that sensational? Have you ever seen cucumbers cut so beautifully? With the famous Morris metric slicer you can slice anything so thin you could get a job with a tobacco company slicing calling cards into tobacco paper . . ."

Can you hear the music? Selling plastic gadgets on the boardwalk; making something out of almost nothing. This was a great slicer of postwar Americana.

"Did you say cabbage, madam? Of course this'll cut your cabbage like no one has ever cut your cabbage before. Not only that, it will make coleslaw, sauerkraut, anything at all that may constitute your cabbage pleasure. But that's not all.

"Let me ask you, ladies and gentlemen, have you ever seen a woman try to slice a tomato? A lady takes a butcher knife, lunges at the tomato, the poor tomato has a hemorrhage before it ever gets to the dining room table. But let me show you how the famous Morris metric slicer slices a tomato. Look at those perfect slices. You can adjust the blade so thin—look at that slice—you could read a newspaper through that slice of tomato. Why, I know a lady in Bayonne, New Jersey, had one tomato last her all summer long . . ."

Then I demonstrated the add-ons: the "rotisserie cutter invented by Peter Nathemelee, dean of the Parisian School of Potato Surgery," a small cutting device that enabled me to cut a potato into a spiral that I could pull out like an accordion, and would snap back when I released it, "so when company comes, spread the potato out; they leave, put the potato back together again"; the incredible "glass knife," a knife actually capable of cutting glass, or at least of scratching it; and most incredible, the Juice-o-matic. The Juice-o-matic was a piece of orange plastic with a sharp edge enabling it to be stuck into a piece of fruit; when the fruit was squeezed, juice would drain out. "Stick this into a lemon and you have juice for a salad, a little lemon for fish, a little lemon for your Tom Collins . . . and some for Mary and Jane Collins too. In fact, there's enough for the whole damn Collins family.

"Sold separately," I pointed out, "these items would be valued at more than five dollars, and that's if you could even find them, but right now"—it had to be right now—"all of these wonderful items, the Morris metric slicer, the rotisserie cutter, the glass knife, and the Juice-o-matic, can be yours . . . not for that five dollars, not for four dollars, not even for the two dollars the metric slicer alone normally sells for, but for only one thin dollar. That's right, you heard me correctly, one dollar bill. But I'm only going to be able to sell sixteen sets during this demonstration, so if you want one . . . Please, not all at once, don't push, here's a man buying two of them, he must be leading a double life . . ."

By the time I finished my spiel, people were throwing money at me. It was not as easy as it sounds. You really had to sell with your whole body. I would work for an hour, then take an hour off, all day, from early in the morning until the crowds disappeared late at night. A long, long day. But during the summer I could earn as much as five hundred dollars a week, a tremendous amount of money in those days, and all in cash. And after deductions for taxes, that was . . . five hundred dollars. In the fall, if I delayed returning to school a few weeks and hit the fair circuit, I could make as much as one thousand dollars a week.

At times the work was dangerous. An integral part of the pitch was the "actual demonstration." I sliced a tomato and I cut a potato. When I introduced the Juice-o-matic, I had a large pitcher of ice water and I made it appear as if all that juice was draining from a grapefruit. I learned how to talk while using my hands, which is tougher than it sounds but became very important when I went into television. During Christmas vacation in 1947 I was in New York City selling slicers from a storefront directly across the street from the Roxy Theatre. One afternoon, as I was trying to cut a frozen potato with the slicer, the blade slipped and cut deeply into my thumb. It was bleeding very badly, but I didn't want to lose the "tip"—the "tip" is the crowd—so I pressed my forefinger against my thumb to stem the bleeding, then put my thumb in the ice water as I began "turning the tip," or making the final pitch. I sold six sets before going to the hospital.

I spent four years as a marine pilot in World War II. I was a flight instructor, I did aircraft-carrier landings, I was a test pilot, and I taught carrier landings. But the injury I suffered selling the Morris metric slicer was more severe than anything that happened to me during that war.

Every pitchman eventually developed a personal spiel. It was an act, and the payoff really was a payoff. Success was measured in one-dollar bills. A lot of very successful people started on the boardwalk. Charles Revson, the founder of Revlon, was a pitchman. Popeil, who I believe is the grandfather of Ron Popeil of infomercial fame, was a boardwalk legend. Lucille Ball's husband, comedian Gary Morton, sold Lanolin a few yards from my spot. Roommates Charlie Bronson and Jack Klugman worked for my father at his Skillo booth, a derivation of bingo, and he used to tell them, "You want to learn how to do this business, go down the boardwalk and watch my son selling vegetable gadgets."

The boardwalk was a wonderful training ground for me. I gained a tremendous amount of confidence in myself and I learned how to think on my feet. And to this day I know that if the television thing doesn't work out for me, I can always make a decent living.

After spending the summers on the boardwalk, I returned to college to complete my degree at Catholic University in Washington, D.C. It was a tough time. I was married and had a child, I was a full-time college student, I was active in the theatrical department, and other than my marine benefits I had no income. I had to find a means to support my family and pay for my education in my spare time. The Morris metric slicer was just about as far as you could go in selling people something they really didn't need, but they were buying my pitch, my show, as much as they were buying a slicer. At Catholic University I found something that people really needed. I started my own dry-cleaning service, Dutch Cleaners.

I knew about as much about dry cleaning as *Teatime Movie*'s Art Fern knew about sophistication. But I knew that the only dry cleaner near campus took a whole week to do a job, which created a real hardship for priests with only one or two black suits, and students with few clothes. So I found a dry-cleaning plant with equipment on the premises near my apartment and negotiated a deal with the owner. I received a percentage of every order I brought in. I couldn't offer potential customers a better price, so I offered better service. I would pick up an order in my Plymouth and deliver the cleaned clothing in only three days. I named it Dutch Cleaners after a very popular household cleanser, Dutch Cleanser. That name was very important; it sounded like an established business, it sounded substantial, it certainly sounded more impressive than "Ed McMahon riding around in a fifty-dollar car." I had business cards printed and began knocking on doors. I'd go to my philosophy class from 9 A.M. to 10 A.M., then pick up dry cleaning until my drama class began at 1 P.M. Many nights I'd be up till 4 A.M. pinning names on shirts and suits. Dutch Cleaners was successful almost immediately, more successful than even I could have imagined, and I had a great imagination. I enlisted a partner, and three years later we had three trucks making pickups and deliveries, and four employees. Dutch Cleaners had helped support my family all those years, so when I graduated I sold my share of the business to my partner for a dollar. Of course, for that same money he could have purchased the incredible Morris metric slicer *and* all the extras.

While I was at Catholic I also answered an ad in the paper promising me that I could make hundreds of dollars in my spare time. I figured my spare time to be between 11:15 and 11:30 P.M., but I always needed money. That was how I began selling pots and pans door-to-door. Actually, it wasn't just any pots and pans; it was the incredible Thermic Ray stainless steel cookware, made with patented copper bottoms that distributed the heat so evenly that food preparation required almost no water or oil.

If I knocked on a stranger's door today, they would probably open it wide and start screaming, "It's Ed! It's Ed! And he's got the check." I suspect Dick Clark—with whom I give away the wonderful American Family Publishers' millions of dollars—and I might be the most welcome surprise guests in America. But believe me, it was quite different in 1947. On occasion someone will tell me they saw me selling on the boardwalk or bought a vegetable gadget from me, but no one ever remembers closing their front door in my face. A lot of people did. I learned quickly never to admit I was selling cookware but rather to explain that I was in the neighborhood, "and I was just speaking with your neighbor, Mr. Rogers, and I showed him some special equipment he is now having installed in his home. May I come in?"

I sold Thermic Ray cookware just like Tupperware. I offered to demonstrate the unique capabilities of these pots and pans by cooking dinner for five or six couples. I actually cooked a full roast beef dinner in their home, giving a nutrition lesson along with my sales pitch. "Now don't peel the carrots, just brush them," I'd explain, "because the healthy vitamins are right under the skin . . ." I'd follow up by visiting the homes of each of the dinner guests to try to close the sale and get additional leads from them. People claim to remember seeing me selling vegetable gadgets on the boardwalk, but no one ever remembers the night I cooked a lovely dinner for them.

I always displayed my shining stainless steel pots and pans on a black velvet cloth under the brightest lights in the house. Under those conditions they sparkled; housewives loved them. Now, the key to closing the sale was convincing a potential buyer not only that he or she had to have these pots and pans, but that they had to have them right now! That minute. So after the equipment was all laid out, looking beautiful, and the customer was wavering, I'd add, "And the nice thing about ordering tonight is that I can give you a handy kitchen fire extinguisher. I don't know if you know this, but almost 90 percent of all fires in the home start in the kitchen, and I noticed you don't have a fire extinguisher in your kitchen . . ." Well, either they ordered right then and there or they didn't sleep soundly until they got a fire extinguisher.

Within months I convinced the owner of the company that we didn't need the demonstration dinner, that we were wasting an entire night cooking when we could be selling. I turned out to be correct. Eventually I became such a fine pots-and-pans man that I began training other salesmen. At one point I had seventeen people working for me. Working part-time at night, I was earning $350 a week. The owner of the company offered me twenty-five thousand dollars a year to leave school and become vice president of marketing. Who knows, if I had accepted, I might have ended up selling pots and pans to the whole country on a cable shopping network.

In fact, I am selling pots and pans on a shopping channel to two countries, the United States and Canada. And as fine as Thermic Ray cookware was in its time, it simply cannot compare with the amazing nonstick Le Dome by Sitram, the largest cookware manufacturer in France. Because you never need to add oils or butter to prevent your foods from sticking to these pans, Le Dome is perfect for the kind of fat-free cooking so vitally important for a healthy . . .

In television, we often thank people for allowing us to come into their homes. It's just an expression used to thank people for watching the show. But when I was selling my cookware door-to-door, I literally did go into people's homes. And some of the experiences I had would make even Dr. Ruth blush. A lot of single women lived in the Washington area because they could get government jobs. My pitch to them was that my cookware was perfect for their hope chest, that it would help them get ready for marriage. It's possible I might even have reminded them that men love women who know how to cook, and pointed out how easy it was to cook with my pots and pans. Cookware, marriage, it was a pretty successful pitch.

By this time the marines had turned me into a man, a nice-looking man, and single women often invited me into their homes. One woman bought a set but asked me to return the next night to meet her roommate, who might also be interested in my cookware. They shared a small apartment, so the three of us wound up sitting on the bed. Her roommate was sitting right next to me; as I began my sales pitch, her robe opened and I couldn't help but notice that she was totally naked. As a fighter pilot I had been specially trained to notice such things. Naturally, it made my pitch a bit more difficult. Talk about a hard sell. "Now, um," I stammered, "I'd like to point out how perfectly this . . . set is matched. You can see how . . . big . . . large . . ." I was very happy the other woman was there. If we had been alone, I don't know how I would have handled . . . things.

When you sell door-to-door you often discover unusual

lives being lived behind those doors. One Saturday afternoon, a seemingly normal married couple invited me into their home. When I sat down I noticed that all the blinds were closed tightly, that only one light in the room was on, and that these people were half-bombed. This was going to be a tough sale. They offered me a drink; I turned them down. They insisted; I refused. At that time my reputation had yet to precede me. The truth is that, with one famous exception, I never drink while I'm working. As I began my pitch, he grabbed her and she started fighting him off. He was grabbing, she was fighting, I was displaying my beautiful pots in the dark. Finally, I suggested, "Perhaps you'd like me to come back at a more convenient time . . ."

When I graduated from Catholic University in the summer of 1949 I sold the dry-cleaning business, stopped selling pots and pans, and gave up the opportunity to sell gadgets during the fall fair season. With just a little luck I would have earned as much as six thousand dollars selling slicers from Labor Day to early October. Instead, I accepted a job working for a new television station, WCAU in Philadelphia, for seventy-five dollars a week.

So much for the value of a college degree.

2

One memorable evening on *The Tonight Show* the great comedian "Lonesome" George Gobel began reminiscing about his career as a pilot during World War II. "I fought the whole war in Oklahoma," he explained, causing the audience to laugh. "I don't know why you laugh. That's evidently where they needed me or they wouldn't have sent me there." But then he added proudly, "We were pretty effective too. Not one Japanese plane got past Tulsa."

I certainly do not want to take anything away from George Gobel, but while he was busy defending the skies of Oklahoma, somebody had to protect Florida. As a United States Marine Corps fighter pilot, that was my job.

Like George, I did not fly in combat in World War II. Instead, I taught aircraft-carrier landings on land. But the government wanted a return on its investment in my training, so just as my career in television was starting to blossom, I was recalled for duty in the Korean conflict. I flew eighty-five missions over enemy lines in Korea. People who had never even seen any of my TV shows were shooting at me.

I don't know why I so desperately wanted to be a marine fighter pilot. Maybe because my distant relative Joe Kennedy was a naval aviator. Maybe because my father made flying seem so exciting. Whatever the reason, while I was a student at Lowell High School I joined the Civilian Military Training Corps, which was the military version of President Roosevelt's Civilian Conservation Corps. For several weeks during two summers I went to a military training camp on Diamond Island in Maine, where I was taught how to march and shoot and follow orders. It was in the CMTC that instructors first recognized my natural leadership qualities and promoted me to sergeant. Those qualities consisted primarily of the fact that I was the tallest person in my squad and had the loudest voice. If I had chosen to enlist in the real man's army, I qualified for a commission as a second lieutenant. But I didn't want to be a soldier, I wanted to be a marine—and not simply a marine but a marine aviator.

In preparation for the war that seemed inevitable, the navy had created the V-5 program. By completing two years of college, a participant could qualify to be an aviation cadet, the first step toward becoming a marine aviator. I wanted to go to the University of Notre Dame, but I couldn't afford the tuition. So one afternoon I drove the large bingo rig with MULCAHEY & DEAN painted brightly on its sides right up toney Chestnut Hill to Boston College and enrolled. It was a colorful and auspicious debut.

My freshman year I did well in all of my courses—physics, calculus, chemistry, biology, and poetry—all except German. As an electrical engineering major I was required to take German because so many of the great mathematicians had written in German. But German was Greek to me. I flunked it my first semester—the only course I've ever failed—and just barely passed it second semester.

Besides keeping up with my studies and holding down

several jobs, I ran for freshman class president. My campaign strategy consisted of handing out ink blotters proclaiming, "Everybody's Sayin' We Want McMahon." Truthfully, no one was really saying it—especially not the coeds—but everyone wanted the free blotter. I won the election.

In the middle of my sophomore year the navy reduced the entrance requirements for its cadet program; I immediately dropped out of Boston College and enlisted. It was then that I heard the four words that since the founding of this republic have become synonymous with our great military heritage: hurry up and wait. I had to wait several months to be inducted. Doing has always been easy for me; I get up, I go, I do. I like the phone to start ringing early and continue ringing till late at night, I like every minute of my day to be filled; waiting is tough for me. The most difficult thing for me to do is nothing.

While waiting to be called I got my first real job in broadcasting. I was hired to be the night announcer on WLLH, the Synchronized Voice of the Merrimack Valley. WLLH was a three-hundred-fifty-watt station that, if the winds were blowing just right, could be heard all the way from Lowell to Lawrence. During the day I worked on a surveyor's crew, starting as a rod boy and eventually becoming assistant crew chief. I had no idea what a rod boy was when I accepted the job, but whatever it was, I knew I could learn how to do it. I've always been a positive person. When I was offered the job as Carson's announcer on *The Tonight Show*, for example, no one had any idea exactly what form the job would take. But I knew from experience that I would figure out how to do it, whatever it turned out to be.

Christmas 1942 was a sad time for my family. America was at war, my father was too sick to work, and I was about to leave for military training. My mother was very upset that I was leaving. Like all mothers, she knew the dangers of sending her son off to fight a war. One night I overheard her on the telephone telling one of her bridge partners, "We're not going to have a Christmas this year. Edward is going off to the navy right after the New Year and I just . . . I just can't handle it."

Christmas had always been a special occasion in my family. Even when my father was struggling, there were always neatly wrapped presents under a brightly decorated tree. As long ago as I can remember, on Christmas Eve, after all the shopping was done, after all the presents were wrapped, my father allowed everyone to choose one present to open. Then we would share a bottle of wine. Later that night we would have homemade chicken soup and chicken sandwiches with beer. It was a warm and wonderful tradition. I knew this was going to be my last Christmas at home for a long time, and as my father had done for me, I wanted to make it special.

The day before Christmas I was working with my surveying crew just outside Bedford, Massachusetts, extending the runway on an army base. As I peered through my transit—my "gun," as surveyors call it—I saw the most beautiful blue spruce I had ever seen directly in my line of sight. It was about seven feet tall with wide, full branches. It was right in our path; it was going to have to be cut down. I must have smiled as I told an assistant, "That one's mine."

I cut it down myself and gently put it in the back of my Hudson Terraplane. As I drove home that night I stopped at a small convenience store and bought their last set of lightbulbs and remaining decorations. It was as dark as a New England night can be by the time I got home, and very cold, and in my memory it was snowing but that might be apocryphal. I put the tree over my shoulder and rang the doorbell. I had a key but I wanted my mother to answer the door. When she opened the door, I told her, "Muth, we're having our Christmas."

And so we did, and of all the Christmases of my life, that's the one I remember most of all.

Six weeks later I reported as ordered to the Fargo Building in Boston to begin a military career that would end almost five decades later. I was one of 150 naval cadets who had passed a series of rigorous tests and physical examinations. Technically a cadet was barely in the navy—"cadet" wasn't a rank, and we were treated with all the respect due that rank. As we stumbled into long lines that first morning, the sergeant called out my name. "McMahon," he screamed at me, "from this minute on you are in charge of this group. You will take them by train to Texarkana, Texas. Do you understand?"

"Yes, sir," I said in my deepest radio voice.

"And McMahon," he added, "you will not lose any of 'em."

I never learned why I was placed in command. Probably those same natural leadership qualities I had displayed on Diamond Island: height and voice. I'd traveled with my parents my entire childhood, I'd traveled with carnivals and circuses, but I'd never before traveled with 149 teenagers, most of whom had never been more than a day from home. For four days I herded this group to Texas. I made sure they got on the right trains and got all their meals; I taught them how to release the lock in the bathrooms and make long-distance telephone calls home. Some of these young people did not even know how to buy toothpaste. Many years later the incredible Jonathan Winters spent a weekend at my home. He climbed all over the furniture, made the most bizarre sounds, and did just about anything possible to entertain my children, but nothing he did even fazed me: I had once been in charge of 149 teenagers for four days and survived.

There wasn't even a military base in Texarkana. We learned to fly at a civilian field, wearing civilian clothes, living in private homes. The closest thing we had to a military uniform was a long white scarf that we wore while flying, the same type of scarf we imagined the heroic pilots of World War I had worn. In Texarkana I flew an airplane by myself for the first time in my life. People who have flown alone have experienced this incredible sense of freedom, and no words can adequately describe it to those who have not. I learned to fly in a lumbering Piper Cub, just about the most basic of all airplanes. From Texarkana, we went to naval training centers at Denton, Texas; Athens, Georgia; and finally to an "E-base"—the "E" standing for "elimination"—just outside Dallas, still as cadets attempting to qualify for the navy flight school at Pensacola, Florida.

In Athens we went through a three-month version of basic training. We spent those months being tested mentally and physically. On *The Tonight Show* we often had demonstrations of unusual physical prowess—people breaking plywood boards with their forehead, jumping off platforms, or performing complicated calisthenics. After one guest had completed his amazing display of calisthenics, Johnny asked me if I ever did that kind of workout. "No," I replied, "I have a man who does that for me."

Not in Athens, Georgia, though. One of those tests consisted of stepping on and off a bench twenty-two inches high for five minutes while carrying a pack one-third your weight—for me that was sixty pounds—to test your endurance and ability to recover quickly. Please, ladies and gentlemen readers, do not try this at home. The publisher cannot be responsible for the results. Now, what stepping on and off a bench while wearing a sixty-pound knapsack had to do with flying a sophisticated flying machine, I had not the slightest idea. But those people who could not do it for five minutes did not get to fly.

At the E-base we flew the Stearman biplane, one of those old-fashioned airplanes with two open cockpits and two wings that are still used in air shows, which we affectionately called the Yellow Peril. We called it that because it was painted bright yellow and the way we flew it put the pilot in great peril. It was used to teach us aerobatics—rolls, loops, spins, turns, steep climbs and dives—because its two wings gave it tremendous maneuverability. The maneuvers we learned to perform in the Yellow Peril would help us survive in combat. All we had to do was survive learning them. Some people did not.

But probably the most important thing I learned from the Yellow Peril was confidence, confidence in myself and my airplane. As an entertainer, each time I did something new—a movie, my nightclub act, a television sitcom—people would ask me if I was nervous. The answer was that, almost without exception, I was not. Flying an airplane to the top of a loop and then reducing air speed until the engine stalls and the plane starts dropping like a leaf makes me nervous; facing an audience does not. The ground is much harder than any audience. The confidence I gained doing Immelmann loops and chandelles and lazy 8s and wingovers extended through the rest of my life.

I had the first of several close calls in the Yellow Peril. During a training flight the plane suddenly seemed sluggish; it just didn't feel right. Pilots trust those feelings. I decided to land in a large field. As I stepped out of my airplane I looked down and there was a single die. It became my lucky charm. I put it in my pocket and carried it with me throughout World War II. It did its job.

One of every three candidates washed out at the E-base. The navy was finally satisfied that those of us who had made it to Pensacola could fly an airplane, and there they turned us into combat pilots. We flew the AT-6, a two-seat trainer in which we learned gunnery and bombing. At Pensacola we also took a battery of psychological tests that would determine the type of aircraft to which we eventually would be assigned. I wanted to fly the Corsair, a carrier-based fighter and just about the hottest piece of machinery in the air. But as I read some of the questions, I knew that if I answered them honestly I probably would not get the Corsair. Among these questions were "Would you strafe women and children in the street?" "Would you shoot an enemy pilot as he parachuted out of a plane?"

I answered them honestly. No, and no. As a result I was assigned to the B-25, a land-based bomber. The navy had decided that if I wouldn't strafe women and children, I'd have to bomb them. A lot of pilots loved the B-25; not me, I wanted fighters. So I requested an opportunity to plead my case before the psychological board.

When I appeared before the board I used every sales technique I knew. "I knew what answers you wanted," I told them, "and if I'd been dishonest and answered the questions that way, I'd be a fighter pilot. But I can't believe the marines want officers like that. I don't believe they want people who are willing to shoot innocent women and children. And as for enemy pilots, why should I shoot down a man in a parachute?"

To make sure he won't fly again, replied one of the board members, and maybe shoot me down.

"Well maybe he might extend the same courtesy to me if I ever have to jump out of a plane," I argued. "I think we all know about the great tradition of honor among pilots."

I got my Corsair. In 1938 the navy had decided to mount the most powerful aircraft engine being manufactured onto the smallest possible airframe. The result was the F4U Corsair, one of the finest airplanes ever made. I was six feet three inches tall and weighed about 180, big for a fighter jock, but that airplane fit me as though it had been cut by a fine tailor. When I slipped into the cockpit I felt like I was home. The Corsair was a gull-winged plane—the wings folded to save space aboard carriers—and it had a maximum speed of 425 miles per hour at twenty thousand feet and a range of fifteen hundred miles. Anyone who ever flew it can probably still tell you all its specs. I loved that airplane.

Of 150 young naval cadets with whom I entered the program, I was one of only two who eventually earned the gold wings of a U.S. Marine pilot. It took me almost two years to earn my wings, and it was worth every minute of it. But I think my training was as tough on my mother as on me. She knew I was stationed in Florida, but if a plane crashed anywhere in America, she was sure I was in it. "I'm in Florida, Muth," I tried to explain. "That plane crashed in Chicago."

"So then you're all right?"

After graduating from Pensacola I was assigned to Lee Field, which was about thirty miles outside Jacksonville, for further training in the Corsair, but first I got to go home. I wanted to surprise my mother. My parents were living in Hartford, Connecticut, where my father had taken a job at the Pratt and Whitney plant in East Hartford. When the war began, the carnival business had pretty much closed down for the duration, so he ended up as a supervisor at Pratt and Whitney—where the Corsair engine was built! My father and I worked out a great plan: I was going to hide at a neighbor's house and he was going to send my mother over there for some reason. When she knocked on the door, I would answer it.

Somehow, she sensed I was there. And she immediately decided that the reason I was hiding across the street was that I had been injured in an accident. "He's hurt, isn't he?" she demanded of my father. He insisted I was fine. "It's his legs; they're gone, aren't they?" She ran across the street in tears, convinced I had been wounded, crippled, or disfigured. Even after a full inspection, she persisted, "You're sure you're all right?"

Of course she had reason to worry. Believe me, flying the Corsair was a dangerous job. The Corsair earned the nickname the Killer because a lot of fine pilots died in that airplane. As was often said, any landing from which you walked away was considered a good landing. At Lee Field we learned how to land on an aircraft carrier. There is only one way to land on a carrier: very, very carefully. There is almost no margin for error. Life and death are a matter of inches. One morning I was practicing carrier landings at a satellite field near St. Augustine. The field was perfect for this job because it was surrounded by water. As I made my approach I kept my eyes squarely on the landing officer, who used flag signals to visually direct pilots onto a carrier. As I decreased my air speed to just about the minimum needed to keep the plane in the air, my engine suddenly started sputtering and I lost altitude much too quickly. I started choking the engine, just as I would have choked the engine on my old Hudson on a cold December morning in Lowell, desperately trying to squeeze a few more feet of air out of that plane. Somehow, I'll never know how, I made it to the very edge of the runway.

When I saw the landing officer a few minutes later, he said, "You know your wheels hit the water?"

I shook my head. I knew how lucky I had been. My approach had been so low that my landing gear had touched water. If my wheels had gone even a few inches deeper, the nose of my airplane would have pitched into the water and the plane would have flipped over. That's fate, that's all it is. If my wheels had been six inches lower, just imagine all the Alpo that never would have been sold.

I qualified as a carrier pilot by making eight landings on the USS *Guadalcanal*. There are two moments that every carrier pilot will remember his entire lifetime: his first take-off from a carrier and his first landing. The takeoff is easier. You rev that engine about as high as it'll go, then release the brakes—and pray. Seconds later the deck suddenly falls out from beneath your wheels, the wings catch the wind, the plane begins to lift, and you're airborne. And very happy about it.

Landing is much more complicated. Very few things in my life will ever be as small as the aircraft carrier on which I had to land. When I was standing on the deck of a carrier, it seemed huge, miles long, like a small city. But it was amazing how fast that deck shrank when I got into the air. I had been flying for more than two years when I attempted my first carrier landing. I had flown several different types of aircraft in various situations. I had spent hundreds of hours in cockpits and thousands of hours in classrooms. I knew every nut and bolt on my airplane, I had studied the physics of flying, I understood aerodynamics. And yet, even with all that training, as I looked down upon the *Guadalcanal* from about thirty-five hundred feet, I thought, are they out of their minds? This is impossible. I remember thinking, Holy God, I gotta get back on that?

If I had spent time thinking about doing it, it probably would have made it more difficult. Instead, I just did it, exactly as I had been taught. My alternatives were limited: I either landed my airplane on that carrier or I found out how good a swimmer I really was. That is called motivation.

While waiting for the first all-marine carrier to be launched, I was assigned to Lee Field as an instructor and a test pilot. Mostly I checked out airplanes that had been repaired to ensure that they were flightworthy. One afternoon my roommate was showing off a bit for his "chicklets," his new class of trainees. He came in very low over the field and started to do a roll, but he didn't have enough power. He mushed in, his wing hit, and his plane cartwheeled down the runway before exploding. They found his body almost two miles from the point of impact. I had to inventory his effects. That was pretty tough. I was ordered to take over his class. "I promise you," I told them, "you're all gonna live through this. Flight safety is going to be the first thing we think about in the morning and the last thing at night."

On our third training mission we flew to the satellite base at St. Augustine. Unfortunately, one of my trainees did a ground loop, meaning that his wingtip brushed the runway as he landed, causing the plane to start spinning. He was not hurt, but his plane was damaged. Mechanics had to take off the wing and repair the operating mechanism. When it was done, they suggested I take it up for a test flight. I had a lot of confidence in these mechanics, they were topflight, and I wanted to get my class into the air as quickly as possible. I tested the plane.

As soon as I got into the air I knew I was in trouble. That plane would not fly level. I couldn't get my left wing up higher than my wheels. It was down at about a forty-five-degree angle. If I tried to land, that wing would hit first, and someone else would have to inventory my effects. I held the stick with both hands and pulled it as far as I could to the side, but the plane would not respond. I made a couple of passes at the field, hoping that miraculously the operating mechanism would suddenly start functioning and I'd land safely. It didn't happen. The flight manual solution to this problem is pretty explicit: jump out of the airplane. The marines had a lot more invested in me than a piece of machinery. I told the tower that I was going to abandon my airplane. I climbed to the proper altitude, set a course for the everglades where the plane could crash without endangering other people, checked my parachute straps to make sure they were good and tight, opened up my canopy, released my safety belt, and got ready to jump.

Then the wind hit my face. Well, I thought, this is a really bad idea. I sat down in the cockpit, closed the canopy, and radioed the tower that I was going to attempt a landing. I made several passes over the field as I tried to figure out what to do. Below me I could see the fire engines and the meat wagons, the ambulances, lining up near the runway for my crash landing.

I probably made a dozen passes over the field as I tried to figure out what to do. Then I had an idea. The Corsair had a plate in front of the wheels that acted as a dive break. When a pilot was making a bomb run, just before he released his bombs he would pop his wheels, which slowed the plane and increased accuracy. I reasoned that the sudden change in airflow might also lift the wing just enough for me to sneak in. I tested it in the air a few times and it seemed to work. It really didn't matter if it was a good idea; it was the only idea I had. Marines never use the word "scared." Instead we say "apprehensive." I think it's accurate to say that I was extremely apprehensive. In fact, I would say I was about as apprehensive as it is possible to be.

I was coming in on the proverbial wing and a prayer. I made my approach with my wheels up. When I was just above the runway, I took a deep breath and popped my wheels. The wing came up and I hit the tarmac safely. Seconds after I hit the ground, the wing dropped again and I lost control of the plane. It swerved wildly across the field before I finally was able to brake. The first sound I heard was the fire-engine sirens racing toward me.

I scrambled out of that cockpit. Someone handed me a big mug of hot coffee, but I was shaking so badly that I sloshed it all over my hand. I may be the only plane-crash victim treated for burns from scalding coffee. When I calmed down I decided against flying back to Lee Field. Instead I rode back to the base in the bus with my students. It was a moment of ignominy—instructors never rode the bus with students—but I didn't care. I was thrilled to be on that bus.

Later in my career I occasionally heard claims that I laughed too easily and too often. Let me ask you, can you blame me?

While I was stationed in Jacksonville, I did something truly daring. Testing airplanes was one thing; getting married took a lot more courage. My years in the Marine Corps had changed me. I wasn't just a pilot; I was a Corsair pilot, a marine fighter pilot. As far as I was concerned, there wasn't anything better. I was very proud and I suspect I showed it. I was confident, cocky, and I knew how good I looked in my pressed uniform. In high school I never had much luck with girls. I told myself I was too busy with my schoolwork and jobs; the truth was that I was too shy. At Boston College I discovered the pleasures of romance, but I was there for less than two years. I tried to make up for that lost time in the service.

There were thousands of single women, the legendary Rosie the Riveters, working in defense plants in the Jacksonville area. Since I was a marine fighter pilot, basically all I had to do to attract some of them was survive. I was an officer and a gentleman and as such I was completely faithful to every one of the women I dated, at least while I was with them.

We were young and single, many of us were living on our own for the first time in our lives, and we were in the middle of the most devastating war in history. We really did not know what was going to happen the next day. So we worked hard during the day and partied hard at night. Admittedly there were times when I might have partied a little too hard. I remember I once found myself dating two women who lived in the same building. However, my problem was not that I was dating two women; no, my real problem was that I met someone else I really liked, and *she* lived in the same building as the other two girls.

Alyce Ferrell was adorable. She was working at the St. John's Shipyards as a secretary. We had met at the Officers' Club, where she was serving as a Junior Chamber of Commerce volunteer hostess, but since she knew both of the women I was dating—in fact one of them was her roommate—I did not pursue her. At least not immediately.

But one night I called for her roommate, who wasn't home, and Alyce answered the phone and we got into a long conversation. One thing led to another and the next thing I knew we had been married twenty-six years and had had four children. Not right away, of course—it took us almost a year before we were married.

We couldn't have been any more different. I was tall; she was small. I was raised in big cities like New York and Boston; she had grown up outside Dade City, Florida. I was a churchgoing Catholic; she was a Protestant. Somehow, though, it worked. There was a sweetness about her that I found irresistible.

I don't think I understood how truly different we were until I visited Alyce's home in Lacoochee. The town was so small that if you put it in a corner of the skating rink at Rockefeller Center, you probably wouldn't notice it right away. It probably hadn't changed too much since the turn of the century. The main road through town had a wooden sidewalk—only on one side. But what I saw there shocked me.

Maybe because I'd grown up around carnivals, where my family had lived and worked with people of different origins, races, and religions, or maybe because I knew all about the signs reading IRISH NEED NOT APPLY, I'd learned to judge people as individuals. In fact, when we lived in Bayonne, several of my friends were Japanese and I spent a lot of time with their families in their homes. That caused me some difficulty during the war. For example, I just couldn't use the word "Jap." I knew it was a derogatory term and I refused to use it. And I couldn't believe that our government would intern American citizens of Japanese ancestry in camps and take away their property. I ended up in a lot of pretty heated discussions with some of my fellow marines. On occasion I was called a "Jap lover," but that didn't bother me. I used to give a speech to each new class I taught, telling them, "This war started when several men went into a room and decided they wanted a war. It's not the Japanese people, it's their leaders. And it's going to end the same way, a few men going into a room and deciding to end the war. Your job is to stay alive until that happens . . ."

Prejudice of any kind has always been difficult for me to deal with. At Catholic University my senior thesis was titled "Against Restrictive Covenants in Housing." In any event, I drove into this town in which my future wife had been raised and just about the first thing I saw was a very small grocery store—the entire store couldn't have been more than fifteen feet by fifteen feet—but it had two doors, one marked WHITES, the other COLORED. It barely had room for a counter, yet it had two doors. Outside was a drinking fountain with a single pipe branching into two spigots, again marked WHITE ONLY and COLORED ONLY. Yet somehow Alyce had managed to break out of this environment, out of this lifestyle. And our four kids grew up completely without prejudice.

We were married on July 5, 1945, in Atlantic City. I was twenty-two years old. I wanted to be married by a priest in a church, but we were not permitted to do so because Alyce wasn't Catholic. Fortunately, we found a loophole in the rules. There was a brand-new Catholic church on a naval base near Atlantic City, so new that it hadn't been consecrated. So it looked just like a church, it felt like a church, but technically it wasn't a church. Because it wasn't a Catholic church, a priest was allowed to marry us in it.

Our first daughter was born the following April in what had once been the dining room of a lovely old home in Dade City. I wanted Alyce to be in the new hospital on the marine base at Cherry Point, but she insisted that her first child was going to be delivered by her family doctor. He had converted a home into a hospital. I stayed in the room with Alyce as long as I could, but after a while I couldn't handle it and waited outside. There was a book made into a movie that greatly affected me titled *Claudia*. Dorothy McGuire played the title role in the movie. It was about a lovely, innocent girl. And so our first daughter was named Claudia.

When Alyce and I decided to get married we knew that as soon as the new marine carrier was ready to be launched, I would be shipping out. A month later my orders to report to the West Coast were issued. Ironically, I received those orders the day the atomic bomb was dropped on Hiroshima. Days later the second bomb was dropped on Nagasaki. My orders were rescinded; the war was over.

I was prepared to go to war, not to peace. I had always been honest with Alyce; I had told her that when the war ended I was going back into radio. But while I was in the service I had started hearing about television. No one knew too much about it—it was still basically considered radio with pictures—but everyone knew it was coming. I had a big decision to make: I could either get back into radio or return to college to prepare myself for television. I really didn't know what to do.

Right after the war ended, NBC hosted a series of welcome-home auditions to try to discover new talent for their vast radio network. The auditions were held on the mezzanine at 30 Rockefeller Plaza, the same building in which we would later do *The Tonight Show*. I remember so well that when the elevator doors opened I saw the beautiful art deco carvings on the wall. I was nervous; when I did this audition I actually heard my knees knocking. I was given a B+ rating and my acetate, a large record, was distributed to all NBC affiliates. I received offers from two radio stations, one in Springfield, Massachusetts, the other in Montgomery, Alabama.

I wasn't used to turning down jobs of any kind, especially jobs on radio. But the prospect of working in television appealed to me. I knew it was a real gamble. I wasn't sure I could make it as a performer on television; I knew my voice was fine for radio, but I had no idea how I would look to TV viewers. Because there was no TV industry, no one knew how to prepare for a career in television. It seemed to me that learning how to act might be helpful. So, I decided to turn down the radio offers and enrolled in a university drama department.

My attitude hadn't changed at all: if I couldn't be a performer, I would be a writer; if I couldn't be a writer, I'd be a producer. But somehow, somewhere, whether it was radio or television or whatever else was invented, I was going to be in broadcasting.

I will now reveal a secret known to very few people. I coulda been a bulldog. I scored very high on the military version of the college entrance boards and was accepted to Yale University. Just imagine, if I had decided to go there, William Buckley's famous book could have been titled *God and McMahon at Yale*. It was not Yale's Ivy League reputation that impressed me but the fact that it was one of the few universities with a full drama department. In fact, I would have returned happily to Boston College if it had had a drama school. Alyce and I visited New Haven and I loved the Yale campus, but I was concerned about finding the kind of work that would enable me to support my wife and child there.

I was also accepted to Catholic University in Washington, D.C. Washington was the kind of big city in which I felt comfortable. It didn't have a boardwalk, but since it was the center of American politics, I knew people there would appreciate a good sales pitch. Catholic University was the seat of Catholic education in America, the only college in the country that offered a degree in canon law. Because the presidents of all the other Catholic universities studied there, it had tremendous power to influence the Church. At various times the leading philosophers of most of the

Catholic orders taught there. It was a very serious place, which is why it was so unusual that it also had such a fine drama department.

The drama department was the creation of an extraordinary man, the Reverend Gilbert Hartke. Hartke somehow managed to convince the good fathers of this august university that drama should be an academic subject equal to philosophy or history, a task no more unlikely than giving a contribution to Jerry Lewis for muscular dystrophy and getting back change. Hartke proceeded to establish one of the premier drama departments in the world. He made it an exciting place to be. Helen Hayes gave her farewell performance in Eugene O'Neill's *Long Day's Journey into Night* on his stage. Walter Kerr, who later became the *New York Times* theater critic, taught my playwriting class—and married one of my fellow students, Jean Kerr.

At Catholic University I learned that the hardest part of acting is being able to act as if you weren't acting. Besides carrying a full course load and working my usual four jobs, I performed in several productions. I played a lawyer in Aristophanes' comedy *The Birds*. I looked like Mercury—I was costumed in tights and a jerkin and my hair was powdered white and combed into a point. In order to make the curtain I had to leave the vegetable gadget stand I was operating in a store in Silver Springs, Maryland, at precisely the right moment. So as I was doing my spiel, "Yes, madam, I certainly will get to the onion slicer, thank you for reminding me," I was constantly glancing at my watch. At the last second I raced to the university, got into my costume and makeup, and walked calmly onstage to deliver my big line: "*I'm* an attorney."

Let me try that reading another way for you; "I'm an *attorney!*"

I played a singing Polonius in a series of Shakespearean-type vignettes Walter and Jean Kerr wrote titled *Thank You, Just Looking*. I made a little extra money during that run by working as an usher. I'd seat the audience, then run back-stage to get into costume.

The play was a big success. I'm sure my fine ushering played no part in that, but eventually the title was changed to *Touch and Go* and the play went to Broadway. Some of the performers went with it, but not me. I'm not sure I was offered my part, but even if I had been, I couldn't have accepted it. At most the part paid seventy-five dollars a week, and I couldn't have afforded to give up my dry-cleaning business just to be a Broadway actor.

I appeared on television for the first time while studying at Catholic University. An original play in which I had a small role was so successful that it was chosen to be used in an experimental broadcast. By 1947 many cities had their own television stations, but since these stations were not connected, there was no such thing as a network. I'm not even sure kinescopes, the very rudimentary videotapes, existed. Finally, several stations from Washington to New York were strung together by something called a coaxial cable. As far as I know, this play was to be the first show broadcast on the coaxial cable.

I played an officer in a play about the military. I suspect I got the part because of my strong audition and the fact that I had my own uniform. We transformed the basement banquet room of the Wardman Park Hotel into our studio and broadcast live on this makeshift network. When I look back on how we had to jury-rig lights and create our own sets, how our director and cameraman were inventing tele-vision as they went along, it seems impossible to believe that little more than two decades later technology had advanced so quickly that every person in America was able to watch Ed Ames toss a hatchet right between the legs of a human silhouette.

Officially I was enrolled in the Department of Speech and Drama, but I minored in scholastic philosophy. I was pretty good at figuring out how, but I wanted to try to understand why. The course I most wanted to take at the university was metaphysics, taught by Father Hart. Father Hart was a brilliant philosopher who had taught Fulton Sheen, and he accepted a limited number of students. I took three philosophy courses in summer school in preparation for this course and finally I was accepted. If I had stayed at Catholic University one more year, I would have taken Father Hart's legendary course, "God and Beauty." Isn't that a beautiful name for a course?

Father Hart was a very demanding teacher and his courses were difficult. At times he would give us the answers to his questions and I was so lost I still couldn't answer them. But I loved being in a classroom listening to him. I just loved it. Father Hart forced his students to wonder about the world. Unfortunately, it convened at ten o'clock in the morning, and on occasion I was so busy collecting dry cleaning that I had to cut it. Twice I was dropped from the class because of excessive absences, but each time I appealed to Monsignor Smith, the head of the philosophy department, and was reinstated.

One morning, just after I'd been put back in the class, Father Hart walked into the classroom, reached up and pulled the string to turn on the overhead lights, and continued to bless himself. "In the name of the Father, the Son, and the Holy Ghost . . . ," he intoned, concluding, "and will Mr. McMahon see me after class today." I didn't know what he wanted, but at least I was in good company.

After class he asked me to walk with him. I was astonished; Father Hart was not known to commune with students. To me, this was sort of like taking a stroll with God. Finally, he sighed and asked, "Why are you doing this to me, Mr. McMahon? Why do you keep cutting my class?"

"I don't want to cut your class," I explained, "but I've got a wife and a child and to pay the bills I sell pots and pans and vegetable gadgets and I have this dry-cleaning business. Sometimes when I go to pick up the cleaning my customers make me wait while they take the hooks out of the curtains . . ." After listening to my explanation, he raised his hand to stop me. "Okay, all right, I understand. You can stay in my class, so long as you keep up your grades and hand in all your required papers. However, Mr. McMahon, let me point something out to you . . ." With that, he stopped and faced me. "Mr. McMahon, philosophy is for the idle man."

Philosophy is for the idle man. Isn't that beautiful? It was precisely the kind of observation that I would have loved to have been able to contemplate; unfortunately, I was too busy.

Father Hart was a large man, big and stocky, not fat, and although he often seemed distracted, he missed nothing that went on around him. One day Alyce was very sick so I had to bring Claudia with me to metaphysics class. She was almost three years old. As we got to the class, I warned her, "Sweetheart, Daddy loves you very much, but if you make one sound in that class, I'm gonna kill you. This is very important to me; I want you to sit on my lap and not make one peep."

I waited until Father Hart was right in the middle of his opening prayer. While everyone was standing and his eyes were closed in devotion, I snuck into the room. One of my classmates was a nun who had been in China for forty years. She was a big woman and I slipped in right behind her. I figured I could hide behind her without being seen. After the class sat down, Father Hart began his lecture. "Babes in arms and suckling babes," he said softly, "none are too young to learn metaphysics."

My grades at Catholic University were very good. In fact, the only reason I did not graduate cum laude is that I flunked one course: German. I took it to fulfill my language requirement, feeling quite confident that since I'd already taken two semesters of German at Boston College I certainly would be able to pass it. Well, I fooled myself right there. Even today German remains a foreign language to me.

I moved to Philadelphia after graduating from Catholic University and immediately—I mean the day I got there—I had my own show on WCAU, the local television station. Television was so new at that time that the television set was the star. It didn't matter what program was on, as long as the TV set was on. So I grew up along with television.

Within two years I was a television star. I was Philadelphia's Mr. Television. I was on the first cover of *TV Digest*, which eventually evolved into *TV Guide*. And perhaps when I returned to Catholic University to visit my old friends, I did walk with a bit of a swagger. As I walked into the office, the girl I'd paid to type my homework papers was operating the switchboard. Big star that I was, I naturally gave her a little kiss. "Guess what?" she said. "I'm working for Father Hart now. Hey, let me call him and tell him you're here."

I didn't want to bother Father Hart, but before I could stop her she had called him and he'd invited me to his quarters. This was really something special, like being invited to the White House—only more exclusive. I didn't know anyone who had ever been in his apartment. I walked into his living room and I couldn't believe it; the room was filled with piles of books, papers, reports, pamphlets, and brochures, tall piles of knowledge. As we sat down, he told me, "I'm glad you're here, Mr. McMahon. There is something I would like to ask you about . . ."

I had no idea what that could possibly be. Father Hart was a respected philosopher, an explorer in the wilderness of ideas. Even those times in class when I couldn't quite follow him, I knew I was being forced to learn how to think. He was someone I admired and respected tremendously. I couldn't imagine what he possibly could want to ask me.

"Mr. McMahon," he finally asked, "what's it like being on television?"

He had been asked to appear on local television shows several times, he explained, and had refused. But eventually he was going to have to do it. So he wanted to know as much as possible about it: how hot the lights were, where the cameras were situated, whether it was always necessary to use makeup. I ended up spending an hour with this great teacher, teaching him about television.

I certainly was qualified to do it. Just as I had been when my daughter Claudia was born, I was standing outside the door at the birth of commercial television. When I started in Philadelphia, we were doing only a few hours of programming every day, inventing television as we went along. I cohosted the first television program I ever saw. I had the advantage of being able to make my mistakes while almost no one was watching. Our programs were budgeted at somewhere between "Ed, you got any change in your pocket?" to "That's way more than we can afford." Our ratings weren't in numbers, but rather by name: "Jesse Stevens over at O'Reilly's Grill saw your show the other night," or "I heard that a friend of my girlfriend's friend watched it." I did talk shows, quiz shows, and cooking shows; I introduced movies; I hosted variety shows and documentaries; I did commercials; I even did a brief humor piece on the evening news. Television was so new that there were no rules, so we didn't have to worry about breaking any of them. We did some wonderfully creative things. On one of my shows, I interviewed a tree trimmer as we sat on the branch he was cutting. No one, I guarantee you, no one turned off that interview.

I was one of the first television personalities in Philadelphia, so as the popularity of television grew, so did my own. And with practice and experience, my work got better and better. By 1952 I was working on several programs, among them a daily morning chat show called *Strictly for the Girls*—that might have been the first morning show on television—and a Saturday morning circus program called *The Big Top*. But I wasn't satisfied just being the biggest clown in Philadelphia—I was determined that someday I would be the biggest clown on network television.

It almost happened. WCAU was part of the brand-new CBS television network, and CBS executives in New York liked my work. They thought I had a comfortable presence on the air, a high "likability." At a meeting in Philadelphia, they suggested broadcasting my morning show regionally and the circus show nationally. This was the opportunity I had been working for since my days in Katie's parlor. I was thrilled. And as it turned out, there was only thing that could keep me from accepting their offer. The Korean War.

At times people mistakenly refer to me as an ex-marine. I politely correct them, explaining that there is no such thing as an ex-marine. "Once a marine," I tell them, "always a marine." I love the United States Marine Corps and I'm extremely proud to be a marine. But, gee, sometimes the Marine Corps does have a terrible sense of timing.

Officially, the Korean War was not a war; it was a "police action." But if the North Koreans knew the difference, they certainly didn't show it. None of us who fought in Korea thought that the North Koreans had invaded South Korea just to screw up our lives, but it was hard not to take it personally. Many of us were World War II veterans and when we received our discharge papers in 1946 we sort of thought the government meant it. Many of us were just beginning to get established when we were recalled. Certainly no one would have objected if we felt our national security was clearly in danger, but Korea was more complicated than that. We tried to keep things in perspective, but there was a lot of bitterness. It was often said sarcastically, "This might not be the best war in the world, but it's the only one we've got."

Being recalled came as a great shock. I was on vacation in Florida with Alyce, Claudia, and our new baby, Michael, relaxing poolside for the first time in years, when I saw the chilling headline TED WILLIAMS CALLED BACK INTO MARINE CORPS. Ted Williams! Ted Williams, arguably the greatest baseball player of that time, was also a marine pilot who had served in World War II. We'd entered the service about the same time, gone through training about the same time, and gotten our gold wings at the same time. The military did everything by the numbers: if they were going to recall Williams at the height of his baseball career, I knew I would soon be packing my bright red circus nose, the nose that lit up and proclaimed HELLO!

The letter arrived several weeks later: "You are ordered to report to the Willow Grove Naval Air Station . . . for duty involving flying. Have all civilian affairs in order. Be in uniform. Bring no civilian clothing and be prepared to transfer."

The person I most worried about was my mother. She had never been a very strong woman, and her health was not good. I was afraid what this news might do to her. My father and I did everything possible to hide it from her until the last possible moment. We hid newspapers, we didn't tell anyone. But after six weeks' training in the Philadelphia area, I was ordered to report to the Third Marine Air Wing being formed in Miami, Florida. She cried for a weekend when we finally told her.

It took me three days to drive Alyce and the kids to Lacoochee. When we arrived, a Red Cross representative was waiting there to tell me my mother had died. Her fears for me had been too much for her heart to bear.

The morale among the troops was awful. Nobody understood what we were doing there—and we were still in Miami. While waiting, and wondering if I was going to be shipped to Korea, I was made the Air Wing's public information officer because of my media background. My job was to keep a lot of bored and bitter people happy. This was a hard job. I organized dances, parties, and concerts. I had my own radio show. I also started a theatrical group and we toured with a play called *Kiss and Tell* that I had produced, directed, and cast. I even started a talent show on Miami television, sort of a military version of *Star Search*. I picked the talent from the base: the singing mess sergeant, the dancing clerical corporal, the bad ventriloquist. I managed a basketball team that won a league championship. I did everything I could think of to keep these people occupied and entertained. But the waiting was devastating, and worse, none of us had the slightest idea what we were waiting for.

After several months I finally got my orders to Korea, by way of the El Toro Marine Air Station in California. This was the first time in my adult life I'd been to southern California, and I wanted to see Hollywood. A friend of a friend was the assistant musical director at 20th Century Fox and he invited me onto the lot. We spent a brief time together and then he asked, calmly, as I remember it—much the same way he might have asked if I wanted a cool drink— "Captain McMahon, would you like to meet Marilyn Monroe?"

Calmly, as I remember it—as casually as I might have acted if he had asked me if I would like to be king of England—I said, "Yeah. That'd be great." Meet Marilyn Monroe? Not a difficult question. I probably could even have answered that one in German. I mean, that's like asking someone if they would like to take their next breath.

Marilyn Monroe was shooting *How to Marry a Millionaire*. When she finished her scene, they brought me to her trailer. They explained to her that I was a TV star from Philadelphia who had been recalled and was on his way to Korea. Her face lit up. As soon as she finished the picture, she told me, she was going to go to Korea to entertain the troops. And then she invited me inside her trailer.

It was just the two of us in her trailer, just Marilyn Monroe and Ed McMahon. We spent a half hour together. Marilyn Monroe in person was as beautiful as she was in the fantasies of every American male. She was dressed casually in a pair of slacks and a loose blouse, but she was radiant. She was also sweet. I don't remember what we spoke about, but as I prepared to leave, she said, "It's so nice to meet you. Now I'll know somebody when I get to Korea. How can I find you when I get there?"

The Marine Corps would know where I was stationed, I replied, then said, "I've got to ask you a favor. If I could have a picture of you I could show the guys in the squadron, I'd be the hero of heroes. They'd go wacko!" Actually, looking back, "wacko" was probably a poor word choice.

"I've got a better idea," she said. "Why don't we take a picture? Let me just fix my hair and I'll be right out."

I waited outside for her. When she finally came out, she was dressed in a gorgeous fur coat. She kind of snuggled in next to me and, as the photographer got ready to take our picture, whispered to me, "You know, Ed, I don't have anything on under this."

So that's why I'm smiling so broadly in that photograph.

A few days later I met Montgomery Clift. Eventually I would meet just about every major celebrity in America, and I'd become close friends with several of them. But at this time the most famous people I had ever met were the host of a local dance show named Dick Clark and a local Philadelphia newscaster named Jack Whittaker. Nice guys, but hardly international movie stars. Marilyn Monroe and Montgomery Clift were major movie stars. I met Montgomery Clift in the Cine Grill of the Hollywood Roosevelt Hotel my last night in the States. I was in uniform and he kept sending me drinks, so naturally I kept sending him drinks. Then he sent me more drinks and I . . . well, eventually we started drinking together and I can't remember a single thing we talked about. Maybe drinking, which would be the reason I can't remember what we talked about.

That was some first week in Hollywood. I can't imagine what Alyce thought about all of this. Supposedly I was leaving for Korea to fight Communism, but then I called and told her that I'd just spent a half hour alone in a trailer with Marilyn Monroe. Now, if she found that difficult to believe, a day later I called to tell her I'd spent much of the previous night drinking with Montgomery Clift. I'm sure she must have wondered what exactly I was drinking.

I arrived in Korea in February 1953. Finally, I was going to do what I had been trained to do ten years earlier: fly in combat. But when I got there I was assigned to a new airplane. The hottest planes in Korea were the brand-new Sabre jets. I hadn't piloted any type of aircraft in eight years and I wasn't qualified to fly jets, so they put me in a small plane, a very small plane, a very small plane with fabric wings, a Cessna. Think of the kind of safe, slow plane people fly out of local airports on Saturday afternoons. That was the Cessna. Now think of that same airplane flying low over North Korean lines with absolutely no armament. That was me piloting the Cessna in Korea.

I would be piloting artillery spotters. We were stationed at a makeshift base about two miles behind our front lines. It was like *M*A*S*H*, but without the great writers. Korea was cold and wet and very dangerous. The Cessna was not much more elaborate than a kite with wings. We often flew through enemy fire, everything from antiaircraft fire to shots from small arms. Sometimes we got bounced around pretty good by the flak. At those times I just couldn't help but think how crazy this whole thing was: only months earlier I'd been hosting television programs in one of the great cities of the world; now I was living in a tent with a mud floor, and complete strangers were trying to kill me. Critics of my work in Philadelphia were tough, but at least they weren't armed.

Avoiding enemy fire required skill, luck, and intuition. Skill meant never repeating a flight pattern. By continually changing altitude and direction, we prevented the North Koreans from getting a bead on us with their radar. They never knew how high we would be flying or when we would turn. The worst thing a pilot could do was get complacent and forget to take evasive maneuvers. Luck was . . . just luck. Intuition—that was interesting. I would be flying a particular pattern and suddenly I'd get a feeling that would cause me to alter my course. There was no reason for the feeling, but I always respected it. We always flew with an artillery spotter, and these men liked to follow a certain pattern because it made their job easier. So we were torn between helping these guys do their job and being cautious. We never knew when we would be fired on. One lovely afternoon, I was flying a relatively straight pattern and suddenly, I'll never know why, I made a sharp turn to my right. "What the . . . ," my observer started complaining. A split second later—*poomp, poomp, poomp, poomp, poomp*—five bursts of flak exploded directly in our former flight path. If I hadn't turned, I would've flown right into them. There's no doubt in my mind that we would have been shot down.

We would fly for six weeks, then have a six-day leave in Japan. Six weeks of danger, six days of pleasure. Near the end of this nonwar, my close friend Chuck Marino, the pilot with whom I flew in rotation, and I took a leave together. We spent six wonderful days in Tokyo, then returned to base.

Our first day back I flew an ordinary two-hour hop over the front lines, then he relieved me. Normally, the transfer of this responsibility was conducted in strict military fashion: the relief pilot would salute and report, "Captain McMahon, you are relieved. I'm up on station now." But a popular song of that time asked the question "What did I do to make you mad at me this time, baby?" to which there was some sort of response, "Well, baby . . ." So instead of the official "You are relieved . . . ," he would salute and ask me, "Captain McMahon, what did I say to make you mad at me this time, baby?" and I would respond with the appropriate lyric.

Two hours later I returned to the station to relieve him. He never came back. He had been shot down. We spotted the wreckage of his plane in no-man's-land, but there was no sign of life. For a time there was some hope he had survived. There were reports that one person had parachuted out of the plane and been captured. That turned out to be his observer.

It didn't seem possible. This was my best friend in Korea. We'd just spent six days together in Japan raising hell. One mistake, one bit of bad luck, and he was dead. Just like that. It didn't take very long for the initial shock to disappear, to be replaced by the terrifying, selfish knowledge that it could have just as easily been me. With his death I lost all my bravado; I lost my belief that it couldn't happen to me. The next few days I flew with white-knuckled concentration. But gradually the routine of daily life in the middle of a war took over, the parties continued, and we fell back into our old habits as we did our jobs.

Unlike in World War II, during which we knew that the entire country was mobilized for the war, the feeling in Korea was that life back home was moving forward without us. In Philadelphia, three people had taken over my programs, and within months all the shows were off the air. In our situation the only way to maintain our sanity was to create our own unique world. Which is why, soon after I arrived in Korea, I decided to build the most beautiful bar ever seen in that war.

When I arrived in Tungaree, as this area was called, the so-called officers' club was in a filthy old hospital tent with dirt floors. It was lit by a single two-hundred-watt bulb, which was the best thing about it, because it made it impossible to see how awful this place really was. I sat there one night, looked around, and decided, "I'm gonna build a great club right here." If I built it, I knew, boy, would they come. Talk about a captive audience.

Everybody thought I was crazy, so I fit right in. With six hundred dollars I had raised from fellow officers, I built a lovely club. The bar was made out of Philippine mahogany; we cut ammunition crates in half, then roped them together to make bar stools, cleaned up the tent, added tables, chairs, and a little jukebox, and covered the floor with the squadron emblem. I paid the Korean kids in gum to collect fresh flowers every day for the tables and installed some subdued lighting. It wasn't the Copacabana, but it was a lot more appealing than a dirty old hospital tent. And if you stayed there long enough, it began to look a little like the Copacabana.

The night we opened for business we had a special treat: nurses! The Red Cross had arranged an exchange of prisoners, and the nurses were there to treat wounded soldiers. As a surprise to my fellow officers, I imported six, count 'em, six lovely nurses for the dedication of this club. And indeed, my fellow officers were dedicated to these nurses. I got the nurses there for the opening. For what happened after that, I bear no responsibility. But I never saw them again.

Because we were so close to the front lines, we were not permitted to sell drinks by the glass, although officers were permitted to keep bottles of liquor. So you could buy a bottle of vodka, but you couldn't order a single martini. I beat that system by cutting out paper chits for individual drinks in the shape of a gin bottle. My customers would buy one of these "bottles," a piece of paper, and trade it for a single drink.

The world-famous "Mactini," famous at least in that little part of the world, was invented in my club. I am a martini drinker; however, I drink martinis only when there is something to celebrate. Often what I am celebrating is the fact that I have a martini to drink. We got our liquor from Tokyo, where it was very cheap. One morning, as a pilot got ready to take off on a whiskey run, I told him to bring back some Noilly Prat vermouth. He returned with six cases. Six cases is enough vermouth to make, I estimate, one hundred thousand martinis. And we made a beautiful martini: we poured vermouth into a shaker filled with ice, then emptied the shaker, and used only the vermouth that clung to the ice to make a martini. Or Mactini, as it became known. We sold them for fifteen cents.

By any name, a martini is a very strong drink. As the great Dorothy Parker once wrote, "I like to have a martini, Two at the very most. After three I'm under the table, After four I'm under my host!" I held the squadron record for Mactinis. Ten. After that I rested on my laurels. Actually, I gently went to sleep on my laurels.

My officers' club was so successful that the NCOs, the noncommissioned officers, asked me to build one for them. After that was completed I built a beer hall for the enlisted men. As mess officer I instituted a system in which soldiers could order breakfast prepared the way they wanted it, instead of having to take whatever the cook piled up. Now, that might not sound like a very important contribution to the war effort, but anyone who has ever had to look at a mountain of cold fried eggs at six o'clock on a freezing cold morning in Korea will appreciate the magnitude of that particular change.

Bob Hope never showed up. Marilyn Monroe came to Korea, but never called. We didn't exactly get the top-name entertainers. We got . . . an accordion player. A famous accordion player who had been a conscientious objector during World War II was trying to make amends by touring the frontline camps in Korea. I was asked to serve as master of ceremonies for the evening. After the accordion player had concluded his concert, somebody suggested, "A lot of people aren't aware of this, but Captain McMahon sings the blues. Let's get him to sing for us."

I don't think anybody wanted to hear me sing the blues. But this was a great opportunity for me; this was my chance to fulfill the dream of every entertainer who has ever set foot on a stage. I was following the accordion player!

It didn't really matter how good or bad I was; I was following the accordion player.

Let me brag a little bit. I can sing the ad-lib blues. I can get up on a stage with a band that knows how to play the blues and make up lyrics that make sense and rhyme. I have no idea where this talent comes from, but I've always been able to do it. I discovered I had this ability as a teenager in Boston. When I would take a date out to the Totem Pole, a dance club, I would make up my own lyrics to whatever music the big band was playing. My girl and I would be dancing close, the band would be playing, and I'd sing my song softly just to her. I remember one song in particular. So why don't you just settle back and let me do it for you? It goes a little something like this:

> *Come on up to my house, baby,*
> *I'll show you my purple room;*
> *That's right, come up to my house,*
> *I'll show you my purple room.*
> *Be careful not to rub against the walls,*
> *They've been painted with perfume.*

Maybe it isn't Doc Severinsen and the NBC Orchestra, but as an ad-lib lyric in the Totem Pole it was very effective.

The song I created that night in Korea was not quite as romantic. At the time, there was a type of infection being spread mostly between American soldiers and Korean women that was called a "nonspecific infection." It was spread by close contact, very close contact. So I titled this song "The Nonspecific Blues."

If you're just now coming over, I've got info for you, dad.
Take the saki and the hot bath, but please avoid the pad.
They'll serve you steak and saki, and wicky-wacky woo,
When she threw that hot bath at me, what else could I do?
I've got the nonspecific blues, those mean old, nonspecific blues.
I was greeted at the doorway by a girl named Lotus Face,
She wore a loose kimono, this must be the place . . .
Well, I flew my hundred missions, I got my DFC,
I'm s'posed to go home Thursday, my wife's expecting me.
She'll be most unhappy when she hears my tour ain't ending,
But since I got that other discharge, lover boy's extending.
I've got the nonspecific blues, oh yeah, those mean old,
  nonspecific blues.

Thank you, thank you very much. Now let's hear the accordion player squeeze a few bars in *his* book!

After I'd flown sixty-three missions, I took R and R in Japan. While in Tokyo, I met the major who was running the Armed Forces Radio and TV Network in the Far East. My timing was almost perfect. He had been offered the chance to run the operation from Hawaii if he could find a qualified replacement to take over Tokyo. He offered the job to me.

It was a really plush job. You got to live in a nice apartment in Tokyo instead of a tent, you spent your time with broadcasters, and no one was shooting at you. The major submitted a formal request through channels that I be transferred to Tokyo upon completion of my flight duty, while I went back to Korea to complete my missions. A complete tour of duty consisted of one hundred missions; I had thirty-seven more to fly. I wanted to get finished as quickly as possible so I started volunteering to fly several times a day. One day I flew five missions and spent ten hours over enemy lines. I flew eighty-five missions. I was on the runway getting ready to take off on my eighty-sixth mission when the fighting stopped. The war that wasn't a war ended without an ending. The fighting just stopped. There was no peace treaty, no armistice, but a cease-fire was declared.

I immediately requested a transfer to Japan. During a meeting with my commanding general, he asked me why I hadn't requested this transfer sooner. "If I had," I explained, "you would've thought I was trying to get out of flying my missions."

He paused to consider that. "You're absolutely right, marine," he said, "but I'm still going to turn you down. This thing is ending; you won't be there long enough to make any difference."

I was terribly disappointed. Head of the Far East Network–Tokyo was a big job. It would've really looked impressive on my résumé. Imagine if I had gotten that job; I could have returned to the States and really been successful in TV.

Instead, he put me in charge of a radio station at a large base. I made myself the all-night disc jockey. I did music with commentary, using my stories to introduce the songs I loved. "It was a long trip on that train taking us from Boston to Texarkana," I'd say softly, "and late at night, when most of the men around me were sleeping, I'd keep changing stations on my radio until I heard the soothing tones of Miss Peggy Lee, singing this great song, 'Why Don't You Do Right?' Ladies and gentlemen . . . Miss Peggy Lee."

I worked all night and during the day floated on a raft on the Yellow Sea.

We were all homesick. While we were fighting the war, staying alive occupied most of our attention, but once the cease-fire began, all we wanted to do was get home and get back to our lives. I had an additional concern. Just before I'd left the States, Alyce had gotten pregnant. As her due date approached and I didn't hear anything from the Red Cross, I got more and more anxious. Finally I got special permission to fly to Tokyo to call the hospital. This was only a few years after the end of World War II, so the international telephone system was only a little better than a tin can and an eight-thousand-mile-long string. There was a long waiting list to call the States; I had to sign up and wait my turn. I waited almost a full day, most of it in the bar at the Imperial Hotel. And as I waited I got more and more nervous. Why hadn't I heard? Something must have gone wrong. Was my wife all right? What about the baby? I worked myself into a state of pure anxiety.

Finally, finally, my number was called. It was about two o'clock in the morning in Florida when I got through to the hospital. It was a bad connection and I was screaming into the phone. The switchboard transferred me to the maternity floor. When the night nurse answered the phone, I yelled, "I'm calling about Alyce McMahon. She's there having a baby. I need to find out . . ."

"I'm sorry," the nurse said, "she's sleeping now. They're both sleeping now." And before I could explain that I was calling from Japan, that I'd been trying to get through for a day, she hung up. No good-bye, no explanation; she just hung up. I had to go back to the rear of the line and work my way back up to the phone. Another day later I learned that Alyce was fine and that our daughter Linda had been born.

I flew eighty-five missions, but it was with my pen that I became a hero in Korea. I was scheduled to be discharged in December, but I wrote a letter to the commandant requesting early release, explaining that the new TV season began in September and that in order to get a job I had to be home by then. Otherwise I might have to wait a whole year. My request was rejected right up the entire chain of command. It was rejected in Korea, rejected in Tokyo, rejected in Hawaii, rejected at Treasure Island in San Francisco, but amazingly, when it got to Washington, it was approved. I received a letter from the Commandant, United States Marine Corps, ordering "that this officer must be in the continental limits of the United States no later than September 10, 1953 . . ."

When other marines heard that I had been successful, they asked me to write similar letters for them. I wrote a letter for Jerry Coleman, the New York Yankees infielder, enabling him to get back to New York in time for the World Series. I wrote letters for businessmen explaining that they had to be home to prepare for the Christmas season, for advertising executives who needed to pitch new accounts, even for lawyers asking to be home in time for the holiday lawsuits.

My career in the marines did not end when I returned home. Although I never flew again as a marine pilot, I stayed active in the Marine Corps Reserve. I completed twenty-three years in the marines and retired as a full colonel. My pride in the Marine Corps has never diminished. The corps taught me to be on time, to have everything I need with me wherever I go, and to leave each place I go as it was when I got there. I've learned that in life, as in the marines, the job is to finish what you start and if you get lucky, as I have, to give something back. I've been asked often how I felt about my career in the Marine Corps. And my answer is that it just pleased the hell out of me.

Including all ten Mactinis.

3

One night, after I'd spent a long day taping a series of commercials for independent banks, making a guest appearance on a quiz show, working out my schedule for our next season with the producers of *Star Search*, finalizing plans to cohost the Thanksgiving Day parade, doing an interview with a reporter about the Muscular Dystrophy telethon, looking at clips for the *Bloopers and Practical Jokes* show Dick Clark and I would be taping later that week, meeting with NBC executives about a Christmas special they wanted me to host, and finally, appearing with Mr. Carson for about the 3,965th time on *The Tonight Show*, I was having dinner with my close friends Don and Barbara Rickles. "You know, Ed," Rickles said philosophically, "you just have to find a way to get on TV more often. If this goes on too much longer, people are going to forget what you look like."

Sometimes I think that the only shows on television that I haven't done are *Sermonette* and *America's Most Wanted*.

In preparation for my career in professional broadcasting, I enrolled in a broadcasting club the summer after graduating from Lowell High. Essentially, this was a thirteen-week course held at Boston's Emerson College in which we learned basic broadcasting techniques. My class met once a week, on Thursday night. The instructor was a former Shakespearean actor who emphasized clear and precise speech and taught us how to modulate our voices so that even the patrons in the back row could understand every word. I began the course by taping my first commercial, a spot for a mythical product called Praise linoleum. In the deepest, most eloquent tones I could muster, I promised, "You'll like the way Praise displays linoleum." Thirteen weeks later I did the commercial again, this time incorporating everything I'd learned. There was no doubt I had improved; I was finally able to sound just as William Shakespeare would have if he had been selling linoleum.

During the daytime that summer I worked on a construction crew building culverts and digging ditches at Ft. Devens. The men on my crew were tough, hardworking middle-European immigrants who enunciated mostly one word, the F-word. The F-word was used in every possible context: it was used as a noun, verb, adverb, adjective, and pronoun; it was used as a preposition and conjunction; it was used in all tenses; it was used to modify itself. At times it would be used five times in the same sentence. As far as I was concerned, using the F-word was proof that I was a man. So all week long I'd use it like an "F-word" sailor, then on Thursday night I'd get out of my filthy clothes, put on a suit and tie, and attend my class. I'd stand in front of the microphone and explain, "Now I would like to show you something rather impressive . . ."

At work, I'd try to practice what I'd learned in class. Instead of saying, "Please tell that 'F-word' guy to get that 'F-word' truck over here," I'd say, "Is it possible that we might have that truck here by three o'clock?" The guys on my crew loved it; they loved to hear me speak good. Whenever a laborer from another crew came by, they'd tell him,

"You gotta hear this 'F-word' guy talk." Then they'd turn to me and tell me, "Do some of that talk."

To which I would respond, "And what is it that you wish me to say?"

"Yeah, that's it. Man, you sure speak 'F-word' pretty."

"That is very kind of you." That summer I stopped cursing. I don't think my kids have ever heard me use foul language. I make one exception, when that word is absolutely necessary in the punch line of a great F-word joke.

With my years of experience in Katie's parlor and my certificate of attendance from the broadcasting club, I was ready to break into big-time radio. Many of the jobs left vacant when men went into the service at the beginning of World War II could be filled by women, but radio sponsors wanted men, whose voices dripped with authority, reading their commercials. A local station, WLLH, held open auditions for announcers in the high school auditorium. Hundreds of males showed up, but I didn't know why they bothered. I knew this job was mine. I had it nailed. I'd been preparing for it my whole life. In my mind I was already a professional.

When I was hosting *Star Search*, this is the story I told those performers who did not win their competition. I went to the audition and, to my shock, I finished second. The station hired a kid named Ray Goulding. I'd like to describe how I felt when I heard the results of the audition, but as I've explained, I had stopped using that language.

As I later discovered, the only reason that Ray Goulding won the job was that he was better than I. In fact, he was so good that he soon got a better job in Boston, where he met Bob Elliott and they formed the legendary comedy team Bob and Ray. When Ray Goulding left WLLH, the station manager remembered that I had finished second and offered me the job. So as I told the competitors on *Star Search*, my whole career is proof that in show business you don't always have to come in first.

At WLLH, the Synchronized Voice of the Merrimack Valley, I was on the air each night for six hours. Just like in my parlor, I introduced records, read the news, sports, and weather, and did interviews, features, and all the commercials. Although it was basically a one-man show, I figured out how to do live remotes from the Hofbrau House, a dance club with a full orchestra eleven miles away in Lawrence. After a nice and easy introduction, I put a sixteen-inch acetate record on the turntable, which would fill about twenty-five minutes of airtime, then got in my car and raced to the Hofbrau House. When the record ended, I'd go on the air to introduce the orchestra: "While Dick Stabile is off in the service of his nation, lovely Grace Barrie takes baton in hand and leads the orchestra in that age-old question, 'Who?'" As the band played a set, I'd get back in my car and race back to Lowell in time to resume programming when they finished.

I was eighteen years old. All it had taken to enable me to break into radio was the greatest war in the history of mankind. Being on the radio was every bit as exciting as I had always imagined it would be. I loved every minute I was on the air. I loved the challenge, the spontaneity, the improvisation, every bit of it. I think I could have—I *know* I could have—very happily spent the rest of my life talking to a small part of the world from a glassed-in studio, but then they went and invented television. I was present at the birth of commercial television. I've spent my lifetime working inside that box, fifty years, half a century. In that time I've hosted or appeared on just about every type of program, and if I haven't actually been on the air more than anyone else, I'm certainly among the top three or four. But after all that, in my heart I still consider myself a radio man.

Everyone in radio was aware that television was coming. One of the most popular attractions at the 1939 World's Fair had been a demonstration of television. But no one really knew what to do about it. No one could even guess what type of programming would be successful, or even whether people would accept it in their homes as they had radio. Some journalists predicted it would be little more than an interesting gimmick. Most often television was described as radio with pictures.

But almost instantly people realized it was much more than that. It allowed people for the first time to bring every entertainment medium that ever existed into their own home. People who had never seen a major league baseball game could watch the World Series. People who hated opera could see as much of it as they desired. When television first became available, the screens were small and often disguised as more traditional pieces of furniture; almost all programming was produced locally and broadcast in black-and-white; and the biggest attraction was Milton Berle, a comedian who, among other things, ran around dressed as a woman.

While I was a student at Catholic University I'm not sure I recognized immediately that television would eventually change the world, but one important thing about television immediately became apparent to me: it was going to be a lot easier for me to get a job in television than in radio.

I got my first job in television the old-fashioned way: my father had a friend in the business. Years earlier my father had been a partner in an Atlantic City boardwalk booth with a wonderful man named John McClay. They used to stage phony arguments over the value of a prize to convince winners that the broken or scratched lamp they'd picked was actually the most expensive prize. John McClay Jr. had been on radio station WCAU in Philadelphia, but when that station decided to make the big move into TV, he had become their program manager. In April of my senior year in college I went to see him to apply for a job, any job, at the station. "When you graduate," he told me, "come on up and we'll find something for you to do around here." That's the way television worked in 1949.

Although I was very excited, I told John that the only way I could afford to take a job in television was to first spend the summer selling slicers on the boardwalk. The real money was in gadgets, not television. When the sun shined I knew I could earn as much as a thousand dollars a week, and if I was careful and saved enough, I could be on television. We agreed I'd start my TV career in the fall.

While I was in Philadelphia I responded to an ad for a place to live. I rode the trolley out to a new development called Drexelbrook and put down a twenty-five-dollar deposit on a beautiful two-bedroom apartment that would be ready to be occupied in September. That was the last twenty-five dollars I had to my name, but as it turned out, that was one of the best investments of my life.

During the summer of 1949 I earned enough money on the boardwalk in Atlantic City to become a television star. In late August John McClay Jr. told me that WCAU was going to try a daring experiment: they were going to broadcast a program during the day and he offered me a job as cohost. Now, you have to understand, no one had ever seen me on TV, no one knew if I had any talent at all, but that didn't matter. My talent was that I was available and I could afford to work for seventy-five dollars a week. That was enough. Besides, putting on a TV program during the day was considered pretty revolutionary; while people were at work or doing something at home they could have the radio on in the background, but it was very questionable that they had time to stop whatever they were doing during the day to watch television. Besides, at that time there were fewer than two million television sets in the entire country; probably a majority of them were in bars, and the bars were mostly empty during the day.

John McClay Jr. told me that the format of the show was

anything that would fill three hours and cost nothing to produce. So the "something to do around here" that he had promised to find for me turned out to be my own show. The station actually had to pay me less to be on the air than to work behind the scenes. That's how fast people became television personalities in those days.

My first show, *The Take Ten Show*, named after the channel number, went on the air at noon, September 12, 1949. Rather than using a catchy stage name, like most other performers, I did something far more daring—I didn't use any name at all. I never identified myself on the air. I'm not really sure why I did that, perhaps to protect my family if I was terrible, but it worked. Scattered viewers began wondering who the guy on that show in the afternoon was.

My cohost was a veteran nightclub and vaudeville comedian named Bob Russell, and we did anything we could think of to fill three hours daily. We did contests, interviews with anybody willing to come on the air—including the tree surgeon who sawed off the branch on which I was sitting during the interview, which ended with my falling onto an unseen mattress—we had local models doing fashion shows; I remember we had a young bricklayer who wanted to be in show business named Al Martino on the show—we introduced him as "the Singing Bricklayer" and we had him sing several songs while constructing a brick wall. We used our imagination and creativity to fill the time. The whole world was open to us, as long as it didn't cost anything. In retrospect, I think it is fair to say that we were the best show on the air during that time period. We were also the only one.

My style in those days was to not have any style, which was a forerunner for later years, when my talent was to make it appear as if I had no talent. Like most television performers in the early days, even though I was the cohost and producer of my own show, I didn't own a TV set. I didn't make enough money doing television to buy a television set. But our neighbor across the street, the bandleader at the Warwick Hotel, did have a TV set. Pennsylvania's blue laws prohibited the hotel from serving liquor Sunday nights, so that was his one night off and he would take his wife out for dinner. I volunteered to baby-sit his kids so I could watch his TV. I don't really remember, but I think the first TV show I ever saw was Ed Sullivan's *Toast of the Town*. I watched Bert Parks hosting the quiz show *Break the Bank*. But the person who most impressed me was Dave Garroway. Garroway wore a bow tie and big glasses and had the most casual style, but most of all he was incredibly polite. I liked that about him, and I decided to pattern myself after him. So I spoke softly and I was very polite and very nice to all my guests. I wanted viewers to feel comfortable having me in their homes.

I had no idea how I looked on television. I wouldn't see myself on television for years because every program I did was live and it was much too expensive to make the rudimentary film known as a kinescope. If Alyce wanted to watch my show, she would have to go into the local drinking establishment and convince the barkeep to turn it on. If a Phillies baseball game was being broadcast, she didn't have a prayer. Often she would bring Claudia, who was almost four, into the place with her and the two of them would sit at the bar watching the show. Claudia had no concept of what television was; to her it was real life, just a lot smaller. Once, for example, I did a duet with a girl singer. We sang "Walking My Baby Back Home," and as we finished the number, we strolled off the set arm in arm. Well, Claudia just started crying hysterically; she thought I'd left her mother for another woman and she would never see me again.

The show was everything the station had hoped it would be, three hours long and cheap. I thought I was doing okay, but after we had been working together for about three weeks, my cohost decided we had to have a serious conversation. We weren't friends; we had just been teamed by the station. We went out into the parking lot and sat down on a barrier. "Ed," he began, "believe me, I'm telling you this as a friend. I'm telling you this to help you. I don't think you're right for TV, I think you should stay in radio . . ." I didn't have the right personality for television, he explained, I didn't seem to have any charisma. I listened to him because he was a TV veteran, he'd been in the business hours longer than I had. And who knows what would have happened if I hadn't been too busy doing the television show to realize I shouldn't be on television.

After several weeks the station gave me my own show. My show, now called *Take Ten,* went on at 5:30 in the afternoon; unfortunately, I was on opposite the most popular show on television, the classic puppet show hosted by "Buffalo" Bob Smith, *Howdy Doody.* The most incredible thing about my show was that there were no strings attached. The station really let me do just about anything I could figure out how to do. These were the pioneering days of television, when anything was possible. We were inventing it as we went along. There was a tremendous sense of creative freedom; viewers didn't seem to care what was on TV, as long as the TV was on. The real star of television was the television set. People would watch whatever was on, and when the broadcast day concluded—the "11 o'clock news" went on at nine o'clock—and the test pattern was being shown, they were so fascinated they would watch the test pattern. I didn't know how good I really was, but I knew for sure I was more entertaining than a test pattern.

This was the ultimate on-the-job training experience. I learned what worked on television by doing it on television. I'd have singers and dancers, Girl Scouts selling cookies on roller skates, fire eaters; I'd do cooking segments and interview authors about their books; we had animals ranging from dogs who balanced plates to baby elephants. One of the first major acts I had on the show was the Clooney Sisters, who agreed to appear on my show to promote their upcoming concert. I interviewed them and then they sang a few songs. Getting the Clooney Sisters was a big coup for me. Only after they appeared did I realize, wait a second, they weren't doing me a favor; they actually wanted to be on television! I just hadn't realized how important a television appearance could be to someone trying to sell or promote something. I mean, it wasn't as important as radio, but it certainly helped. Until that time I didn't even know what a public relations person did, and I didn't know how important they could be to me. Eventually PR people began offering me their clients as guests on my show—I didn't even have to plead with them.

It was on *Take Ten* that I did my first commercials. I think that the first television commercial I ever did was for a pants presser. The gimmick was that you would insert this device inside your pants and it would stretch your pants enough so that while they were hanging in the closet all the wrinkles would come out. To figure out how this thing worked I had to go downtown to Wanamaker's department store to watch the salesman demonstrate "this amazing new product that actually stretches the wrinkles out of your pants while you are sleeping! Forget about steam irons . . ."

Certainly among the most memorable segments on *The Tonight Show* were the things Johnny did with animals and reptiles and insects. For me, that started in Philadelphia. A small circus was in town and we were going to have a performing bear on the show. Before the show, I was rehearsing a commercial for Dole pineapple juice when the bear's trainer mentioned to me, "Oh, he'll probably want some of that."

I stopped. All the instincts that had been honed in the

carnival suddenly sharpened. I asked, "You think the bear'll drink this?"

"Oh sure, he loves it," the trainer said, then added, "He can even hold the glass."

There *was* a God. "You're kidding me!" This was just too good to be true. This cute bear drank the sponsor's product. If I had had this bear working with me on the boardwalk, I would've been a millionaire. Viewers would enjoy it and the sponsor would love it, and if the sponsor loved it, the station manager would love it and I would love it. We rehearsed the spot with the bear, and sure enough, he actually drank the pineapple juice from a glass. It was unbelievable.

I rewrote the commercial to feature the bear. "Our wonderful bear, Rosco, would just love some of that delicious pineapple juice," I said when we were on the air, "wouldn't you, Rosco?" I poured a glass of juice and he picked it up with his paws and drank it. "See, even bears know . . ." And then Rosco let out the loudest, deepest growl I had ever heard. Rosco wanted more juice. I mean, he *really* wanted more juice. I leaped out of the way. The bear growled again, louder. I held up the juice can and tried to look sincerely into the camera, as I had been taught, and said, "I guess you'll find that one glass isn't enough . . ."

Today almost all programming is produced by independent production companies, but in the early days of television the local stations produced most of their own programming. The performers worked directly for the station, and often appeared on several different shows. So after *Take Ten* proved to be a success, WCAU began assigning me to some of its other shows. Six months after my first appearance on television I was starring on four different shows, which ran twelve times a week; I was actually on the air seven hours and forty-five minutes a week. Another six months later I was doing thirteen different shows a week, had been honored as Philadelphia's Mr. Television, and the local chapter—actually the only chapter—of the Ed McMahon Fan Club had almost one hundred active members. It was just about impossible to watch television in Philadelphia for more than a few minutes and not see me.

It's nice to know that some things never change.

I did just about every type of show on the station. Several nights a week I hosted the *Million Dollar Movie,* and just like Johnny Carson's *Teatime Movie* host Art Fern, I would do six minutes of commercials after five minutes of an old movie. For forty-five minutes every morning of the workweek I hosted the breakfast show, *Strictly for the Girls.* At noon each day I played the role of Aunt Molly's mischievous nephew on the homemaker's program *Home Highlights,* a role that consisted of my sampling Aunt Molly's cooking and asking silly questions to our guests. Wednesday nights I served as emcee for a quiz show with musical entertainment called *Cold Cash,* during which I stood in front of a freezer filled with Birds Eye frozen foods and the station's cash; viewers would phone in to win that cash by answering questions. Saturday mornings I was the chief clown on the station's most popular program, a circus show called *The Big Top.* And Sunday nights I hosted a series about submarine warfare called *The Silent Service.*

Strictly for the Girls was the first breakfast show in television history. Breakfast chat shows had been very popular on radio, but nobody knew if viewers would be interested or have time to watch TV in the morning. I produced, wrote, and starred in the show, which really served as a prototype for the local morning shows produced in just about every major city. We had a little combo, a set divided into several different areas in which I would do interviews or commercials or our guests would perform, and several regularly appearing members of WCAU's morning family. At that time one of the most elegant shows on TV was a talk show broadcast from New York's famed Stork Club. That show opened with a shot of champagne being poured into a glass and an engraved place card inviting the viewer into the club. *Strictly for the Girls* opened with a similar shot, except that we showed steaming hot coffee being poured into two big mugs bearing the name of our sponsor, Horn & Hardart cafeterias, and a handwritten card welcoming viewers to the show. And then I would sing a song with our band.

That's correct, I would sing. And I could do it without building a brick wall! I was sort of a saloon singer; the more time you spent in the saloon, the better I got. I might not have had the most beautiful voice in the world, but I could carry a tune across a stage. In fact, years later I would star in several musicals in summer stock. When I played Buffalo Bill in *Annie Get Your Gun,* I got to sing the show business anthem "There's No Business Like Show Business." My breakfast show audience seemed to like my singing, although admittedly people don't require music in the morning to be as good as music later in the day.

At first we lured an audience into the studio with free coffee, donuts, and prizes, but the show very quickly became hot and we actually had people fighting for tickets. And the prizes. My favorite segment on the show was called "The Big Three," in which I would sit around a table and interview three preschool-age children. For example, I would ask these kids, "When should a girl marry?" Their answers might include, "If she ever kisses a boy," "Not until she's six years old," and "I hate girls and I'm never gonna get married."

Once I asked a little boy, "Do your mommy and daddy take care of you?"

"Well," he replied, "it's mostly my mommy."

"Well, does your daddy help?"

"Sometimes," he admitted, "but my mommy's mad at him because he pees in the bathtub."

The Big Top was my first network show. It was created by Charlie Vanda, who had been one of the creative giants of radio and had been hired to make WCAU a major television station. Originally Charlie hired me to be the ringmaster, which was just perfect for me. Having spent several summers touring with carnivals and circuses, I knew how to be a ringmaster. I even went out and bought a red coat, top hat, and whip. But a few weeks before we were scheduled to go on the air, Charlie took me out for dinner and broke the bad news to me: the CBS network had a commitment to give Jack Sterling, who was very hot on radio, a television show. The network wanted him to be the ringmaster. Charlie knew how disappointed I was, and said something like, "Ed, I've seen a lot of your work. Have you ever thought about being a clown?"

So I became a sad clown. That's a character description, not a comment on my disappointment. Was I really disappointed? Absolutely. I think everyone wants to be the ringmaster, the person who cracks the whip, rather than one of the clowns. I'd been a leader my entire life. In college I had been freshman class president; I ran my own bingo operation before I was eighteen; I was the youngest salesman on the boardwalk; during military training I was the platoon leader; and I'd become a marine officer and a hotshot fighter pilot. I wasn't used to being second. But it was a good job and it gave me an opportunity to be on network television. So I became a clown, and I probably vowed to myself that I would never take the number-two spot again.

Little did I know.

Clowns are made up, not born. My character consisted of a bald wig with a fringe of red hair, big round white eyes and a white mouth, a painted-on brown beard, thick black eyebrows, heavy glasses, and, most important, a big bright-red nose that blinked on and off and read HELLO! HELLO! I wore an emerald green opera cape with scarlet lapels, the traditional oversize trousers held up by huge suspenders, and different colored shoes on each foot.

A lot of people mistook me for Clarabell, the clown on *The Howdy Doody Show,* who "spoke" by honking a horn. Now, I had a nose that lit up and blinked HELLO! HELLO! and I was wearing a green opera cape. How easy could it have been to mistake me for someone else?

The show opened with a shot of my bald head, on which was printed THE BIG TOP. As I raised my head, I turned on my nose. Originally the nose was also going to carry the CBS logo, but perhaps a blinking nose did not precisely fit the image William Paley was trying to create for his TV network.

I believe it was William Shakespeare who noted that there were only thirty different clown bits in the world, but somehow I had to come up with fifty-two three-minute gags a year. I was the leader of the clown troupe Ed McMahon and His Merry Band of Clowns. I wrote and produced all the clown bits. If we had to cut the bit to fit the time slot, I directed it as we did it. Like all the classic clown acts, we did only sight gags, so our bits would not have worked as well on radio. My partner in mime was a wonderfully talented actor named Chris Keegan and, basically, he was the pratfall guy. I was the victor; he was the victim. If a rock fell in the pool right in front of me, the water splashed on him twenty feet away; if he moved over and stood next to me and dropped another rock in the pool, it would still splash all over him.

If I was holding a ladder and turned around, he got hit in the head with it. If we were both eating a banana, the gorilla ate his banana. If I fell off the high wire, I fell on him. Once we did an elaborate gag about finding the surprise in a box of cereal. It was supposed to end with Chris's finding a pony in the box. The first box supposedly contained cold cereal; when he opened it up, it was filled with steaming dry ice. The second box supposedly contained hot cereal; when he opened it up, it was on fire. The third box contained a ton of cornflakes, as well as another clown sitting on a pony; when he opened it up, the cornflakes fell on him and the pony ran over him. In rehearsal it worked perfectly. But when we did it on the air, the flames in the hot cereal caused the cornflake dust to ignite. While we were running around stamping out the fire, the pony panicked. It ran out of the box and knocked over both me and Chris. I fell and my nose started blinking on and off. But somehow Chris saved the gag—he managed to get buried by the cornflakes.

I wore my nose proudly for eight years on *The Big Top*. I rarely had fewer than four shows on the air in Philadelphia. In addition to the shows, I was also doing commercials for local car dealerships and banks and supermarkets, so I got to be pretty well known in the city. I was the big cheese in Philadelphia, although in Philly it is probably more appropriate to call me the big cheesesteak. For the first time in my life I was a little bit of a celebrity. Well, there are no classes in how to be a celebrity. You just do the best you can, try to be nice to everyone, and hope that you don't get run over by the pony in the cereal box.

I've always been so pleased that people enjoy my work enough to want my photograph or signature that I always find the time to pose for a picture or sign a piece of paper. But one evening in Philadelphia, after I had started doing five minutes of commentary on the eleven o'clock news broadcast, I was having dinner with my close friends Bob and Marti Gillin when a pleasant woman approached our table and explained, "I really enjoy watching you on the air."

"Thank you very much," I said modestly. "That's very kind."

"You went to college with my brother," she continued, "and I was just wondering if you could come over and say hello to some people."

Well, I always try to please people, so I walked with her

over to her table. As she introduced me, she added, "He went to school with my brother at St. Joe's . . ."

I kept smiling. I knew exactly what had happened. The sports reporter on the newscast was a talented kid named Jack Whittaker, who *had* graduated from St. Joseph's University in Philly. And Whittaker looked a lot like me, except for our height, weight, and hair color. I nodded to the group and began doing what I call tap dancing; I moved lightly around the subject without ever getting into specifics. "St. Joe's was a wonderful place to go to school," I agreed.

But all of a sudden she looked at me and drilled me with the question, "Who'd you have for philosophy?"

"Well, you know," I began, fumbling for an answer, "I had a lot of different teachers at that fine school. It was a while ag—"

Sternly, she said, "You never forget your philosophy teacher."

Now everyone at the table was staring at me and I knew I had to respond to this woman. I had to stop dancing. As warmly as I could, I said, "I'm afraid you've made a little mistake. People make it all the time. They think I went to St. Joe's but I didn't. My friend Jack Whittaker went to St. Joe's and . . ."

She said very evenly, "You didn't go to St. Joe's?"

"Oh, believe me, I would've loved to go there. It's a wonderful place. But see, I wanted to go to drama school . . ."

"You don't even know my brother, do you?"

"No, I don't, but if I met him, I'm sure . . ."

With a sneer in her voice, she continued, "I suppose somebody as important as you went to one of those big fancy Ivy League schools like Harvard or Yale. Catholic schools weren't good enough . . ."

I wanted to dive into a hole. "No, no, that's not true at all. I went to Catholic University. I didn't go to St. Joe's, but I really would've loved to have gone there . . ."

As I walked away from that table I heard people muttering words like "liar" and "stinks" and "big shot." This incident upset me; I don't like to see anyone get their feelings hurt, even if I had nothing to do with it. And, in fact, in poor lighting, on a seven-inch screen, I could see how it might be possible to confuse me and Jack Whittaker. But what I still couldn't understand was how people could mix me up with Clarabell.

I don't think anyone anticipated how rapidly television would become an integral part of our lives, make radio seem obsolete, and just about destroy the movie business. Edward R. Murrow accurately described television as "the five-ton pencil." It had the kind of mammoth power to create stars overnight, to shift public opinion, to educate, to inform, and, mostly, to entertain. The people working in television in those early days didn't have time to worry about doing it right; we were much more concerned with just getting it done. With very small budgets, we had to be creative, find ways of using the unique technical opportunities television offered. On the news programs, for example, we had neither the time nor the money to film stories, so what the producers did was put still photographs on easels and pan, or move the camera, from right to left or up and down to give the illusion of motion, or a stagehand would flip through a series of photos as the newscaster read the story.

Everything on the East Coast was done live, not just the breakfast shows but even the most prestigious dramatic programs like *Playhouse 90*. The most popular programs were kinescoped and these grainy films were flown overnight to be shown the next day on the West Coast. Doing live television meant there was no going back: if you made a mistake, you lived with it and did your best to make something out of it, developing the technique to deal with whatever happened. Many performers currently on television never had to learn how to do that. Dick Clark was doing a live special a few years ago and one of his guests, a well-known television actor, flubbed a line. Instead of continuing, he turned to the director—now this was on live TV—and said, "Let's stop and do it again."

Television became sophisticated very fast. The difference in the way things could be done in 1949 and the way they had to be done by 1952 was enormous. In 1949 we were the new kids in town, just looking to put on a show and hoping somebody would watch. Three years later we were a serious business. As soon as it became obvious how profitable television would be, the radio networks just poured money into its development.

I was one of the biggest stars on television in Philadelphia, one of the nation's top five media markets, by the time I was thirty years old. But just when the network decided to transmit my show beyond Philadelphia—CBS was going to broadcast *Strictly for the Girls* throughout the Northeast—I was recalled to serve in Korea.

When I returned I didn't exactly have to start all over again—I still had my blinking nose and mismatched floppy shoes—but every other program of mine was off the air. WCAU ran a big campaign advertising my return: "Guess who's back? Ed McMahon! And look who's got him! WCAU!" But they had almost nothing for me to do. Television had grown substantially during the time I was gone. The normal broadcast schedule now ran the full day, from early morning till late at night. The eleven o'clock news was finally being broadcast at eleven o'clock. The station's programming was built around network sitcoms, westerns, and dramas. Some of the biggest stars of television, like Milton Berle and Howdy Doody, were not as popular as they had been. So WCAU created a late-night show for me titled *Five Minutes More,* which they broadcast during the last five minutes of the eleven o'clock news.

Basically, it was my playtime. I had five minutes to do

absolutely anything I wanted to do. I could do serious or humorous pieces, I could interview guests, I could start a fund-raising campaign, or I could simply do an essay about whatever was on my mind. It was my show and doing it every night was about as much fun as I've ever had on television.

As always, I had a very small budget. About the only thing I could afford was creativity. Once, I remember, Ginger Rogers was in Philadelphia to publicize a new movie. In those days the movie studios were terrified of television and most of the big stars were contractually prohibited from appearing on TV. But I had always been a big, big Ginger Rogers fan and I wanted her on my show. Finally I convinced her husband, Jacques Bergerac, to allow her hand to come on the show. Not Ginger Rogers but Ginger Rogers's gloved hand. When we went on the air, viewers saw me sitting on a stool holding a white gloved hand that protruded from behind the curtain. "This is the hand of Ginger Rogers," I said softly. "Look how delicate it is, how graceful. It is the same kind of grace we've become accustomed to seeing when she dances . . ." Viewers never saw Ginger Rogers, she never said a word, but the entire five minutes was all about her.

Five Minutes More was as much like a daily television column as I could make it. I wrote and produced the entire show myself, but I tried to make it as much as possible like a visual Robert Benchley piece. For example, I opened the show one night with the camera slowly panning a photograph of the famed Philadelphia Mummers' band marching in the annual parade, as the band's music was heard playing in the background. "This is a Mummers' marching band," I said solemnly, "and this year this incredible group of musicians will mark the tenth consecutive year they have marched in the Thanksgiving Day parade . . ."

As I began explaining that the Mummers were a very special charitable organization, my stage manager, a great man named John Heatherton whom I often used on the show, came out wearing headphones and interrupted me. "Sorry to bother you, Ed," he said, "but what do you want me to do with that band that's waiting out in the hall?"

I stared at him for a moment, then gently placed my hand on his shoulder and asked, "Now, John, how long've you been in this business?"

"Almost four years."

Searching for the proper words, I explained, "See, I know what you saw on the monitor made it look as if there was a band in the studio, but actually it was just a photograph and a recording."

"Oh, yeah" he replied, nodding, "I get it. That was just a recording. That was great the way you did that. It sure sounded real to me. So, what do you want me to do with that band out in the hall?"

"John," I sighed, "let me try to explain this to you. There is no band in the hallway. See, in show business you try to create an illusion, you try to create an atmosphere, and if you do it well enough, people will believe. So when I told the viewers that they were looking at the Mummers' band and played a record, the idea was to make people believe the entire Mummers' band was right here in this studio. But they're not here. Look around, do you see them?

"No, I don't . . . ," he said.

"Of course you don't . . ."

". . . 'cause they're out there in the hall."

That was it; I'd had it with him. "Okay, John, have it your way. The entire Mummers' band is here. If you want to believe that, it's fine with me. I hope that makes you happy."

"So then you want me to send them home?"

"Yes, John, please," I agreed. "Why don't you just go out there and tell the band to go home."

96

He turned and yelled offstage. "Okay, go ahead and send them home."

I faced the camera. "I'm sorry for that interruption, ladies and gentlemen, but sometimes in doing this program . . ." and as I continued, the Mummers' band, in full regalia, marched across the stage playing loudly.

That didn't stop me. I just raised my voice above their music and continued to explain about how difficult it was to create an illusion successfully.

Sometimes I didn't know what I was going to do on the show an hour before airtime, but I always managed to come up with something. One night, when I was really desperate, I did a variation of an old vaudeville joke: I interviewed a talking bull. As it turned out, though, this animal was bull-headed. I explained to my audience that just before the show he had had an argument with his owner and had decided to get even with him by not speaking. Naturally, the owner and I were terribly embarrassed, and we finished the show with a sincere apology. Then the owner walked out of the studio.

But just as we were going off the air, the bull shouted at the owner, "If you don't come back right now, I'll never speak to you again."

I was always searching for something new. One night I did a remote interview with a singer outside the studio. As we discussed his career, a faked shoot-out took place right behind us. I never noticed it; I just continued with the interview. People were running, ducking behind cars, firing at each other, and I was asking calmly, "So how did you decide to become a singer?"

Actually, we had a problem with that bit because someone called the police, who arrived in force ready for a fire fight.

I used a lot of photographs. Once, to illustrate an essay about the beauty of a woman in motion, I mounted a sexy photograph of Marilyn Monroe on a piece of paper and jiggled it at the right time. That's where imagination became important—I was hoping people would imagine she was actually moving. I opened a show about handicapped people overcoming their disabilities with a photograph I'd cut out of a magazine of blind pianist George Shearing's hands. "These are the hands of George Shearing," I explained. "He has never seen them."

Alyce, our kids, and I were still living in Drexelbrook. I'd become extremely friendly with the builder and owner of the complex, the great Dan Kelly. It was from Dan Kelly that I learned about generosity and grace. Dan Kelly's joy in life came from sharing his success with others. Dan owned racehorses and on occasion would give me a solid tip. Once, he gave me the proverbial sure thing, and I was so excited about it that I went on the air and shared that tip with my listeners. It is possible I asked them not to tell anybody else. But approximately half the entire population of Philadelphia bet on the horse, which drove down the odds. The horse won, and paid about a quarter.

Once, I organized a campaign to outlaw the lyric to "Muskrat Ramble." I went as far as to propose a law making it illegal to write or perform the words to any Dixieland tune. I also organized a fund-raising campaign to save Admiral Dewey's flagship, which was rotting in the navy yard. My five minutes of whimsy at the conclusion of a serious newscast became very popular. I tried to give people something a little lighter, something that would contrast with the often sad news stories they had just heard, with which to end their day. The whole program, with John Facenda and Jack Whittaker doing the news and my hosting the last five minutes, worked very well and was very successful.

But as much as I enjoyed doing *Five Minutes More,* it wasn't enough to keep me busy. At most it took only a couple of hours a day to write the show and gather whatever props I needed. As everyone in the entertainment industry knows, once you pick up the stuffed elephant, there just isn't too much else to do. So I started commuting to New York City, the center of the television industry, to meet talent agents, make the rounds of the big advertising agencies, and audition for commercials. I didn't really know how to advance my career in television, except to keep doing exactly what I had been doing but to try to do more of it.

Several talent agents encouraged me. They told me they thought I had "it," although they couldn't describe precisely what "it" was. But whatever "it" was—a genial manner, an Irish wit, an amiable personality—apparently I had a lot of "it," and it seemed like only a matter of time before I found the right opportunity to use "it."

Several months after I began my daily train trips into New York, I got my first network job. I was hired to replace the host of *Bride and Groom,* which was canceled almost immediately after I was hired. Like so many television shows of that period, *Bride and Groom* was based on a successful radio show. Although NBC had already canceled it when I was hired, the network had to run it for six weeks until a replacement was ready. People got married on the show, and we gave them all sorts of great gifts; a TV set, a refrigerator, a two-week Caribbean honeymoon. In fact, one couple got married only for the gifts, and the staff joked that their marriage ended before the kinescope aired in Hawaii. My job was to interview the happy couple, their relatives, and guests at the wedding. One of my more probing questions was "How did you meet?"

On radio it was simple to create a fantasy wedding, the peaceful chapel somewhere in a wooded glen, the beautiful bride and handsome groom of a listener's dreams . . . but the harsh reality of television's bright lights destroyed the fantasy. The set was a cheap imitation of a chapel, some of our happy couples were less than truly beautiful, and it was difficult to maintain the ethereal atmosphere when I had to remind our viewers, "We'll be right back with our happy couple after this word from Drano."

Making it just a bit more difficult for me was the producer, who hated the show and continually made bawdy comments into my earpiece as I conducted interviews. "I'm here with the proud groom . . . ," I began.

To which the producer might have added, ". . . who married that horse for her money."

Or, "And we're very pleased to give our newly wedded couple their first gift. A beautiful . . ."

". . . paper bag he can put over her head, 'cause that's the only way he's gonna . . ."

Years later people wondered how I could sit with Mr. Carson and deal so comfortably with some of the surprises with which we were confronted. The answer is, I learned on shows like *Bride and Groom*.

As a favor to Dan Kelly, I used the experience I'd gained in Korea creating clubs to turn his struggling restaurant into the exclusive, very successful Drexelbrook Club. We served good food, we offered good music and good dancing, and most important, because we were a private club we could legally serve liquor on Sundays. Eventually I hired my father to be in charge of the liquor supply. He kept track of what the club had on hand, did the ordering, and supervised the bartenders. It was great for both of us: he felt useful and was able to spend time with his grandchildren, and I knew he was safe.

Drexelbrook was an ideal place to live. There were about twelve hundred apartments, most of them occupied by young successful families. Dan Kelly liked me and when I was recalled by the marines he'd promised to have a place for me when I was discharged. When I got back to Philadelphia, he had saved one of the best apartments in the entire complex for my family. It was a beautiful three-bedroom apartment on the end of one building, open on three sides, with a beautiful view. But this particular apartment turned out to be so important in my life primarily because the guy who lived in the adjoining apartment was Dick Clark.

Dick Clark had begun his career in television as a newscaster in Utica, New York. But when he moved to Philadelphia, TV executives thought he looked too young to be taken seriously, so they offered him a job as a radio disc jockey. His local program, *American Bandstand,* became so popular that ABC decided to televise it nationally. By 1950 Dick Clark was doing seventeen hours of live television weekly—a music show in the morning, *Bandstand* in the afternoon, and commercials at night. Two years later he made his first ABC network appearance, doing a Tootsie Roll commercial on *Paul Whiteman's TV Teen Club.*

By the time I moved in next door, Dick Clark's dance show, *American Bandstand,* was the hottest show on television. Every teenager in the country watched it every afternoon, including my lovely daughter Claudia. But of all the millions of teenagers in the country, only Claudia McMahon's bedroom wall was flush against Dick Clark's bedroom wall. Claudia attended a Catholic girls' school that forbade its students from going on *Bandstand;* just imagine how frustrating that was for her. But she would baby-sit for the Clarks and each week Dick would bring home the top ten records for her.

Alyce and I got to know Dick very well. I remember in those days he looked so young, so very young. And maybe I'm making this up, but I seem to remember that there was a portrait of him hanging over his fireplace, and in that painting he appeared to be just a little older than he was at that time. But Dick was so popular that the legendary journalist Edward R. Murrow interviewed him on his program, *Person to Person. Person to Person* was sort of the 1950s version of a Barbara Walters interview program. Each week, from an easy chair in his studio, bathed in cigarette smoke, Murrow would interview a well-known person in their own home by remote control.

The technology was not like it is today. There were no such things as lightweight minicams or mobile units; the CBS crew practically had to install a studio in Dick's apartment, so we had thick cables and wires and big cameras all over the place. It was a very big deal at Drexelbrook. All the Philadelphia newspapers were doing features about the show. Dan Kelly, who thought the daily mail delivery was a sufficient reason to throw a party, figured this would be great publicity for the club, so after the show he threw a big party for Dick Clark's family and the CBS crew. And if a few reporters happened to wander in, that was not a bad thing either.

During the party Dan asked me to get up onstage and entertain his guests. Me? Entertain a group of CBS television producers and a crew? Naturally, I was a bit shy about it, but somewhere, from some deep hidden reservoir, some place so deep I didn't even know it existed, so very deep that . . . It's a good thing that no one was standing in the direct path between me and the microphone, so there were no serious injuries. "Ladies and gentlemen," I began, "our wonderful host, Dan Kelly, felt this evening would not be complete without something in the way of entertainment . . . so if there's anything in the way of entertainment here right now, let's get it out of the way and start the show."

Several talented performers living at Drexelbrook performed, I told some jokes, bantered a bit with the audience, led some sing-alongs, and everyone had a fine time. Now, besides the daily *American Bandstand*, Dick Clark hosted a Saturday night network dance party from New York. The producer of that show was a man named Chuck Reeves. After the party Reeves complimented me on the easy way I handled the show and asked, "Have you ever thought about going to New York?"

"Just about every second of every minute of every hour of every day," I said, "but other than that . . ."

Chuck Reeves promised to keep me in mind. Now, in show business lingo, that meant one of two things: either I was never going to hear from him again, or he was going to introduce me to this skinny comic genius from Nebraska with whom I would work for the next thirty-four years. I figured it was more likely I would never hear from him again.

Dick Clark's Saturday night show was broadcast from the Little Theatre on West Forty-fourth Street. During the week, a half-hour quiz show titled *Who Do You Trust?*, starring Johnny Carson, was broadcast from that studio. Chuck Reeves's office was down the hall from the office of Art Stark, *Trust*'s producer. Soon after the *Person to Person* party, Reeves overheard Stark telling Carson that his announcer, Bill Nimmo, was leaving to host his own game show and they had to find a replacement right away. Reeves remembered me. As legend has it, Reeves leaped up and yelled to Stark, "I got the perfect guy for you! He's in Philadelphia, but I'll have him here tomorrow." At least that's the way the legend is told in my house.

Reeves didn't know how to contact me, so he phoned Dick Clark. Ironically, a few days earlier we had moved out of Drexelbrook into our own home in a place called Gulph Mills. Dick Clark did not have my new phone number. It was unlisted, but Dick, a wonderfully talented man who continues to complain that he got me a job that lasted thirty-four years and never got a commission, asked if there was a listing for Claudia McMahon. For her thirteenth birthday, I had gotten Claudia her own phone. Dick called that number and one day later I was walking into Johnny Carson's office in the Little Theatre.

I don't think I had ever seen *Who Do You Trust?*, but I had seen Johnny Carson. After graduating from the University of Nebraska, where he had starred in a fraternity production of the classic drama *She Was Only a Pharaoh's Daughter, But She Never Became a Mummy,* Carson had hosted a show, *Carson's Cellar,* first on WOW-TV in Omaha, then on KNXT in Los Angeles. After that show was canceled, he hosted a quiz show called *Earn Your Vacation,* and when that was canceled he was hired as a writer by Red Skelton. In rehearsal one day, Skelton suffered a minor concussion and could not do his live show that night. Carson went on in his place—and was so good that CBS gave him his own prime-time variety show.

Sometimes while I was rehearsing for *Five Minutes More,* we'd have a TV on in the background. No sound, just the picture. So I saw Jell-O presenting *The Johnny Carson Show* for several weeks before I ever heard his voice. I was fascinated by his facial expressions and body language. Perhaps because he was one of the greatest monologuists and ad-libbers in comedy history, Johnny Carson has always been underrated as a physical comedian. But as I watched him on the monitor—even before he hired me, which enabled me to have a wonderful career during which I have earned millions of dollars, for which I will be eternally grateful and never say anything but the most loving things about him—he reminded me of some of the great comedians of silent movies.

Eventually I turned on the sound. From the very first time I heard him, I knew he was an original talent. I remember watching as he opened his show by auctioning off the television camera. "You can throw away your old Brownie," he explained. "Shoot your own TV programs, and then complain about them."

The first full sketch I ever saw him do was set inside the Trojan horse. He was with two other Greek soldiers; they were wearing those big metal helmets with feather plumes, shields, boots with buckles, and their mission was to rescue Helen of Troy. The punch line was such a non sequitur that most people still don't get it. As one of the soldiers got ready to leave the horse, Carson stopped him. "Not that way," he said. "Go out the rear end."

The soldier looked at Carson and said, "You tried a chicken and the chicken didn't work. You tried a pig and the pig didn't work. What makes you think a horse will work?"

I can still hear Carson's voice as he replied, "You know, a horse they just might go for."

It was so dumb that I couldn't stop laughing. *The Johnny Carson Show* was eventually replaced by *The Arthur Murray Show* and ABC hired Carson to host the afternoon quiz show *Do You Trust Your Wife?* Apparently the answer was no, because the format was changed and the title became *Who Do You Trust?*

Johnny Carson was very much the same person the day we met in 1958 as he was when we did the last of thousands of shows together in 1992. The interview was brief and totally professional; he was direct, polite, and private. When I walked into his office, he was standing with his back to the door, looking out the window at the Shubert Theatre directly across the street. Four giant cranes had blocked Forty-fourth Street and were hoisting a new marquee for the theater, which was replacing the traditional tivoli lights that spelled out the name of the current production. I stood at the other window as workmen started hanging the title of a new play, letter by letter. "Times Square'll never be the same after this," he said, indicating the marquee. "This is gonna be the new look for everybody."

Gradually, we realized the marquee was announcing the arrival of JUDY HOLLIDAY IN THE BELLS ARE RINGING.

Finally, Johnny Carson turned to face me. In the thirty years Mr. Carson and I did *The Tonight Show* together, I most enjoyed the first segment, a five-minute slot during which Johnny and I would sit at his desk and chat about absolutely anything of interest. It was never rehearsed. I just loved that spot. It was an opportunity for me to engage in witty repartee with the most clever, accomplished performer I had ever seen, in front of about ten million viewers. I had to be ready for anything. And this was the very first conversation we ever had. "So Ed," he asked, "what are you doing down in Philadelphia?"

I told him about all my shows.

He nodded, then asked, "Where'd you go to school?"

"Catholic University," I said, "in Washington, D.C. I studied speech and drama."

"That's great," he said, "very interesting. Hey, thanks for coming up. I really appreciate it." We shook hands and I walked out of the office. I've waited for elevators for a longer time than this meeting took.

Producer Art Stark took me into the studio where rehearsals were in progress. Carson came in a little while later and they put the two of us on camera to see how we looked together. I looked tall, he looked smaller. "Thanks for coming up, Ed," Stark said. "We'll get in touch with you."

I got back on the train to Philly convinced I'd blown the audition, although I didn't know what else I could have done to impress them. Maybe I shouldn't have been so tall? I was disappointed. It was obvious to me that Carson was a rising star, and I thought it would have been fun to work with him. Besides it was a paying job. *Who Do You Trust?* figured to be on the air for another two seasons at least. A broadcasting year is similar to a dog's year; it's a multiple of a normal year. The life span of most television programs is less than four years, so two good years on a national program was very desirable. I went home convinced I had been rejected.

For three weeks I didn't hear from anyone. That is the

loudest silence you will ever hear. It meant I had not gotten the job. At the same time, one of the companies in Philadelphia for whom I did commercials had chartered a plane and was giving away trips to Europe as a sales promotion. The gimmick was that Alyce and I would be along on the trip. But Alyce didn't want to go; we had just moved into our new home and she had too much to do. We decided I would take Claudia. For some reason, though, I just didn't feel comfortable about making the trip. It didn't feel right. The day before we were to leave, a Friday morning, I decided not to go. Literally minutes after I'd made that decision, Art Stark called and said casually, "Ed, we'd like you to wear suits because we want to emphasize your size. The fact that you're a big guy, you know, will play well against Johnny. Johnny's kind of slight, so he likes to wear sport clothes . . ."

I was a little confused. "What are you talking about?" I asked.

"Didn't anybody call you?" he continued. "You got the job. You start Monday."

All of which is how putting down my twenty-five-dollar deposit on an apartment in Drexelbrook when I didn't have any money proved to be the shrewdest move I've ever made in show business.

On October 13, 1958, I went on the air with Johnny Carson for the first time. My job was to introduce the contestants, do the commercials, and occasionally have a brief conversation with him at the beginning of the show. I don't remember being the slightest bit nervous when the show went on the air. It didn't even occur to me that it might lead to something else. My biggest hope was that it would lead to a paycheck every other Friday.

The first time I walked onstage to introduce our next contestants and hand the questions to Johnny, he established the nature of our television relationship, which would last more than three decades. At that time one of the most popular comic strips was "Mandrake the Magician," and Mandrake had a big, big manservant, a gentleman's gentleman, named Lothar. When I came out Johnny pretended not to see me and then turned suddenly and jumped back, as if I had surprised him. "Lothar," he said, "you startled me."

That was it: big guy and little guy, boss and employee, star and announcer. One night on *The Tonight Show*, I remember, he started discussing a newspaper column that had described him as cold and aloof. This was something we never discussed, but I knew this kind of criticism bothered him. "You see that thing in the paper today?" He complained, "They're writing the same old thing. Johnny Carson is cold and aloof. Ed, how long have we been together?"

"It'll be twenty-one years this October."

"That's right, so you know me pretty well. Tell me the truth, really now, do you think I'm cold and aloof?"

To which I responded, "No, my Lord." Now, that line descended directly from the first thing he ever said to me. The audience laughed because . . . because it was funny. And it was funny because it described completely the TV relationship between us that began on *Who Do You Trust?*

The game was the least important aspect of *Who Do You Trust?* Exactly like Groucho's quiz show, *You Bet Your Life*, it was simply a vehicle that allowed Johnny Carson to show off his genius. The format was simple: a couple was asked three questions of increasing difficulty and value and had to agree on an answer. The most they could win was about $150. For example, they might have been asked, "Which mountain is taller, Mt. Everest or Mt. McKinley? Who do you trust?" Believe me, our contestants were not chosen for their intellect. We had people on the show who were so nervous that they were stumped by questions like "How many children do you have?"

The quiz was really nothing more than an excuse for

Carson to conduct interviews with unusual people and participate in demonstrations. The stranger, the better. Among the contestants we had on the show was a woman who dressed her parrots in historical costumes—Napoleon squawked—we had lots of singing pets; once we had a woman who tossed alligators. Several contestants claimed to have been abducted by Martians or were themselves Martians. Johnny loved people with strange tattoos in unusual places. Inventors were always coming on with unusual inventions. One contestant had invented panties for cows. Another man had invented padded pants with a built-in derriere; he brought a special large size for Johnny, who made a perfect model. Another inventor demonstrated shoes with springs attached to the bottom and Carson bounced across the stage. One of our most memorable contestants was the owner of Hubert's Flea Circus, a Times Square emporium. He brought with him a complete miniature circus, including his star, Gypsy Rose Flea. I mean, he had this tiny little trapeze, little swings, an invisible high wire. You should have seen these little fleas, because nobody else did. "Look!" he told Johnny, as he supposedly put his fleas through their act. "You see that? That was unbelievable! A triple flip. He's never done that before."

Carson admitted he'd missed it.

One of the few performers turned down for the show was a singer named Tiny Tim. He came into the office for an interview wearing lipstick, eye shadow, heavy makeup. Art Stark thought he was much too strange even for our show.

Who Do You Trust? was perfect for Johnny Carson. It gave him the chance to work out so many of his memorable expressions and reactions. No matter how strange a guest was, no matter how ridiculous his story, Johnny played it straight, as if he were talking to a perfectly normal person. About the furthest he would go to express some doubt about a guest was raising his eyebrow. He was just great at finding the humor in the most ordinary things. Just after the big quiz show scandals erupted, when it was discovered that contestants on big shows like *The $64,000 Question* were being given answers, one of our contestants tried to give Johnny a little doll. He recoiled as if the doll were on fire. "A little bribe, huh?" he said. "Five years on the show and I knew something had to happen . . ." Then he sort of whispered to her, "See, all that stuff is given backstage . . ."

Carson was willing to do just about anything for a laugh. He was very athletic and really knew how to use his body. If he had to be skinnier for a bit, somehow he became skinnier. On every show we had at least one demonstration in which he participated. We had an archer who shot an apple off Johnny's head, a karate expert who taught him how to break a board with his forehead, weight lifters, people trying to break hula-hoop records, a woman contortionist who tried to set the world record for supporting her weight on her hands with her feet behind her head—then tried to twist Johnny into a pretzel. We had a gymnast who showed him how to jump on a trampoline—and Johnny jumped straight out of the top of the TV screen.

The thing about Carson was that he was good at this stuff; with a little practice he could pretty much master whatever it was he was doing. I learned very quickly that he was the most facile, accomplished man I'd ever met. He could do a little bit of everything. When we would be talking in his dressing room he might be drumming with two pencils, rolling a half-dollar between his fingers, hiding cards. He could even tap dance a little; few people know this, but he once won an Arthur Murray jitterbug contest. Sometimes he seemed a little apprehensive about doing things, at least he played it that way, but he always ended up doing it. We had an expert fly caster on the show try to drop a lure inside a tire, and he was so nervous he missed—so Johnny showed him how to do it.

Long before Ed Ames tossed his famous hatchet between the legs of a silhouette on *The Tonight Show*, one of our contestants taught Johnny to toss a battle-ax, and Johnny hit the center of the target with his first throw. He was terrific with kids. Kids used to come on and demonstrate how to hop around on a pogo stick or ride a unicycle, and naturally Johnny failed in the funniest ways possible. Then he would just glare at those kids with his steely blue-eyes glare. I'm telling you, if there was a tub of water around he would fall into it, if our guest was demonstrating how to make a pizza we would end up in a flour fight, and no pie ever went unthrown.

This show also gave us the chance to develop our characters and our on-air relationship. Even then Johnny looked like the naive choir boy from the Midwest who had innocently wandered into the big city. He was often shocked, oh, terribly shocked, at some of the things people said. He loved double entendres, sexual innuendos, anything he could get away with. That was the main reason we had couples as contestants. I remember one couple we had on who confessed they had met while she was on her honeymoon with another man. The great singer Rudy Vallee came on with his new bride, who was much, much younger than him. She was a beautiful, very sexy girl, and when Johnny asked her what it was like being married to an older man, she admitted, "Oh, it's great, I keep him up all night."

Almost immediately he made me his foil and by doing so made us a team. On the air I became the big guy who drank too much and ate too much, the good-time guy, hail-fellow-well-met. I was "Big Ed," then "Big Ed, who is the announcer on this show only because he never passed the bar. In fact, Ed has never passed any bar." And just off camera he was always doing little things to cause me problems, things like setting my script on fire. I did a billboard at the top of the show; each of the six sponsors that day had a copy line: "Swans Down cake mixes, the cake mixes you can swear by." But the sponsors changed all the time, so I had to read this opening from a script. And almost every day, as I started reading, he'd set fire to the bottom of my script. I had to get through the opening before my script burned up. I had to read as fast as I could. Some days a copy line like "Nabisco crackers are so good and salty you can eat the whole package" was reduced by fire to something like "Nabisco crackers. Eat 'em." By the end of the opening I was trying to read charcoal.

Who Do You Trust? was as much a training ground for me as it was for him. I did all the commercials live, and I learned how to deal with just about anything that could happen on the air. And Carson made sure anything that could happen did happen. One afternoon, just as I was ready to demonstrate how easy it was to use cake mix, he walked by my prop table and "accidentally" hit the leg, knocking my bowls and mixers and cake mix on the floor. Now, I am not saying that Mr. Carson hit that table leg intentionally, which resulted in prolonged laughter from the studio audience, but I wouldn't bet my Bud against it.

Most of the time, I was able to get through my commercials. I had my professional dignity to uphold, but occasionally even I would make a mistake. I was doing a spot for StayPuff softener. This was long before Pampers had been invented, when mothers had to pin diapers on their babies. Mothers always had to be very careful not to stick their baby with the pin when putting the diapers on. I had two piles of diapers; the pile washed in StayPuff was much fluffier. I was supposed to say, "StayPuff makes it so easy to pin these diapers on . . ." Well, I don't know what Carson had done to distract me—actually that might have been the day he crawled under the camera and gave me a three-match hotfoot while I was doing the spot—but whatever he did, I wasn't paying attention and I said, "StayPuff makes it so easy to pee . . ."

Well, in those days you couldn't say that word on TV. The censors were so strict that if you read the alphabet you were supposed to leave out that letter. Carson was laughing so hard he left the theater. But I'll tell you how he would have described this scene. In his most innocent tone, he would have said, "The organist was laughing so hard he couldn't play his organ . . ."

I understood that my job was to support Johnny Carson. I didn't tell the jokes, I set up the jokes. I didn't get the laughs, I helped him get the laughs. Johnny and I never discussed this; we didn't have to. We were smart enough to see how well our relationship worked. At times I had to consciously stop myself from responding to something he said; I'd always had my own shows, I'd always been free to say whatever popped into my mind. But after a few weeks I had slipped quite comfortably into the role of straight man, his second banana. And as he got to trust me more and more, he gave me more to do. He began to depend on me, and my role expanded greatly.

We became great pals. When we started working together he was living in Harrison, New York, about an hour outside the city, and his first marriage was breaking up. So, often, after the show instead of going home he'd suggest we get something to eat and drink. And drink. And sometimes toward the end of the week he'd ask me to spend the weekend with him in Ft. Lauderdale. I believe there is a word for people who say no when the boss suggests dinner—and that word is "unemployed." Besides, my marriage wasn't doing all that well either. Alyce was very unhappy about all the time I was spending in New York. She would much rather I had remained Mr. Television in Philadelphia and not tried to expand my career in New York. I remember negotiating with her on the phone, telling her that Johnny wanted me to go to Florida with him and that the producer thought it was a good idea.

That was a tough time for me, too. I was a practicing Catholic, I often went to Mass on my way to New York, and I believed completely that as a Catholic I married once and for life. But gradually my marriage to Alyce was breaking down. If I have one regret in my life, it is that often my career prevented me from being with my kids. I always tried to be there for important occasions, but the truth is I missed a lot of the day-to-day family life. I wasn't there when my son Jeff was born, for example, because we had just started taping *Who Do You Trust?* and we were doing two shows that day. Jeff was born between shows.

Johnny and I spent a lot of time together, much more than we would in later years, but our friendship was forged then. We'd spend nights going from restaurants to bars, places like Michael's Pub and Danny's Hideaway and Sardi's and Jilly's and P. J. Clarke's. We had the adventures that two young successful guys on the town in New York City who enjoyed a bit of libation might have, actually a lot of libation, we libated all over the city. And at times the fact that I was big and, as a marine, in great shape prevented us from having even more public adventures. We got to know each other very well; we learned a lot about each other's feelings and values, what hurt us, what made us happy. We came to understand how each of us thought, and most important, we really liked each other, we had a good time together. The intimacy that developed during the four years we did *Who Do You Trust?* was essential to the success of *The Tonight Show*.

Who Do You Trust? was pivotal in my career. As soon as I started appearing on a daily network program in New York, I began getting all types of offers for shows and commercials in Philadelphia. One of the most interesting was an opportunity to do my own late-night show. NBC was getting very nervous that Jack Paar, the controversial *Tonight Show* host, was going to quit. So the network requested that each of the O & Os, the local stations that they owned and operated, find a potential replacement for Paar. The NBC affiliate in Philadelphia picked me, and I created a late-night show titled *McMahon and Company*. I did the show for six or seven months, while commuting to New York. Which is *not* the story of how I ended up on *The Tonight Show*.

4

One evening the actor Fernando Lamas, who had quite a reputation as a ladies' man, was a guest on *The Tonight Show*. Johnny Carson liked him a lot. He said that he thought it had been very brave of Lamas to come to America without speaking the language and try to make it in the motion picture industry. After praising him for his courage and dedication, Johnny asked him why he pursued such a difficult career.

Lamas told him, "It was a good way to meet broads."

Johnny laughed, nodding his head as if the answer had been obvious, then said, "You know, Nietzsche couldn't have said it better."

Nietzsche? Nietzsche! After the show I went into Johnny's office and asked him, "Where the hell did Nietzsche come from?"

Johnny just shrugged. "Who knows?" he said. "It was just back there somewhere."

I worked with Johnny Carson for thirty-four years. During that period I think the longest we ever went without doing a show together was four weeks. Besides four years of

Who Do You Trust? we did 6,583 *Tonight Show*s. And the guy never failed to surprise me or entertain me.

Sometimes I think television was invented just to display the talents of Johnny Carson. No one has ever mastered it as he did, and it was my privilege to be sitting by his side in the swivel chair that didn't swivel, and then move down one seat onto the couch as the big movie star came on to promote a picture, then move down another seat when the zoologist came on and put the Goliath beetle on Johnny's hand and watched it crawl up his arm, and then another seat when Johnny brought out the farmer who created jewelry from animal droppings, and finally move onto a folding chair when the author came out for the last three minutes, for all those years.

NBC's *Tonight Show* dated back to 1951, when it debuted as a late-night variety show titled *Broadway Open House,* hosted by comedian Jerry Lester and his pulchritudinous sidekick, Dagmar. Maybe television was really invented for entertainers like Dagmar, whose two biggest talents could not be appreciated on radio. As Johnny once ad-libbed about a guest during a commercial break, "She could have nursed Wyoming." Then Steve Allen hosted the show for almost four years, introducing great performers like my friends Steve Lawrence and Eydie Gorme, and Andy Williams, and doing parody sketches like "What's My Pain?" When he left, the network didn't have any idea what to do with the time slot; after experimenting with Ernie Kovacs for a few months, they created a really terrible news, interview, and gossip show called *America after Dark,* with Jack Lescoulie and Al "Jazzbo" Collins. That failed, so in desperation they hired Jack Paar. Paar, a low-key comedian who had hosted several radio and summer replacement television programs, described himself as "Lawrence Welk without music." Paar saved *The Tonight Show,* and maybe all of live late-night television.

Paar made *The Tonight Show* the hottest program on the air. People started staying up to watch the show because they knew the next day everybody in their office would be talking about it. He brought together a wonderfully eclectic mix of talent, combining an offbeat group of regular guests, people like Cliff Arquette playing a folksy character named Charley Weaver, pianist-curmudgeon Oscar Levant, and "ditsy" comedienne Dody Goodman, with great young performers like Jonathan Winters, Joey Bishop, Diahann Carroll, and Carol Burnett, and still managing to attract big stars like Jack Benny, George Burns, Red Skelton, and Jerry Lewis. Part of Paar's appeal was his unpredictability. You didn't want to miss his show because you never knew what he might do. He made front-page headlines for weeks, for example, when in the middle of a show he announced he was quitting, then walked off the stage because network censors had cut out a joke in which he had used the phrase "WC," meaning a water closet or bathroom, without consulting him.

His return got one of the highest ratings in television history, even if the entire history of television was then only about fourteen years. My show in Philadelphia, *McMahon and Company*, came on right after Paar. He was a tough act to follow, particularly on my limited budget. The "and Company" was my piano player and whomever I could convince to sit for an interview. My guests ranged from the legendary actress Helen Hayes to an elderly woman who played her head; she actually banged her hand against her skull to produce an identifiable version of "I'm Looking over a Four-Leaf Clover."

After hosting *The Tonight Show* for five years, "the King"—as Jack Paar called himself, explaining, "overstatement is very funny"—decided to quit for real. "You can only work a field for so many seasons in a row before it becomes barren," he said. "I don't think Paar's half acre is completely worn out, but it has gotten a little dry lately."

Paar was so popular and controversial that the media

doubted anyone could really replace him, but Paar himself decided that Johnny Carson, who had filled in for him as host on occasion, was "the one man who could or should replace me." Paar retired at the end of March 1962; NBC hired Carson to succeed him starting the following October. While Carson fulfilled his *Who Do You Trust?* contract at ABC, a succession of guest hosts including Bob Cummings, Jan Murray, Joey Bishop, Merv Griffin, Jerry Lewis, Arlene Francis, Groucho Marx, Soupy Sales, and Art Linkletter filled in during the summer.

To this day I don't know how I got the job as Johnny Carson's *Tonight Show* announcer. I've never asked him and he has never told me. I do know how badly I wanted the job. We had become very close friends, but I think one of the reasons for that was that we rarely, if ever, spoke about business. We just had a good time together. After it was announced that Johnny Carson had been hired to replace Paar, I heard all kinds of rumors about who his announcer would be. The story that seemed most plausible was that NBC was pressuring Carson to keep Paar's announcer, Hugh Downs, as a way of making viewers more comfortable with the change, whereas Johnny wanted to take me and producer Art Stark from *Who Do You Trust?* Apparently a deal was made—again this is all rumor—allowing Carson to hire me if he agreed to accept a producer already under contract to the network. This was NBC's way of maintaining some control over the show. So Perry Cross became producer of *The Tonight Show*, Hugh Downs replaced Dave Garroway as host of *The Today Show*, and I got the announcer's job.

I found out about it late one night at Sardi's. Johnny and I were sitting at the bar celebrating . . . celebrating the fact that we were sitting at the bar, when he said casually, "You know, Ed, I've been thinking, when we take over the show . . ."

"Whoa," I said. "Now just back up a little bit. Did you say, when *we* take over the show?"

"Yeah, of course. Of course you're going with me. Didn't you know that?"

I looked at Johnny gratefully and said those four lovely words most appropriate at a moment like that: "I'll drink to that!"

There had been several announcers on *The Tonight Show:* Gene Rayburn had worked with Steve Allen, Hugh Downs with Jack Paar, and each of them had fulfilled quite a different role on the show. I had no idea what I was supposed to do beyond showing up on time wearing a clean shirt. About the only thing I knew for sure was that I would be doing a lot of live commercials. I'd learned while working on the boardwalk that the best way to make something look natural was to rehearse the hell out of it, that the more you did it, the less it looked like you'd ever done it before. I'd met Hugh Downs while he was cohosting a morning home-makers' show, *The Home Show,* with Arlene Francis, and he graciously invited me to spend time with him in studio 6B at Rockefeller Center, the studio in which *The Tonight Show* was done.

For several weeks I went over there in the afternoon and rehearsed that night's commercials with him. I got to know the crew, and I learned the very complicated, technical aspects of doing commercials, like where to stand. I mean, there really was no training period for this job; I just had to do it. All those Thursday nights I'd spent at the Emerson College Broadcasting Club really had very little value— unless, of course, we got Praise linoleum as a sponsor.

No one knew what *The Tonight Show* with Johnny Carson would be like, including Johnny Carson. The show had changed completely with each host; Steve Allen was great in sketches, Paar was a terrific interviewer. In late summer Johnny took producer Perry Cross, all the writers, his brother Dick Carson, who would direct the show, and me to Ft. Lauderdale, where we sat around the pool and planned the show. Actually, I sat around the pool; they planned the show. Johnny Carson didn't just show up to do the show; that was my job. He created and produced it. He wrote jokes for the monologue, worked with the writers, planned the sketches. I don't think viewers ever realized how completely the show was a reflection of his personal vision.

During that Florida trip, some of television's most wonderful characters—*Teatime Movie* host Art Fern, Aunt Blabby, the great mentalist El Moldo, and the seer from the East, Carnac the Magnificent—came to life. My contribution to this meeting was primarily to get a great tan.

On October 1, 1962, Johnny Carson and I did *The Tonight Show* for the first time. I can assure you, that first night we did not think that we were going to become "part of the fabric of America," as Pulitzer Prize–winning poet Archibald MacLeish later claimed, or that we were to become "history's most effective contraceptive," as journalists wrote. Which, by the way, is one of the rare times that calling someone a contraceptive is meant as a compliment. In our wildest fantasies that first night, we never dreamed that the show would generate one hundred million dollars a year in advertising revenues, accounting for one-fifth of NBC's annual profits, and become so much a part of American culture that Johnny would cause a national shortage of toilet paper simply by mentioning that supermarket supplies were running low.

No, that first night all we were hoping for was that we would be good enough to be renewed. Paar had done the show for almost five years, and from the vantage point of the first day, that seemed like an impossibly long run. The network didn't seem to have too much confidence in us; they didn't bother to upholster parts of our set. The set was built on a platform several inches high, and for several years the front of that platform was bare, revealing the nails and hinges that held the whole thing together. I was so insecure about the show's staying on the air that for the first two years I continued to commute from Philadelphia, and even after I finally moved to New York, I rented a house for two more years instead of buying. Just in case.

Johnny and I never discussed my role on the show. But the afternoon of our first show, as we were going down to the stage, I said, "John, I want to discuss something with you. How do you see my role down here tonight?"

"Ed," he told me, "I don't even know how I see my own role. Let's just go down there and entertain the hell out of them." That was the only advice I ever got from him and, in retrospect, it was probably the best possible plan. The show, and our roles on it, evolved over time. About the only thing I can think of that didn't change at all from our first show to our last show was my introduction of Johnny Carson.

Very few performers in history have been linked forever to one phrase. George Burns, for example, will always be remembered for his line "Say goodnight, Gracie." Quote the phrase "And that's the way it is," and everyone knows you're quoting Walter Cronkite. Jimmy Durante was known for his mysterious closing, "Goodnight, Mrs. Calabash, wherever you are." "It's always something" immediately brings to mind the great Gilda Radner. Well, I've probably been associated with more phrases then anyone in show business, but the first one, the best known, and the line I am continually being asked to repeat is . . . "Heeeeere's Johnny!"

As a spokesperson for American Family Publishers, I have the pleasure several times a year of calling people to tell them that they have won several million dollars. Sometimes they refuse to believe either that I'm Ed McMahon or that they've won a fortune. So when that happens, I ask them their first name. Richard. "How 'bout this," I say, "Heeeeere's Richard!" *That's* when they believe me.

While preparing for the first show, I was trying to think of a way of opening that would be distinctive, something that would set me apart from other announcers. Normally, the only opportunities an announcer has to make his presence known are the opening and closing of the show. Hugh Downs, for example, had a great phrase, ". . . and I'm yours truly, Hugh Downs." But I just couldn't come up with a good gimmick for myself. Then, literally about five minutes before we went on the air, it came to me. I used to host the NBC radio show *Monitor,* and one of our correspondents was the fine reporter Robert Pierepoint. When I introduced him, I would elongate the *r,* Rrrrrobert Pierepoint. So I decided to do the same thing when I opened the show. And it stuck. It was immediate. On my way to the studio the next day, literally the next day, people recognized me and imitated that phrase. But in all the years Johnny and I were together, he never mentioned it.

The second phrase instantly connected with me is the mellifluous rallying cry "Hi-yoooo." John Paul Jones rallied his sailors with the memorable phrase "I have not yet begun to fight." Nathan Hale became immortal with his last words, "I regret that I have but one life to give for my country." Me? I got "Hi-yoooo." And when I walk down the street, I still get it . . . over and over and over and over. It wasn't even my phrase. It came from our associate producer, John Carsey. One night after we'd been doing the show for about six or seven years, we had a terrible audience. It happened sometimes. Fortunately, no one reading this book was there that night, so I feel free to be critical. But these people . . . I don't know where they came from. Maybe *The Merv Griffin Show.* During the first commercial break, Johnny and I exchanged glances; we knew it was going to be a grim night. But Carsey, standing off camera behind me, suddenly gave a slight rallying cry, the kind of upbeat, energizing, thrilling cry that the old wagon master, John Wayne, might have given to signal the hundreds of covered wagons to begin the great trek westward over tall mountains and through fields of . . . Carsey said, "Hi-yoooo." I picked it up and repeated it loudly and the audience responded immediately, and that night that audience was miraculously transformed from a sad, dull group to a wonderful audience of which any of us would have been proud to have been a member. It became the rallying cry of the *Tonight Show* audience. I used it often, but especially on those rare occasions, those once-in-a-great-while moments, when one of Mr. Carson's witticisms received a less than favorable response. I would cry out, "Hi-yoooo," knowing that my cry would be echoed by the entire audience, that their voices would rise as one to remind Johnny how much he was appreciated, even if his joke really smelled up the joint.

I just didn't realize I'd have to hear it several million times. Or more. I loved it, I loved the fact that it allowed the audience to participate in the fun, to be part of the show. And I still enjoy hearing it. One of the nicest moments of my life took place when I served as the grand marshal of the Orange Bowl parade. I was introduced at the game and as I walked out onto the field at least fifty thousand people greeted me with the loudest, most affectionate "Hi-yoooo" anyone has ever heard.

Of course, as soon as I appeared on television informing viewers, "You may have already won ten million dollars," "Hi-yoooo" practically disappeared and people began greeting me by asking, "Hey, Ed, where's my money?"

Johnny and I did the show for thirty years. Just imagine that, thirty years. That's seven different presidential administrations. The Kennedy assassination. Watergate. The entire space program. The Vietnam War. Seven marriages between us. And not a single world championship for either the Boston Red Sox or the Chicago Cubs. The world changed drastically while we were on the air. When we started doing the show there were no such things as color televisions, portable telephones, personal computers, microwave ovens, or VCRs. By the time we left the show, people all over the world were able to misplace the remote control for their color televisions, couldn't figure out how to replace the batteries in their portable phones, had no idea why their computer insisted it had no memory left, kept burning popcorn in the microwave, and were totally unable to program their VCRs.

Hi-yoooo!

It wasn't just that new things were invented during that period; there were fundamental changes in American society, and one of the reasons *The Tonight Show* remained popular for so long was that we were able to change with the times. When we first went on the air we weren't permitted to use words like "pregnant." We had to use phrases like "with child." Once when Johnny and I were doing a question-and-answer bit, I said to him, "Now here's a query from . . . ," and I got a memo from standards and practices, the network censor, telling me not to use the word "query" because it sounded too much like "queer."

I'll tell you how much television had changed. Decades after that incident, Jane Fonda was on the show one night and said to Johnny, "I've got to ask you something. You were just talking about Zsa Zsa Gabor. My son said she was on your show one time, she came here with a cat on her lap, and she said to you, 'Do you want to pet my pussy?' My son said that you said, 'I'd love to, if you remove that damn cat!' Is that true?"

Johnny nervously drummed his pencil on his desk until the laughter had subsided, then said with a sigh, "No, I think I would have recalled that."

My role on the show never was strictly defined. I did what had to be done when it had to be done. I was there when he needed me, and when he didn't, I moved down the couch and kept quiet. The farther down the couch I moved, the quieter I was. I did the audience warm-up, I did commercials, for a brief period I cohosted the first fifteen minutes of the show with our orchestra leader, Skitch Henderson, and I performed in many sketches. On our thirteenth-anniversary show, Johnny and I were talking at his desk and he said, "Thirteen years is a long time."

Long enough for me to recognize my cue. "So," I asked, "how long is it?"

"That's why you're here," he said, probably summing up my primary role on the show perfectly, and then he continued, "It's so long that when we started Gladys Knight was using training Pips." My job was to be the straight man, the sidekick, a role honored in show business tradition as the second banana. There is an old story that a straight man was walking along the beach when suddenly he heard someone screaming, "Help! Help! I'm drowning." And when he heard that he stopped and turned and said, "You mean to say that you're *drowning?*"

I had to support him, I had to help him get to the punch line, but while doing it I had to make it look as if I wasn't doing anything at all. The better I did it, the less it appeared as if I was doing it. When you're a performer there is a great desire to try to please the audience. Even though I understood and accepted completely that my role on the show was to support Johnny, I still wanted to hold my own. I've often been asked how I felt about being Johnny Carson's sidekick, his second banana. The answer is that I wanted to be the best damned second banana it was possible to be. I wanted to do the job better than anyone had ever done it before. I wanted to create a role that no one could duplicate. If I was going to play second fiddle, I wanted to be the Heifetz of second fiddlers.

Playing straight man to Johnny Carson was a privilege. I'm an intelligent man. I knew how talented he was. I knew

I couldn't do so many of the things he did so easily. I couldn't play that range of characters. I couldn't create Carnac. I couldn't do imitations. I didn't want to jump off platforms or let tarantulas crawl up my arm. I didn't mind playing a supporting role. In fact, I relished it, I loved it.

In all honesty, I think I did it well too. Anyone who has ever tried to play this role knows how difficult it is to do. Basically the only rules of the job are that the sidekick never gets the girl or to shoot the bad guy. The most difficult thing for me to learn how to do was just sit there with my mouth closed. Many nights I'd be listening to Johnny and in my mind I'd reach the same ad-lib just as he said it. I'd have to bite my tongue not to say it out loud. I had to make sure I wasn't too funny—although critics who saw some of my other performances will claim I needn't have worried. If I got too many laughs, I wasn't doing my job; my job was to be part of a team that generated the laughs.

In fact, it was much tougher for me to work without Johnny than it was to be with him. When we started doing the show, we were on the air from eleven-fifteen P.M. till one A.M. Then Johnny found out that many local stations didn't pick up the network feed until eleven-thirty. So for the first fifteen minutes, he couldn't use his best material. Finally he decided not to do that segment at all. Skitch Henderson, our natty bandleader, and I cohosted the show for those fifteen minutes. Years later, when Johnny was having problems with NBC, or negotiating his new contract, he came down with a bad case of the NBC flu about an hour before we went on the air and was unable to work that night. I had to host the show. Most of the time I didn't even know who was going to be on, much less have time to prepare.

That was the toughest job in the world. I had to be good, but I couldn't be too good. I had to make it look as if I was enjoying myself, but I also had to make it clear I wasn't enjoying myself that much. My goal was a lot of loud smiles. If the producer complimented me, I never knew if he meant I had been funny or had been just not funny enough.

I can remember only one time when I was working with Johnny that I went too far. In fact, I'll never forget it. One night Johnny carefully explained to me that scientists at Cal Tech had just completed a multimillion-dollar study about mosquitoes and they had found that for some reason mosquitoes were particularly attracted to extremely "warm-blooded, passionate people."

Instinctively, I said, "Whoops, there's another one," and slapped my wrist.

I knew even before my wrist stopped stinging that I'd gone too far. Johnny was glaring at me with his steely blue eyes. "Well, then," he said, reaching down and picking up a can of insect spray the size of a fire extinguisher, with which he had intended to spray himself, "I guess I won't be needing this five-hundred-dollar prop then, will I?"

It was obvious to everyone in the audience exactly what had happened. And they enjoyed it a lot more than I did. Johnny had managed to salvage something from the setup, but I knew how angry he was with me. Not so much because I'd gotten the laugh, but rather because I'd ruined the bit. And he was right to be. After all the years we'd worked together, it should have been obvious to me that he was setting up a joke, a joke that was not written for me to get the laugh. Now, that was not the only time Johnny got mad at me; when you work together as closely as we did for as long as we did, it is inevitable that there will be some bad times. I'm sure there must have been some shows when he thought I was too strong, I'm sure of that, but when that happened I knew it too. There were nights when I asked myself, did I go too far? Did I step outside my role? Never for one moment in thirty years did I forget that it was Johnny's show.

Our relationship survived a lot longer than several of our

marriages. The amazing thing is how many really good nights we had together. All kinds of stories have been written about our relationship, but the simple fact is that Johnny and I liked each other and respected each other. Maybe the fact that two men who worked together liked each other didn't make very exciting headlines, but it was true. When Johnny was between marriages, for example, he would occasionally spend a weekend at my house. He slept in Claudia's room so often that he gave her a picture on which he'd written, "To Claudia, Some time you must sleep in my bed." Johnny and I could not possibly have worked so well together on the air if we didn't genuinely like each other off the air. The viewing audience is too smart to allow us to fake a friendship for any period of time.

The audience knew that Johnny was the boss, and the rest of us were employees. And since almost all of our viewers had bosses of their own, they understood and identified with that relationship. We had the same problems with our boss on national TV as they had in the office. And that served as the foundation for a lot of humor. For example, one night Johnny and Doc Severinsen got into a discussion about the correct pronunciation of the poinsettia plant. Johnny contended it was pronounced "poin-set-e-a," while Doc claimed it was "poin-set-a." The next night Doc brought a note from a noted professor of linguistics supporting his claim. Johnny took it very well. "That's very interesting," he told Doc, "but do me one favor. Why don't you ask that expert if the correct pronunciation is '*un*employed,' or 'unem*ployed*'?"

On one of my favorite shows Johnny and I got into a very silly conversation that ended with my taking a pair of scissors and actually cutting off the bottom half of his tie. It was exactly what so many viewers must have dreamed of doing to their boss, but they also knew there were consequences. Johnny just looked at me, looked at the remains of his tie in disbelief, looked at me, again at the tie, all the while waiting for the audience to stop laughing. He got every laugh possible out of that long pause. When they finally quieted down, Johnny said to me, as if there were only one possible explanation for this behavior, "Oh, you must have just sold a pilot film."

After more laughter, he added with incredulity, "I've been wearing this tie for seven years."

"Well," I told him confidently, "you'll never wear it again."

Johnny never objected to someone else getting the laughs—in the right situations. On *The Tonight Show* each of us had a primary role to play; Johnny was the host, ready to welcome a variety of talented and interesting people and pretty much willing to try anything. I was the big party guy who did the commercials and ate a lot and drank a lot and occasionally put down the boss. For example, in his monologue one night, he told the audience, "Ed only drinks on special occasions. Like when he sees wall-to-wall carpeting." Once, when he was actually donating blood on the show to remind people to give blood, he lifted his head and said, "Ed's is the only blood with a ten-minute head on it." My drinking was always good for an ad-lib; once, when a kinkajou started sniffing at my leg, Johnny decided, "He's obviously attracted to the scent of olives." On another show, Joan Embry from the San Diego Zoo brought on a bear, who started sniffing at the cup of iced tea I always had. But as the bear started lapping at it, Johnny warned Joan, "You better get him away from that or he'll go into hibernation for a year."

Our first NBC orchestra leader, the great Skitch Henderson, was kind of a fop, always well dressed, allowing Johnny to kid him about his sartorial splendor. In contrast to Skitch, Doc Severinsen, who eventually replaced him, was an extraordinarily talented trumpeter who wore outrageously loud and sometimes bizarre outfits, which allowed Johnny to tell the audience, "I wouldn't wear that outfit to fondle Randolph Scott's saddle horn," or, "I wouldn't wear that outfit to a whale's hysterectomy." Tommy Newsom was the bland band member with absolutely no personality. As Johnny once explained, "We received the report today on Tommy's autopsy. There was no foul play; he died of natural dullness." These roles evolved over time and Johnny knew how to use them. Once, we did a parody of *This Is Your Life*, a popular show on which celebrated people were surprised by friends and relatives from their past. We did *This Is Your Life: Tommy Newsom*, but when the people from his past were brought out from backstage, they'd look at him, say, "No, that's not him," then turn around and leave.

These character traits were based on real life but magnified. Believe me, in real life Doc did not wear bright orange-and-yellow shirts with skintight paisley trousers. And in real life I didn't drink either . . . well, at least Doc didn't really wear those kind of clothes.

Hi-yoooo! I see those jokes still work.

Johnny created a character for himself just as he did for the rest of us. He was Peck's Bad Boy, the wide-eyed midwesterner in the big town who might sometimes be naughty, but never nasty. And, just as with the rest of us, it was a character based loosely on fact. Being that character allowed him to get away with sexual innuendos that no one else on television could possibly have gotten away with. The same lines coming from me or almost anyone else would have seemed raunchy. But this behavior was acceptable from him; it was cute. Everybody understood that he wasn't really serious when he made outrageous remarks. One of the first nights Dolly Parton appeared on the show, she wore a revealing outfit, and she had a lot more to reveal than most other women. It was about as possible to overlook her breasts as it would have been to overlook the Grand Canyon. "People are always asking me if they're real," she told Johnny.

Not Johnny. That would not be polite. "I would never," he protested, "I would never . . ."

"I'll tell you what . . . ," Dolly continued.

" . . . I have certain guidelines . . . ," Johnny continued, then admitted, "but I would give about a week's . . . make that a year's pay, to peek under there."

Amply endowed women were such a staple of the show that we probably could have telecast highlights of their appearances as *The Breast of Carson*.

All together now, Hi-yoooo!

A beautiful actress named Carol Wayne appeared on the show semiregularly, playing the role of the sexy blond in sketches. Once, in a *Teatime Movie* bit, she came out carrying a model of a house in front of her chest, allowing Carson as Art Fern to ask the audience, "How would you like to get your hands on one of these?" Moments later she reappeared holding up several insurance policies, as supersalesman Fern suggested, "Take a look at what we cover with these policies," and then, with a twist of his mustache, added, "And then take a look at what we don't."

With Johnny, sex was always funny. On the show, I mean. His material was always suggestive, the kind of jokes boys would tell each other. "A wise man who has no chin," he once explained, "should learn to stroke something else." Or, "Here's a tip for women. A man is sexually interested in a woman if he stares up at her—from underneath a glass coffee table."

Carson understood how to use this character. He knew just how far he could go, how much he could get away with. A perfect example of that was his introduction of Lucille Ball at a dinner. As he told the audience, he had been asked to avoid the kind of suggestive remarks he often made on *The Tonight Show*. "And so," he concluded, "it gives me great pleasure to introduce our guest of honor tonight, Miss Lucille Testicle."

Maybe because we had spent so much time together, or maybe just because we were together so long, the fact is that Johnny trusted me. He knew I wasn't going to lead him down a bad path or steal his thunder or go for the jugular or take a cheap shot. Often during the show he'd glance over at me to see what I thought about whatever he was doing. Was the bit working? Should he keep going? And just as had happened on *Who Do You Trust?* my role on *The Tonight Show* expanded as it became clear that the audience enjoyed the relationship and repartee between Johnny and me. They were in on the joke: he was always the boss and I was always the employee, so when I did manage to get in the last word, all the millions of employees in the audience just loved it. I knew I had the greatest job in the world, I loved it, but my favorite part of the show was just after the monologue, when Johnny and I sat down at the desk. I would be in the swivel chair—that chair hadn't swiveled in a hundred years but it was always called the swivel chair—and we would ad-lib for five minutes. I loved waking up in the morning knowing that later that day I would be sitting with Johnny Carson in front of about ten million people and we would ad-lib five minutes of great entertainment and comedy.

I never knew what he was going to throw at me and I loved the challenge of trying to hold my own with the master. One night, out of nowhere, he started discussing a story he had seen on a *National Geographic* documentary. It was about a bird, the swit. "Listen to this," he said. "The swit flies its whole life, it's in the air the whole time. It just keeps flying. It mates in the air, it has babies in the air . . ." He went on and on about this little bird.

When he finished, I said, "Well, that's very interesting, but what about the shark?"

"What are you talking about, the shark?"

"Maybe the swit flies all the time," I continued, "but finally it lands on a branch and says, 'Whew, I'm glad that's over.' But the shark never stops swimming. The water has to flow in and out of its gills. If the shark stops swimming, it stops breathing, it dies. That's why sharks are so mean, they never get to stop swimming."

Johnny didn't know if I was kidding him or not. "Wait a second," he said. "You mean to tell me that at night the shark doesn't stop and rest?"

"John," I said, "how would a shark know night from day?"

Only twice in our years together did I intentionally disrupt a bit. One night we had a jaguar on the show and Johnny was supposed to feed it ice cream from a big ladle. Johnny was really terrific with animals and sometimes during these bits he would look as if he was really scared. Let me tell you the truth, sometimes he was really scared. These animals could be very unpredictable. I was amazed at some of the things he did. But this night, just as Johnny was scooping out the ice cream, I noticed blood dripping from the trainer's hand. He was trying to hide it, but I saw three deep bloody scratches. Interrupting Johnny, I said, "I don't think this cat is hungry."

Johnny glared at me. Actually, he glared right through me. The expression on his face was clear: are you out of your mind? What the hell do you think you're doing?

I indicated the trainer's hand. "I think he had some ice cream before the show." At first Johnny didn't understand and insisted on feeding this animal. "John," I said forcefully, "I don't think he wants ice cream."

Finally, Carson saw the trainer's hand. "Oh yeah," he said, "maybe he has had too much ice cream."

The second time I disrupted him was right in the middle of his monologue. Or rather, his attempt at a monologue. He was dying. Now, normally nobody died better than Johnny. As far as I know, he was the first comedian to make a joke out of the fact that his jokes were so bad. Maybe his best monologues were his worst monologues; certainly no one has ever been funnier about not being funny. In fact, the jokes he would make about his jokes were often much better than his jokes. But one night nothing was working, the jokes, the jokes about the jokes, the man was standing out there on what we called "the star mark" dying a slow death. Normally no one would walk into his monologue area; that was his sacred place. But I just couldn't resist. Like a coach helping a battered fighter, I went over to him and grabbed him by his shoulders and turned him toward me. Obviously he was very surprised. "You can do this," I said earnestly, "I know you can. You're better than this . . . ," I pointed to the audience. "Don't let these people get you down. You're funnier than this." I gave him a gentle punch in the shoulder. "Now go ahead and do it!"

"Thanks," he said, laughing, "I needed that."

Johnny knew I was always there behind him. And the more dangerous the animal on the show, the farther behind him I was. In fact, the most persistent criticism I received through the years was for laughing out loud. Some people thought that I faked my laughter just to be supportive of him, that it was part of my job. That's absolutely not true. If I could fake that much laughter, I'd be the finest actor in the world. I admit it, I laughed a lot, and there was a reason for that: I thought Johnny Carson was very funny. Sometimes I did laugh very loudly at something other people did not find funny. But there was a good reason for that—and no, it was not my paycheck. Through the years Johnny and I spent a lot of time together offstage, and many of the things he said or did on the air, or some of his expressions, were funny to me in the context of our relationship. We did share some private jokes. For example, when we did a bit in which Johnny replied to viewer mail, I often told him, "Here's a letter from a little boy named Gordon from Linden, New Jersey." Now Johnny knew that the train I took to go home to Philadelphia went right past the Gordon's gin factory in Linden, New Jersey.

So Johnny would laugh whenever little Gordon wrote, adding, "He writes a lot, that kid, doesn't he?" I doubt anyone except me and Johnny got that joke, but we loved it.

Johnny and I had a little tradition: right before the show, I'd go into his dressing room for seven or eight minutes. Before every show. Sometimes Freddy de Cordova, our producer, or Bobby Quinn, the director, would be there, but a lot of the time it was just the two of us. We rarely talked about the show; we'd talk about anything else—marriage, divorce, sex, religion, science, the World Series, the world situation—but whatever it was, Johnny had something funny to say about it. Carson has the incredible ability to find humor in just about anything. He doesn't just say funny things; his normal way of thinking would be considered funny by most people. Now, sometimes during those conversations a risqué remark might accidentally have slipped out of his mouth or my mouth. Sometimes, in fact, the whole conversation was downright risqué. And so when we were onstage I might well have laughed at something other people didn't find that funny, but that laughter came from knowing him so well, from something private between us, or from what he'd said only moments before in his dressing room.

A lot of material that started in his dressing room would later show up on the air. When Johnny's divorce from his second wife was settled, one of the tabloids reported in a bold headline, CARSON'S EX TO GET $65,000 A WEEK. So I figured out how much that came to per hour. When I went into the show that afternoon everybody was scared to death to go near his dressing room. In all honesty, I must admit I wasn't looking forward to our daily meeting with great anticipation either. But at the usual time, I opened the door and kind of peeked in. He was sitting quietly behind his desk. "I figured it out," I said. "It's about $380 per hour, waking or sleeping."

"You so-and-so," he said, kicking his lamp off his desk. Under the circumstances, I thought that was a pretty reasonable thing to do. But then he started laughing. Eventually that became a running gag on the show. Whenever the subject of marriage or divorce came up, one of us would look at the other and say quite distinctly, "Waking . . . or sleeping."

"Waking . . . or sleeping" became an inside joke that just about everybody in America was in on. But there were a lot of points of reference like that between us, and often what I was laughing at on the air referred to something that had happened in private.

I think the best way to explain why I laughed so easily at Mr. Carson is the line he had inscribed on a lovely watch he once gave me, the meaning of which will forever be known only to the two of us: "Don't look up, Mrs. Thompson."

Besides, why wouldn't I laugh? I had the best job in the world. I never went to a production meeting. If I wasn't involved in a sketch, I didn't even go to the rehearsal. I'd get to the studio in time to run through any commercials I had to do, but that was really all the preparation my job required. In fact, most of the time I didn't even know who our guests were going to be until I walked by the dressing rooms on the way to my office and saw their names on the doors. Before the show, I would check with Freddy de Cordova to see if there was anything I needed to know about that night's show; he'd tell me, for example, that Johnny was going to set fire to the studio in the third segment and that I should not try to put it out. But otherwise everything that happened on the show was completely fresh for me. And for that I was paid a wonderful salary. So I think the real question should have been, why didn't I laugh more?

One thing I did do for only the first twenty-seven years was the warm-up. Just before a TV show begins, someone, usually the announcer, comes out and spends a few minutes familiarizing the audience with the studio and getting them excited about what they are about to see. For example, I'd point out the APPLAUSE sign and explain that when it was lit they should applaud loudly, and then confide in them that Johnny had told me that when he retired that was the only thing from the set he wanted to take with him—and he intended to hang it in his bedroom. The job, as I tried to do it, was to turn a lot of individuals into a responsive group. I likened it to taking five hundred pearls and turning them into a necklace. However, on rare occasions, it turned out to be a noose.

Only once in my broadcasting career have I been fired, and that was because of something I said during the warm-up. When I was doing *Five Minutes More,* the wonderful schoolteacher-turned-comedian Sam Levenson appeared on my show several times and we became friends. When Sam was hired by Mark Goodson to host the quiz show *Two for the Money,* he hired me as his announcer. This was a big opportunity for me, a network show, as well as a regular paycheck.

During the warm-up one night, I told the audience, "Sometimes when you see a show like this you're a little tired, maybe a little shy, and you don't want to laugh out loud. If you were home watching, you'd be laughing. If you were on a bus with your sister, you'd be laughing. But since you're in a strange area, you don't know the people sitting next to you, you try to hold your laugh in. I must warn you about that. That's a very dangerous thing to do. Tonight, when you feel a laugh coming on, you must let it out. Please, do not hold your laugh in. It is a well-known medical fact that if you hold a laugh in, it will settle in your lower colon and that can be quite painful. Just the other night, for example, we had a lady here, a very large lady, in fact she was a very fat lady, she made the serious mistake of letting a laugh settle in her lower colon. It took four ushers to carry her out and I'm still waiting to hear from the hospital about how she's doing. So I implore you, ladies and gentlemen, do not let that happen to you. I am legally bound to tell you that we cannot be responsible if you hold in . . ."

Mark Goodson fired me because I said it was a fat lady. He thought that was disrespectful to the audience. I couldn't believe it. Several years later I hosted two quiz shows for Goodson and Bill Todman. Fortunately, I didn't have to do the warm-up on either show.

On *The Tonight Show* Freddy de Cordova would greet the audience and introduce me. "Here is the gentleman who is a big star of the show," he'd say, perhaps exaggerating a bit there, "a great friend and a man who has been known to take a drink. Watch now, you'll see him stumble out here . . ."

I was always greeted warmly by the audience. They felt that I was their guy on the show, the person they could sit down with and have a drink. Or two. *Tonight Show* audiences were always very excited. In many cases, they'd written months in advance for their tickets; they might even have planned their whole vacation around the show. They were always surprised by the set, and couldn't stop talking about it. It was much smaller than it appeared to be on television, the curtain was higher, the band was squashed into a small area. So, unlike many other shows, the purpose of the warm-up was not to get the audience involved but rather to calm people down.

The *Tonight Show* audience also had a role to play on the show. Members of the audience knew their lines. When Johnny said, for example, "This is a very strange audience," they recognized their cue and responded, "How strange is it?" Which allowed him to reply, "I'll tell you. Just before the show, a sweet, elderly lady came up to me and said, 'I'd like to capture you on canvas.' I said, 'You mean you'd like to paint my portrait?' She said, 'No, I've got an army cot in my Winnebago.'" At times, during his monologue, someone would yell out and Johnny would respond with a look or an ad-lib. He'd often refer directly to the audience, drawing in a deep breath, raising his eyebrows, tilting his head, and deciding, "You people are tough tonight. You're the kind of people who would send an Arrow shirt to General Custer." My job was to get everybody relaxed and comfortable, to make them feel welcome, but also to remind them to be on their best behavior because they were going to be seen by millions of people. "So if you're here with somebody you're not supposed to be with . . ."

I've always felt that the thing that made our audience so loyal is that they knew they were in on our big jokes. I used that knowledge to make them feel welcome. I'd tell them, "I'm really glad to be here 'cause just a little while ago I didn't think I was going to make it. I just felt so bad and I didn't want to come on and do a bad show for you folks. But the funniest thing happened. I called across the street to El Toritos, a little Mexican place, and they sent over the most delicious yellow soup I've ever tasted. Unfortunately, it was probably quite hot when they made it, but by the time they got it across the street it was quite cool. Funny, the way they'd seasoned it, they'd put the salt all around the edge of the container. A very nice girl named Margarita brought it over. I drank the whole thing down. I can't wait to get more of their soup . . ."

Every audience worried that Johnny wouldn't be hosting the show that night. "Boy," I'd begin, "I don't know how to tell you this, but we have a real mix-up tonight. The girl who does the scheduling went out to lunch and had three martinis. When she came back to set up the schedule she got the whole thing screwed up. So Johnny, Doc, and I are all here on the same night."

The more personal the warm-up seemed, the better the audience responded. If someone coughed, for example, I'd pause and sympathize with them. "Oh, that's a terrible cough," I'd say. "I'm sure we must be selling something for that. Oh, we're selling Formula 44 tonight, we'll get you some. Formula 44 . . . You ever wonder what went wrong with all the formulas from one to forty-three?"

Finally I'd introduce Doc Severinsen. "I call him Tiffany Lips, he calls me Golden Throat. Tommy Newsom, what can I say about Tommy Newsom?" I would wonder and then pause as if I were trying to think of something, then pause a little longer, then start to say something but stop. "Well, nothing actually." The band would play, and we would open the show.

Doc, Tommy, Skitch, Freddy, the band, the crew, our guests, the writers—we all played important roles in the show's success, but *The Tonight Show* had the longest run of any entertainment program in television history because of one person, and that person was the beautiful and gracious Aunt Blabby, the amazing El Moldo, the incredible Carnac, the frenetic Art Fern, the sincere Floyd R. Turbo, and the innocent and slightly naive man from Nebraska, Johnny Carson. Johnny brought to *The Tonight Show* a blend of extraordinary abilities. He was a terrific stand-up comedian, a fine interviewer, a great ad-libber, and he had perfect comic timing, and he built the show around these abilities.

Johnny did not write his monologues; with everything else he had to do that would have been impossible. The writers would submit fifty or sixty jokes and he would pick the jokes he wanted, find a thread, and weave them together. But the jokes really just served as a starting point for his nightly conversation with America. Generally, the monologue included jokes from several different categories. For example, there were always a few topical jokes, allowing Johnny to comment on the day's news. "Teachers in Newark, New Jersey, are striking for higher pay," he'd explain. "I don't know, I think they need it. Apparently they have to pay for their own bullets."

He did a lot of political jokes, but he was an equal opportunity comedian. Even after watching him for three decades, people still didn't know his politics. When Republican president George Bush attempted to relate to inner-city kids by showing them how to fly cast, for example, Johnny said, "He also showed them how to signal from their schooners when they run out of Grey Poupon." And when Democratic Speaker of the House Jim Wright was forced to resign because he'd circumvented House rules by making thousands of dollars selling his book to supporters, Johnny suggested, "Part of his deal was that he would resign if the committee bought ten thousand copies of his book."

You didn't appreciate that joke? As Johnny would say in this situation, "You're the kind of people who would give condoms to pandas."

The targets of his monologue were often things viewers could relate to in their own lives, from the company cafeteria—"I asked the waitress what was on the menu today. She said it was a dead fly"—to the company itself—"I got a Christmas card from General Electric today. It said, 'In lieu of a gift, a GE employee has been laid off in your name.'" After the laugh, he added, "I guess that joke blows my chance of being employee of the month."

And somewhere in just about every monologue, he'd make reference to me or Doc or Tommy. "Ed drinks a lot but he never gets in trouble," he told the audience one night. "If he gets a little loud, a friendly bartender pours two warning shots over his head."

When a joke or several flopped, which happened on occasion, the audience would groan or, on occasion, even hiss. That was their role in the monologue. It's difficult to explain a groaner. But if you heard one, you'd groan. Johnny would respond, "Hoo-kay," and continue bravely ahead. "Never buy jokes from people on the street," he might explain after several jokes had died. "Give 'em a quarter, but never buy a joke from 'em."

And each night, he'd finish the monologue with one of TV's best-known and imitated gestures—a golf swing. I have absolutely no idea why he started doing that golf swing. Maybe he thought it would help him beat Paar.

Now you know how to recognize a groaner.

The thing that made Johnny such a good interviewer was that he listened to his guests, whether he was speaking to Martin Luther King or Tiny Tim, and he responded directly to their answers. He didn't just ask a list of questions, he had a conversation. Before the show, a talent coordinator would interview the guests and suggest what we called "islands of conversation." For example, "Ask him about the night he slept under a pregnant elephant." But most often, Johnny wouldn't get to these notes; he'd find something that interested him and go to that. When guest hosts would ask me how to do the show, I'd tell them, "In hosting this show you have to have the curiosity of a child and you have to listen, because your next question is in the last answer. And if you don't ask it, the audience is going to feel deprived." The first night a legendary comedian hosted the show, our guest was the brilliant Scatman Crothers, who was then starring in *Chico and the Man.* He was the perfect guest; he'd been in show business for two hundred years, he'd performed at Lincoln's inauguration, and he was a great storyteller. So he told the guest host, "Boy, I'm nervous tonight. You know, in my career I've done just about everything. I was in vaudeville, I was in burlesque, radio, television, I've done just about everything you can do in show business, but you know what, until tonight I was never nervous."

That is technically known in the world of professional straight men as a slam dunk, the perfect setup. There is only one possible response to that statement. And obviously Scatman Crothers had his answer ready for that question. He may have had a whole routine built around that question. But we will never know because the nervous host asked him, "So how long do you think *Chico and the Man* will go on?"

Like so many guest hosts, this comedian was so concerned about his next question that he just didn't listen. Johnny listened, which allowed him to deliver the perfect ad-lib. I'm going to tell you a show business secret: some ad-libs are more ad-libbed than others. Sometimes ad-libs are actually scripted, but Johnny rarely resorted to prepared material. He didn't need it. Most of the funniest things he ever did could not have been planned. I'll give you an example. The first time Muhammad Ali appeared on the show, when he was still known as Cassius Clay, he was in training for his first major fight at Madison Square Garden. No one knew too much about him, but his brash personality, his poetry, his ability to name the round in which he was going to knock out his opponent, and his insistence that he was the greatest had made him very controversial. Johnny asked him what he would do if his opponent, Doug Jones, beat him.

In his own shy, humble way, Ali replied, "If Doug Jones beats me, I'll get down on my hands and knees, crawl across the ring, kiss his feet, tell him, 'Man, you are the greatest,' then go to the airport and get the next jet out of the country."

By the time the laughter had died down, Johnny had the perfect response. "Yeah, but you just can't go in that ring with all that insecurity. I mean, you do that, and he'll kill you."

Johnny could get more out of less than any performer I've ever seen. One night we had a woman accordion player on the show and just as she was about to perform, she confided to Carson, "Well, Doc said . . ." Then she looked over to the band and asked Doc Severinsen, "You told me I could call you Doc?"

That's all Johnny had to hear. "He's not a medical doctor," Johnny explained. "Did he tell you he was a medical doctor? Did he try that old routine about being a medical doctor again? We've had some problems about that here in the studio . . ."

People generally agree that Jack Benny, whose character was the cheapest man in the world, got the longest laugh in radio history when he replied to a robber's demand, "Your money or your life . . . ," with complete silence. And then more silence. The longer the silence lasted, the louder the laughter. Finally, when the robber began repeating his demands, Jack Benny interrupted him and said, "I'm thinking it over."

I think Johnny Carson got the longest laugh in TV history the night Ed Ames, who played an Indian named Mingo on the series *Daniel Boone*, demonstrated how to throw a tomahawk. Ames was supposed to teach Johnny the correct way of tossing a hatchet by throwing it at the outline of a man drawn on a large wooden board, then Johnny would try it. But when Ames threw his hatchet, it landed right where a man should not be struck. I mean, bull's-eye. Let me describe it this way: if it had been a bull, after this it no longer would have been. These were the kind of moments Johnny just lived for. The audience was hysterical; I looked at him and I could almost see his mind whirling. It was like a computer searching for the proper response. Ames immediately began moving forward to retrieve his hatchet, but Johnny grabbed him. Johnny was holding two hatchets, and he stood there sharpening those hatchets as he waited for the laughter to subside. His timing was impeccable. Finally, at just the right moment, he told Ames, "I didn't even know you were Jewish." That started the laughter all over again, and when that wave quieted down, he announced, "Welcome to *Frontier Briss*."

Eventually the audience calmed down, and an obviously embarrassed Ed Ames asked, "You want to try it?"

Johnny shook his head no, saying, "I couldn't hurt him any more than you did."

Not all of Carson's ad-libs were verbal. He did a lot of great physical humor on the show. I remember one evening when things got completely out of control. Believe me, none of this stuff could be planned. Johnny got into an egg fight with Dom DeLuise, which ended with Carson dropping an egg down the front of DeLuise's pants and then breaking it. Johnny then turned around and started throwing eggs at me. At me! Finally Burt Reynolds came out with a can of whipped cream. After spraying just about everything, Reynolds put the can down the front of Johnny's pants and squirted whipped cream straight down. Now here was Carson's genius. When he took the can from Reynolds, I'm sure everyone expected him to squirt it down Reynolds's pants. I know I did. But instead, he put it down his own pants and, with a big smile on his face, squirted it again.

I don't know how many people can say, as I can, that for thirty-four years I looked forward to going to work every day. When I started in television in Philadelphia, we were thrilled simply to be on the air. All the programming I did was live and anything was possible. Television really wasn't so much of a business in those days as a wonder. Of course, that changed very fast. By the time we started doing *The Tonight Show*, TV had become a very profitable, professional business and every minute of every show was carefully planned and rehearsed. What made *The Tonight Show* so much fun for me as well as for our audience was that we treated it like a live show. Even though we taped in advance, we rarely edited anything out of the tape. Most of the things that happened on the show weren't planned and weren't rehearsed. I think Johnny probably expressed it best one night when expert Jim Fowler brought a marmoset, a monkey, on the show. As this monkey climbed to the highest ground on the stage, in this case Johnny's head, Johnny said, "Name me one other place in this entire world of four and a half billion people where a man is sitting with a marmoset on his head . . ."

To which I added, being completely supportive, "If you turn sideways the tail is extended and it's very cute."

And after doing the show for all those years, when I look back on it, I really have only one thing I want to say to Mr. Carson: Nietzsche?

5

The only things scripted on *The Tonight Show* were commercials and sketches, so most of the time I too had to ad-lib my part. And as I look back over those wonderful years, I remember with great happiness some of my favorite ad-libs. For example, how could I ever forget, "That was terrific, Johnny." Or, "No kidding?" And, "Yes, I do, all the time." Here's one from the early days of the show: "Really? That's amazing." One that the audience loved was, "Boy, right on this show." Then there are the classics like, "How big was it?" "How high was it?" and "How cold was it?"...

As we all know, sometimes life isn't fair. While Johnny got to sit and talk with Raquel Welch, I got to hold up a can of Budweiser. No one ever successfully defined my role on the show. Originally I was hired to do announcements and live commercials, but the job expanded quickly. Besides the billboards and commercials, I did the five-spot with Johnny, I was there when he needed someone to play off, I acted in sketches, and for most of our run I worked with our guest hosts when Johnny took the night off. For someone who seemingly had very little to do, I did a lot of it.

A rare photo of my father
(left), two friends, and me
(right) on the beach in
Atlantic City. It's rare we were
on the beach rather than
working on the boardwalk
seen in the background.

My grandmother Katie Fitzgerald McMahon
and grandfather Joe McMahon on the back
porch of their home in Lowell. It was there
that I practiced being a radio broadcaster—
for better or verse.

On leave in Lowell,
Massachusetts, with my
parents.

Aviation Cadet
McMahon

As I learned early in my career, television can be an extraordinary means of conveying important ideas— and the important idea I'm conveying as host of the Miss Philadelphia Contest for the Miss Universe Pageant is that nothing attracts a larger audience than beautiful women in bathing suits.

As usual in our clown act on *The Big Top*, my partner, Chris Keegan *(left)*, proves to me that bad things happen to good clowns—otherwise there is no act.

One night, when I walked into the *Million Dollar Movie* vault to get that night's film, the crew closed the door behind me—forcing me to walk around the rear of the set and seem to magically appear through a wall.

When I met Marilyn Monroe on the set of *How to Marry a Millionaire*, she told me, "You know, Ed, I don't have anything on under this." But, of course, I saw right through that. Hi-yooooo!

When I was hosting my late night show *Five Minutes More*, Jack Benny came to Philadelphia for a concert. He was so pleased I didn't ask to be photographed holding my ears as he played his violin, he agreed to pose with me doing my version of the famed "Benny take."

Just about everything I did on *McMahon and Company* was made up as we went along; but rarely did we actually do any making-up on the air as pictured here.

Just exactly what is it that makes a good quiz show host? Is it just debonair good looks, the ability to ask questions and control the game, or does it also require the skills to entertain the audience?

Was it really possible for me to work on the *Tonight Show* every night while hosting daily afternoon quiz shows like *Snap Judgment* and *Missing Links*?

Whodunnit?, the first attempt to broadcast a quiz show in prime time since the scandals. How silly would I look in a Sherlock Holmes cap? (courtesy of NBC/Globe Photos)

From the NBC radio studios, not-so-high atop Rockefeller Center in the heart of New York City, I fulfilled my lifelong ambition to be a radio announcer as host of the feature program *Monitor*. *(courtesy of NBC)*

When the producers of my special *Ed McMahon and Friends at Cypress Gardens* told me they wanted me to do a Superman takeoff, I thought they meant an impersonation. *(courtesy of NBC/Globe Photos)*

When my syndicated show Star Search moved to the Disney-MGM Studios at Walt Disney World in Orlando, Florida . . .

. . . we discovered future stars like Sinbad . . .

. . . although, unfortunately, we still had to reject many people, like that kid Rodney Dangerfield, "Still getting no respect." *(courtesy of Walt Disney Company)*

In this 1977 magazine ad I prove the old adage "Two 'Eds are better than one." *(courtesy of the Anheuser-Busch Corporation)*

My good friend Dick Clark and I were cohosting *Bloopers and Practical Jokes* when Johnny surprised us. "Ed's got three other jobs tonight after this," he complained. "He's doing 'Celebrity Mud Wrestling,' 'Bowling for Towels,' and a week ago I opened my front door and there was Ed in a dress, claiming he was the Avon Lady." *(courtesy of NBC/Globe Photos)*

D'Arcy president Tony Amendola *(left)* gave John Wayne *(center)* a million dollars to produce and star in a ninety-minute variety show, *Sing Out, Sweet Land,* at the time the most expensive TV show ever done— and the highest-rated variety special.

The only palace I ever played was Caesar's, but I presented an award to Princess Grace of Philadelphia and Monaco as John B. Kelly and Eddie Fisher looked on.

And I did emcee a show for Queen Elizabeth on the set of M*A*S*H, featuring show business royalty Frank Sinatra, Dionne Warwick, and George Burns.

On the *Tonight Show*, I worked with guest hosts of all sizes and shapes and species, ranging from Orson Welles to someone who lived at the bottom of a well, Kermit the Frog. *(courtesy of NBC/Globe Photos)*

Bob Hope appeared
on the show more
frequently than any other
guest, 132 times.

Johnny's door was always
open to big stars, like
Elizabeth Taylor and
Michael Douglas.

Our musical guests ranged from Paul
McCartney to Tiny Tim. Even I sang one
night to promote my nightclub act. Tiny
Tim's 1969 wedding to "Miss Vicki" drew
forty-five million viewers, our largest
audience. (courtesy of NBC/Globe
Photos)

The biggest stars often visited the show. On one of our anniversary celebrations Jack Benny, Joey Bishop, and I are dressed to the nines, while Don Rickles is dressed to the . . . twos. But the biggest star ever to appear on the show was Wilt Chamberlain, at 7'1". *(courtesy of NBC/Globe Photos)*

Two years after Johnny, Doc, and I finished our run, I appeared on *The Tonight Show with Jay Leno.* We did a bit in which I was supposed to read a real advertising slogan and he would then explain what it "really meant." "Oh," I said, "I do the setup and you do the snapper. So nothing's changed."

Me and "The Master."

It was my job to ask the great mentalist El Moldo, "What am I holding in my hand this TIME?" and listen to crabby Aunt Blabby complain. "Not only can't I get a date, men come into my house to steal my calendars!" and be told by Carnac, "May a herd of crazed decorators wallpaper your sister's tent!"

We shared the stage with bandleader Skitch Henderson until 1966, when the great Doc Severinsen assumed the podium.

Our childhood photos make it obvious that
we were destined to work together
(Nate Cutler, Globe Photos).

From our first *Tonight Show*
together on October 1, 1962,
to our last appearance thirty
years later on May 22, 1992,
Johnny Carson and I spent
6,583 *Tonights* together.
And how I wish we were
starting all over again.

And one of the great men, Father Herbert A. Ward, at St. Jude's ranch.

In this photograph, taken at the Horatio Alger Foundation dinner in 1997, everyone is a marine. I want my epitaph to read, "He was a good broadcaster, but a great marine."

One of the great moments of my life, as Jerry Lewis and I celebrate the announcement that we've raised more than fifty million dollars for the first time on the Muscular Dystrophy telethon.

The plaque at the Michael McMahon sports complex at St. Jude's ranch.

Michael Edward McMahon
(1951–1995)

Michael McMahon and Dad

(ARE YOU MIKE McMAHON?) | YEP.....THATS ME! | (YOU WON FIRST PRIZE IN THE BABY CONTEST!) .....AWWWW | (YOU WIN $200 CASH OR A T.V. APPEARANCE!)

.....WHEW!! $200!!.. | ....MONEY MAKES ME NERVOUS...! | ...WHADAYOU THINK DAD?.. | .....WE'LL TAKE THE MONEY!!

Jeff, Michael, and Lex

The McMahon Family Album

With Jeff and Claudia

Me and my best friend, Charlie Cullen, with our sons, Bill and Mike

Katherine

Jeff and Martha

Linda and Peter

"Brace yourself, he's cooommmi-innng!" My grandson, Matt

My son Lex

Pam and me, and our best person, Katherine, on our wedding day, at the Ed McMahon Child Care Center at St. Jude's ranch.

Claudia, Martha, and Linda

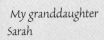

My granddaughter Maggie

My granddaughter Alex

My granddaughter Sarah

Pam and me at her first major New York fashion show.

Tom Arnold with me as I nervously watch Pam's show.

Pam and me (Michael McCreary)

Ed and Pam at their Christmas party

Left to right: Peter Schmerge, Michael, Linda, Cap'n McMahon, Pam, Jeff, Claudia, Alex, Katherine, and Sarah

The Skipjacks return from our annual unsuccessful fishing excursion: (left to right) John Millar, Bob Gillin, Art Williams, Jake "The Mouse" Moran, Bob Haley, and me.

As the famous troubadour Steve Martin sang during his first appearance on the show, "We're gonna have a lot of fun. We got laughter, we got surprises. We got forty-seven minutes of commercials . . ." Admittedly, at times *The Tonight Show* seemed to be one long commercial interrupted occasionally by entertainment, but that's why it's called show *business*. The importance given our sponsors on the show is probably best exemplified by my greeting to the forty-five million viewers of Tiny Tim's wedding to seventeen-year-old Miss Vicki in 1969. "We cordially request the pleasure of your company at the marriage of Tiny Tim and Miss Vicki right here on *The Tonight Show*," I told the largest audience we ever had. "But right now, here are some words of wisdom from Pepto-Bismol tablets."

I can't begin to estimate how many commercials I did for how many products on the show. But the most amazing thing is how few of the thousands of demonstrations I did went wrong. When I started doing the show, like every commercial spokesperson, every salesman, I was afraid that something would go wrong on the air. That happened for the first time about three or four years after we started doing the show. And the sponsor's reaction really surprised me. The product was a tape recorder, I think the company was called Voice Magic, and we had to get special permission from the Federal Communications Commission to record my voice on the air, then play it back. In rehearsal it worked perfectly. But on the air something went wrong; the recorder didn't work. So I fumbled around with it, then started doing the spot all over again. It just didn't work. It was supposed to be a sixty-second commercial; by the time I was finished, it probably ran about five minutes. I felt awful. This poor sponsor was paying a lot of money to demonstrate this wonderful product and somehow I had screwed it up. That's the end of that sponsor, I thought.

I was completely wrong. The company loved the attention, they loved the fact that everyone was talking about the commercial that didn't work. They got more name recognition because the spot failed than they ever would have gotten had it worked. Instead of canceling, they extended their commercial commitment.

I don't think we ever lost a sponsor because something went wrong. On those rare occasions when a demonstration failed, I tried to correct it immediately. One night, for example, I was doing a spot for a plastic wrap and to show how this particular wrap sealed so tightly, I was to fill a glass with red wine, stretch the plastic over the mouth of the glass, and then turn it upside down to show that no wine spilled out of the glass. Again, it worked perfectly in rehearsal. But when I did it live on the air, I accidentally overlapped the wrapping, creating a ridge, so that when I turned it upside down, the wine poured out. The audience thought it was hysterical. I was laughing, but only on the outside.

I knew it was my fault and I intended to correct it. So I picked up my plastic wrap, my wine bottle, and my glass and I walked over to Johnny's desk. I poured the wine in the glass and put down the bottle. Then very carefully I took the plastic wrap and stretched it over the mouth of the glass. As I did this, Johnny was watching very closely; he wasn't really sure what I had in mind.

Then I held the glass over Johnny's head and turned it upside down. Not a drop spilled. "Thank you very much, ladies and gentlemen," I said. "I think I proved my point." Now, that was a pretty brave thing to do. Suppose the wrap leaked again? Oh sure, when I went to look for my next job I would have had two minutes of great television, but . . .

It wasn't always my fault when something went wrong. One night, for Lipton tea, I believe, I was supposed to show viewers how simple it was to brew a cup of instant tea. Unfortunately, our propman forgot to fill the pitcher with water. When I went to pour the water in the glass, the pitcher was empty. I laughed, the audience laughed, and I explained that if I had water, I would have shown viewers how easy it was to make this delicious drink in their own homes, and then I added, "In fact, it's a drink our propman could be enjoying in his own home tomorrow night, because he certainly won't be here."

Certainly the best-known commercial we ever did was for our wonderful longtime sponsor, Alpo dog food. Whenever possible I liked to test a product before I agreed to do their commercials. That worked just fine in the case of Anheuser-Busch, for example—actually the cases of Anheuser-Busch; however, with Alpo, I took our dog's bark for it. I always had a warm spot in my heart for Alpo. The name came from the fact that it was invented in Allentown, Pennsylvania. It was just being sold locally when I started in Philadelphia and it was one of my early sponsors. I loved the fact that I started doing Alpo commercials when it was a small company and grew with it as it became the largest-selling dog food in America.

Alpo was one of our first sponsors when Johnny and I started doing *The Tonight Show*. The spots never changed very much; as I read my copy, a very hungry dog would demonstrate just how much dogs loved Alpo by gulping it down. Now, the truth is that we made sure that the dog would love Alpo by giving him only a small taste of it during the afternoon rehearsal. By the time we did the show in the evening, I guarantee you, that dog was hungry. Although we used all kinds of breeds, for a long time our regular was a beautiful English sheepdog named Patrick. One night Patrick must have had other plans, because we were using a beagle named Hernandez. The commercial started normally enough; I was sitting on a chair on a raised platform holding up a can of dog food. "Alpo is the only one of the leading dog foods that has real beef . . . ," I began, and at that point the dog was supposed to run to his bowl and

start eating. But Hernandez had stage fright. As I continued, "The real beef could be the reason Hernandez here . . . ,"
Hernandez walked away. I tried to coax him back,
"Com'ere, come on, come here, here it is, come on up,
come on . . ." He took one bite, then turned and walked
away. The audience started laughing, but I persisted. I took
my commercials seriously. "He's a little frightened," I apol-
ogized for the dog. "Come on, come on, dog . . . well, Hernandez is a little . . ."

And then I saw Johnny come into my little commercial
area. He got down on his hands and knees and came over to
me. "Come right up, nice Hernandez," I said as I started to
pet Johnny. Nice boss, I was thinking as I pet him on the
head, nice boss. By this point the audience was hysterical.
Carson wagged his rump to show how much he loved Alpo. I
just kept going. I was going to get my commercial done. "The
next time you're looking at the canned dog food . . ."—he
rubbed his cheek against my leg— ". . . nice Hernandez . . .
reach for the can that contains real beef . . ." Johnny got up
on his knees and started begging for more. I started petting
him again . . . and then he licked my hand. Good boss, good.

And I still managed to conclude, gratefully, "And doesn't
your dog deserve Alpo?"

Maybe what surprised me most when I saw Carson was
that he was trying to help me. Normally, when I did commercials, he did everything he could to cause me problems,
from giving me a hotfoot to setting my script on fire. I did
the commercials in a little area backstage. This commercial
area was just behind the main set. To get there, I had to walk
around the end of the set beyond the couch. Going that way
enabled me to leave while Johnny was still on the air without being seen. It was a walk of about fifty feet, so it took
only a few seconds to get there. Whenever I had a live spot
to do, I'd leave about thirty seconds early to get ready. But
one night—as it turns out, it was a live Alpo spot—Johnny
wouldn't let me go.

As I quietly got up to leave, he asked, "Where are you going?"

"Nowhere," I said.

Now, he knew exactly where I was going. The entire audience knew where I was going. "I thought you were getting up," he said.

"Oh, no, no, I'm staying right here," I told him. "I wouldn't leave you. You're the boss. You want me to stay here, I'll stay right here. What time do they close this place?"

"Oh, okay, good," he decided, then returned to whatever he was doing. And as soon as he did, I'd start to leave.

He stopped me. "*Now* where are you going?" he demanded. "Can't you sit still?"

"I'm right here, right where you need me."

Of course, Johnny was making a big deal out of watching me from the corner of his eye, and in that way directing the audience's attention on me. "As I was saying . . ." I got up to leave again. "Now what is your problem tonight?"

I have spent my entire life being on time. Maybe it's my marine training, maybe I learned it from my father. But when I am scheduled to be somewhere at a certain time, I am there. It really bothers me when I'm even a few minutes late. This commercial was scheduled to run at a specific moment; I intended to be there. "Well, John," I admitted, "I'm just going to take a little walk backstage and see, maybe, you know, maybe there's a little dog back there I can talk to. Maybe he's lonely. Maybe he's hungry. Maybe I can find a can of dog food for him . . ."

"Well, why don't you just sit there," he said. Once again he started speaking, then stopped in the middle as if he'd caught me.

I held up my hands. "I'm right here. See. I'm not going anywhere. I'm staying."

"You're sure?"

"I'm sure."

"Good," he said, then faced the camera, held up a can of dog food, and said quickly, "and now, here's Ed with a message from Alpo."

Carson wasn't the only one on that show trying to cause me problems. He was just the ringleader. One night I was doing a serious spot, I think it was for a life insurance company, and I looked up to see Buddy Hackett standing right next to the camera. And as I looked into that camera and started speaking to viewers in a somber voice, he started taking his clothes off. I mean, all his clothes: his shirt, shoes, pants, shorts. I am here to tell you, my friends, that is not a pretty sight.

Buddy Hackett's body looks like a large lump of silly putty acting really silly. Perhaps for the first time, as I looked at his body, I understood the derivation of the phrase "belly laugh," because it was almost impossible to look at that belly and not laugh. I tried to remain serious, I tried not to laugh, particularly when I had to say phrases like "taking care of your family." And I did it. Everyone has his own definition of professionalism. Mine has something to do with getting through a complete commercial while Buddy Hackett is doing a striptease right next to the camera.

I take great pride in my professionalism. I'm always on time, prepared, and ready to go to work. Very rarely have I allowed anything to distract me while I'm working. But there is one night on *The Tonight Show* that comes to mind. Again, it was an Alpo spot. By the time this happened, I had been doing Alpo commercials for years. The copy changed a little, but the commercials were all pretty much the same. Because I was busy filming the movie *Fun with Dick and Jane* with Jane Fonda and George Segal in the afternoon, I didn't have time to rehearse this commercial. I really wasn't the slightest bit concerned, I'd done thousands of commercials, I figured what could go wrong? But because I wasn't at rehearsal, I didn't know they were using a new dog.

That night, at the right time, I slipped around the end of the set and ran toward the commercial set. And as I did, the woman in charge of the commercials said casually, "Watch out for this dog, Ed." I turned and saw this big German shepherd sitting quietly. A big shepherd. I immediately stopped running. I walked very gingerly to my chair and sat down. I didn't want to disturb him. As the commercial started, I had several thoughts in my mind, none of them having anything to do with the commercial: why exactly should I watch out for this dog? What's wrong with him? What's he doing? When it came time to push the bowl of dog food closer to him, I did it very carefully. I mean, I never took my eyes off this dog. I finished the commercial, but it was not one of the more convincing spots I've ever done.

When the commercial ended, I couldn't wait to get off the set. But I didn't rush. Not with Rex the killer dog still eating. I stood up slowly and walked casually away. When I was far enough away, I asked, "What the hell was that all about? Why did I have to watch this dog?"

"Oh, it was nothing," she replied. "He played an attack dog in some movie yesterday, but they deprogrammed him this morning."

Nothing? A big, hungry attack dog? I asked, "Does the dog know he's been deprogrammed? How do we know that he knows he was acting?" Well, at least that dog ate his Alpo.

Johnny and I did rehearse the sketches we did together, but most of the time what we did on the air was not what we rehearsed. In one sketch, for example, I played a reporter interviewing the world's oldest living man. Johnny was dressed in a zebra-skin loincloth, he was carrying the long staff of life, and his makeup was terrific. In fact, his makeup was the best thing in the sketch. The jokes were awful. The funniest thing about it was that a few jokes into the sketch Johnny and I, as well as the entire audience, realized it wasn't funny, and it wasn't going to be funny. It was filled with bad jokes and single entendres. Finally, Johnny, still in character, said to me, "You know what I'm going to do?"

"Well no," I said, "I don't."

"I'm going to get out of this sketch." And with that he turned around and walked back into his cave, leaving me out there all by myself.

I didn't hesitate. I yelled, "Take me with you!" and followed him as fast as I could.

We always tried to maintain our professionalism during these sketches, but sometimes we'd get so far away from the material that it was just impossible to get back. Often we just ended up giggling like two little kids. One night when things were completely out of control, it might have been the sketch we did about the famous nude bowler who had special bowling ba . . . well, I'll let you finish that joke. Johnny, who was wearing his bowling . . . equipment, looked at me, shook his head, and said in wonder, "Do you believe that two grown men . . ."

To which I added carefully, "Graduates of major universities . . ." From that night on, whenever things got out of control Johnny would look at me and say it again. And again.

I never knew what Aunt Blabby was going to do to me. Oh, sweet, dear Aunt Blabby, the lovable old lady who would happily run me over with her motorcycle if I stood between her and a handsome man. One night while wearing golf shoes, she accidentally stepped on my toes with her spikes, causing me to limp for a week. We've probably all got Aunt Blabbys in our families, particularly those of us who come from really dysfunctional families. I think it is fair of me to say that the team of Blabby and McMahon will take its place among the many wonderful man-and-woman teams in show business history, teams like Burns and Allen and Lucy and Ricky, and that place is way down at the bottom, way, way down. My role with Aunt Blabby can probably best be described as tormentee. One night, for example, Aunt Blabby told me she was seeing an analyst. "Oh really," I said, as if that were a surprise, just as it was written. "I didn't know you were seeing an analyst."

To which she replied, and this was not written, "I just told you I was . . . Why don't you listen to me? Bert Parks"—the perennial host of the Miss America pageant—"is available 364 days a year, you know that? One day a year he works, he can be here every night. You know, I've been depressed lately?"

I recognized my cue. "Depressed?"

"Yessss, depressed. Why do you repeat everything?" she scolded me. "I could go to Taco Bell for that . . ."

Johnny enjoyed putting me on the defensive in our sketches, knowing that the audience enjoyed it too. So when he found something that worked, he never hesitated. We were doing Aunt Blabby one night, I think she had just returned from Club Med—she went accidentally, she thought it was Club Men—and very early in the sketch, either by accident or on purpose—and I have my suspicions—she hit me with her cane in the crotch. I jumped back. That was a mistake on my part; I should have remembered that old show business adage, never show weakness to Carson in an Aunt Blabby sketch. He knew he had something going, so he hit me again. And as I jumped back again, he said, "Where are you going?"

"Nowhere," I said, backing up. The cameraman was shooting this from the waist up, so viewers at home couldn't see what was going on. But the audience in the studio was hysterical.

"Why are you walking away from me," she asked, swinging that cane again. "If you want to do the interview, stay here."

I backed up a few more feet.

"See, there you go again. Do you want to talk to me or don't you?" Boom. Again. I wonder if there is an organization for abused straight men?

I think our most popular sketches were the visits of Carnac the Magnificent. Carnac was a psychic who would give the answers to questions sealed in an envelope. My role in Carnac developed over time; originally all I was supposed to do was introduce him. But I improvised some things and the audience liked them and they became important elements in the sketch. What was supposed to be a brief introduction eventually became "Ladies and gentlemen, it is now time to introduce that wonderful visitor from the East. We have not seen him for many a fortnight and it is now time for his return. And so, I am pleased to introduce the famous sage, seer, soothsayer, the all-knowing, all-seeing, all-omniscient, and former dress designer to Janet Reno—or former tax adviser to Governor Reagan, or former campaign adviser to George McGovern, or former musical director of the Sex Pistols, or whatever—Carnac the Magnificent!"

Johnny would come out dressed in a shawl and turban, take two steps . . . and trip right over the stair. I would try to help him and he would push me away. "Welcome," I began, "welcome, old—"

"Not so old," he would correct me. Eventually he would settle down behind his desk. My job was simply to hand him sealed envelopes, but I began embellishing on that and it too became an important part of the skit. "I hold in my hands the envelopes," I announced seriously. "A child of four can plainly see that these envelopes have been hermetically sealed"—I have no idea where any of this stuff came from—"and they have been kept in a mayonnaise jar on Funk and Wagnall's porch since noon today. No one knows the contents of these envelopes, but *you*, oh great Carnac, in your magical, mystical, and borderline divine way, will ascertain the answer to the question, having never before heard the question. Is that about it?"

I'd hand him the first envelope. He would hold it against his forehead, as if trying to mentally read its contents. And when he did, I would repeat, "Hermetically sealed . . . ," and laugh.

He'd glare at me. "Please, I must have absolute silence."

Which was always my cue to respond, "Carnac has had that many times before . . ."

Then Carnac would reveal the answer. "Hi, diddle diddle."

And I would repeat that answer, seriously, as if it had been carved in stone. "Hi, diddle diddle."

And as I did, Carnac would tear open the envelope, blow into it to puff it open, then withdraw the question to which he'd just given the answer. In this case, "How do you greet your diddle in the morning?"

Those were the jokes, folks, and we still lasted thirty years! I will be honest, sometimes Johnny and I were laughing at the quality of the jokes rather than at the jokes. "Executive action" was a typical answer, to which the question was "What does the president look for in a singles bar?"

" 'Breaking Away' and 'Here's Boomer' " was Carnac's answer to the question "What are two really bad names for a laxative?"

During the multibillion-dollar savings-and-loan scandal, the answer was "A nail, a board, and an S & L customer," to which the question was "Name something that's hammered, something that's sawed, and something that's screwed." And when Richard Nixon's attorney general, John Mitchell, went to jail, the answer was "A dove, a canary, and John Mitchell," which answered the question "Name a lovebird, a songbird, and a jailbird."

"Sis, boom, bah" was the answer to the all-time favorite question of Carnac's fans, "What is the sound made by an exploding sheep?"

The audience had a role in Carnac too. At the end of the sketch I would hold up the final envelope and announce, "I hold in my hand the last envelope . . . ," and the audience would cheer loudly. "I hold in my hand the last envelope . . ." became another line that people love to hear me say that always gets a laugh and thunderous applause.

Carnac responded to that line with an insult, "May your only son become a Kelly girl," "May the Tunisian army invade your sister's closet," and that would end that visit from Carnac.

My favorite character, who we really didn't do that much, was El Moldo, the mentalist. This was a parody of performers like Dunninger, who supposedly could read minds. I played his accomplice. El Moldo was very different from Carnac. Carnac had to figure out what was in the envelope, whereas El Moldo was blindfolded and had to figure out what I was holding in my hand. Big difference. Admittedly, on occasion I would give slight hints to El Moldo. For example, if I was holding up a watch, I would ask, "El Moldo, what am I holding up this . . . *time?*" Or, I'd hold up a pencil and urge him, "El Moldo, hurry on this, you know, get the *lead* out." It didn't matter; he would never get the correct answer.

El Moldo was no less suggestive than Carnac. "El Moldo, I have a woman in the audience . . . ," I began.

"Good, get me one too."

"And she is holding something in her hand that . . ."

He laughed, "El Moldo not touch that one or El Moldo be off the air."

Sometimes though, even the great El Moldo actually did get something right. One night he guessed, "Is there someone in the audience wearing a shirt?"

"Well," I replied sarcastically, "of course there is."

"El Moldo's off to a good start . . ." El Moldo was scripted, but that didn't matter very much. I mean, if I missed a line, who would notice? And who would care? This wasn't like Burns and Allen, where if George missed one of his setup lines, Gracie's punch line would make no sense. This was two guys having fun. We were explorers in search of laughter. We started on a trail, the script was our map, but when we heard a laugh, we turned in that direction. And we followed the laughs, wherever they led us. Believe me, there were many times when we had no idea where we were or where we were going.

We would often do a little bit in which Johnny read a short excerpt from a book or a newspaper item in which there was a list of suggestions or some advice, and then he would add some additional suggestions or advice that had been created by our writers. For example, "Do not marry a girl who's had a fungus named after her." My job was to occasionally shake my head in wonder and amazement and improvise responses like "That's terrific," "No kidding, I didn't know that," and "Wow." Perhaps you'd like to read that last line again, "Wow." Thank you.

Most people don't believe that I took an acting lesson until they read my delivery of those lines. Look, it's tough for a straight man to get laughs, even with big lines like that. But as in everything else Johnny and I did, my little role in this bit grew until it became an integral part of the sketch. People laughed in anticipation of laughing. They knew the setup. For example, Johnny would read a list of things a good driver should know from an auto magazine. When he finished, I would begin, ad-libbing as I went along, my voice growing louder, "Johnny I don't know how you do it. You're as busy as anyone I've ever known. You've got the Oscar telecast coming up, millions of people are going to watch you on that show"—this is known in the straight-man trade as "milking it," or, technically, "sucking up to the boss"—"and yet you have time to go to the library and find this amazing book. Because when I go to the library I don't find them. But you have found a book that clearly delineates all you should know about driving a car. It's amazing, it's not a very big book. It doesn't have a lot of pages. From where I'm sitting it doesn't look like it could be more than ninety pages long. It's not a book that would jump right off the shelf. But you found it. I just don't know how you do it, but somehow you find these things and bring them in to enlighten our audience and it's a wonderful thing . . ." Here comes the big loud finish, ". . . Because when you read that book to our audience, I can say right now that *everything you ever want to know* about driving a car is listed in that thin little book."

"Wrong!" Mr. Carson would respond immediately, and then follow with an insult, "bumper breath." Or Methuselah breath, manifold breath, mooseface, six-cigarette, three-martini-lunch breath. Thirty years we got away with material like this, thirty years!

"You mean there's more?" I said, shocked, thus proving my acting lessons had not been wasted. "I can't believe it." He would then read the new list. "You know you've done something wrong if a pedestrian is waving to you . . . from the hood of your car." That's where my "Wow!" proved valuable.

Johnny often said, "We started doing this show on October 1, 1962. The second night they ran a *Best of Carson*." Wrong! Boss breath. I've been waiting a long time to write that. When we started doing the show, we were on five nights a week for an hour and forty-five minutes. But as the show became more successful it was shortened. In 1967 it was reduced to ninety minutes, and in 1980 to sixty minutes. Eventually Johnny began working only four nights a week and we used guest hosts. And then we used more and more guest hosts. And then he worked three nights a week. We were in the enviable position of being paid more money to work less. With that in mind sometimes I wonder why Johnny bothered to retire. If things had kept moving in the same direction, eventually we wouldn't have had to be there at all, for which they would have paid us a fortune.

We used so many guest hosts that in my warm-up I would ask the audience for volunteers to be the guest host. And then I'd give them a date. It seems as if at one time or another just about every major star in show business hosted the show. The record for serving as guest host most often belongs to Joey Bishop, who filled in for Johnny 206 times, far more than anyone else, at least until NBC started using permanent substitutes. Sometimes viewers forget how many major stars sat in Johnny's chair: my friend Frank Sinatra did it twice; Harry Belafonte, Rickles, and Newhart; Jerry Lewis filled in for a week; Flip Wilson, Groucho, David Brenner; Joan Rivers became a permanent guest host until she . . . left; Roger Moore; Sammy Davis hosted for a wonderful week; Leno and Letterman; Dick Cavett; Bob Hope had a young singer named Barbra Streisand as his guest; Alan Sherman had a young comedian named Bill Cosby; even Kermit the Frog hosted the show.

For many years I worked with every guest host. NBC wanted me there to provide continuity when Johnny wasn't working. In later years that became a problem, because Johnny wanted me there when he was there and the network wanted me there when he wasn't there. And I wanted to start taking a little more time off. NBC finally decided I would continue to work with guest hosts. Fine with me, I said cooperatively, then I'll take my time off when Johnny's there. But just one thing, I added, please, you tell that to Mr. Carson. So they told Johnny and it worked out fine: for the last few years of the show I worked only with Johnny.

Working with so many different guest hosts served to remind me how brilliant Carson was. Night after night Johnny made it look so easy; he made it look as if anyone could do it. But it wasn't easy; it was a job with extraordinary pressure. Hosting a program being watched by ten million people without a script is a very difficult thing to do. My friend Don Rickles, for example, hosted several times. There are few people in show business with more courage than Rickles. Rickles once told Frank Sinatra, "Frank, be yourself. Stand up and hit somebody." But whenever he hosted the show, he got so nervous that he would perspire more than anyone I've ever seen. Buckets of sweat poured off him. By the time he got to "Good evening," he was soaking wet. He used to kid about it himself, saying, "Don't mind me, I'm working on Guam." And at every break during the show he would ask me, "Was that good? Was that funny?"

Naturally I was as reassuring as I could be to my good friend. "Excuse me," I'd say supportively, "did you say something?" Or, "That was great, Don, much better than anything Kermit the Frog did."

To some degree every guest host was nervous. Most of them expected to be nervous and knew how to inject that nervous energy into their performance. Bob Newhart used to say that the only time he really got nervous was when he wasn't nervous. But usually movie actors, people who were not used to performing live, got the most nervous. The most nervous of them all was Roger Moore. Roger Moore was at the height of his success as James Bond when he hosted the show. I mean, he was the epitome of sophistication. James Bond personified. Before we went on the air, he grabbed me by the arm, dug his fingers into my skin, and asked, "Ed, please, don't leave me alone out there. Please stay with me." He was absolutely frantic. But on the air, his professionalism took control and he was wonderful.

When working with a guest host, I did feel more responsible for the show than I did when Johnny was there. The guest hosts looked to me for security, for direction, and I had to provide it. They thought of me as the guy who knew where all the bathrooms were. Just as when I was working with Carson, I tried to be there when needed and be quiet when I was not needed. It's just that the guest hosts needed me more. One night, for example, when Newhart was hosting, his good friend Robert Morse from *How to Succeed in Business* was his guest. Both of them are very talented, very funny men, but together nothing happened. They were having a wonderful time, they were breaking each other up, but the audience was just staring at them. It was about as exciting as the narration for home videos. They did two segments, about ten minutes, without getting a laugh. Finally, mercifully, the segments ended and we went to a commercial. Coming out of the commercial Bob Newhart was supposed to introduce the musical act, an organ player.

Unfortunately, and sometimes things like this happen, the organ caught fire. I don't mean the organist was great; I mean smoke started rising out of it. Freddy de Cordova told Newhart, "The organ's on fire. Do two more segments with Morse." This was a real problem. The two of them had already done their best material and that hadn't worked at all. Now it really got bad. They were just filling time. Newhart had this forlorn look on his face; he knew how bad it was going. Finally, I had to step in. After one of them finished another long uninteresting story, I laughed, but only politely, and suggested, "Gee, have you two ever considered putting out a book of these stories?"

I think when Johnny took a night off he knew he was leaving the show in good hands with me and Doc and Tommy and Freddy. I mean, the man took an occasional night off once or twice a week, what could really happen? I mean, what was the guest host going to do, insult the pope? Well, actually, there was that one night when the host David Frost and his guest Robert Shaw were discussing Pope Paul VI's position on abortion. "Well," Frost said, "there's supposed to have been an occasion in the nineteenth century when [the Pope] said in the afternoon, 'I'm not infallible.'

And then at seven o'clock he said, 'I'm sorry. I made a mistake. I am infallible.'"

As the only graduate of Catholic University on the show that evening, I declined gracefully to get involved in that one. I just did my job, knowing for sure that no one could debate the virtues of Alpo. But I did wonder exactly how Johnny must have reacted when someone told him that everything on the show had been fine, except for that little comment that alienated the entire Catholic Church.

Sometimes the guest hosts did use the show to discuss serious social topics. When Harry Belafonte hosted the show for a week in 1968 he invited many of the greatest black entertainers to be his guests, but also people like Senator Robert Kennedy and the Smothers Brothers. Tommy Smothers, whose criticism of President Johnson and the Vietnam War was well publicized, admitted that he believed President Johnson was indisputably the best president that the country had at that moment. Later in the show Belafonte mentioned that he'd enjoy appearing on the Smothers Brothers' controversial show, to which Tommy Smothers replied, "I'm sorry, but we don't allow any of that interracial stuff."

Of all the guest hosts I worked with, the one I most enjoyed was Muppets star Kermit the Frog. That was one of the few times we had an interspecies host. At least Kermit did not break out in flop sweat like some of our other hosts; instead he broke out in warts. That was the night I really had to use everything I'd learned in my acting lessons. I decided to deal with Kermit as if he were a real frog, as if I were talking to a real frog. Not that I would normally discuss anything of importance with a real frog, but I treated Kermit as if he were a real frog who could speak. And it worked very well. But during the show I did hope that one of my old marine drinking buddies would tune in and see me conversing pleasantly with a frog. I knew if they did, one of two things would happen: either they would think I had finally flipped because I was talking to a frog, or it would look to them as if I were speaking to a frog and that hallucination would cause them to quit drinking.

During one segment, Kermit read a few household cleaning tips from a book, enabling me to say, "You know, it's not a fat book, I mean the pages are tiny but . . . by golly, that's a great book for a frog to be reading because *everything in the world you'd ever want to know* about household hints is in this book."

"You are wrong, dishwater breath," Kermit replied, marking the only time in my life that I have been insulted by a puppet, although admittedly in Philadelphia I was outrated by Howdy Doody.

During his monologue on our twenty-ninth-anniversary show, Johnny, who was suffering from a bad cold, quoted the classic line "The show must go on." Then he turned to me and asked, "Who said that?"

"The man who owns the theater," I suggested. *The Tonight Show* did go on for almost thirty years, through marriages and divorces and earthquakes and wars, and during that time just about every significant actor or performer appeared on the show, as well as numerous politicians, experts, and ordinary strange people. And when you've done thousands of shows as Johnny and I did, and had thousands of guests, and performed in thousands of bits, the shows begin to run together in my memory. Sometimes, when I watch *The Carson Comedy Classics* I see myself doing things I have absolutely no memory of ever doing. And sometimes I laugh out loud when I hear myself laughing out loud. So it's very difficult for me to recall favorite moments or favorite shows. But there are days and nights that stand out in my memory.

For example, no matter what some people have said, I really don't claim credit for making Richard Nixon president of the United States. Oh sure, perhaps I helped a little. Politically, I would call myself an American, meaning I've always voted for the candidate rather than by party affiliation. In 1968, when Nixon ran against Hubert Humphrey, a man I greatly admired, I voted for Humphrey. But when a potential candidate for the presidency asked for my help, I was pleased to give it. And believe me, if you're ever in that situation, feel free to call on me.

In 1968, when I was living in Bronxville, New York, one of my neighbors, a delightful man named Clint Wheeler, was working as an adviser to Richard Nixon. This was before Nixon had announced he was going to run; it was even before Lyndon Johnson had announced he would not run. In the first televised presidential debates, in 1960, Nixon looked tired and unshaven compared to the handsome Jack Kennedy, and claimed later that his poor makeup cost him that election. Well, by 1968 politicians understood the importance of looking good on television. So when Nixon was scheduled to appear on *The Tonight Show*, Wheeler asked me to meet with him and offer some advice.

We met in his Fifth Avenue office. It was the middle of summer, and although the air-conditioning was on, there was a fire burning in the fireplace. "I'm going to be on your show," he explained, "and I just wonder if you have some ideas how I can make sure I come across well."

Today media consultants are paid thousands of dollars to answer that question. But this was a subject on which I was an expert. I'd been in television almost as long as there had been television. "The most important thing to do when you're on television is to include everybody," I advised Nixon. "Make contact with the people who are watching at home as well as those people in the studio. This isn't live theater; you have to play to the camera. Include everybody. Try to find common emotions, things that people watching at home can relate to. If Johnny asks you how you feel about something, you might tell him that you have the same feelings that every person in the audience has felt at one time or another."

Here I was, trying to teach Richard Nixon how to be warm. "And when you do," I continued, "point straight into the camera, because you're pointing to ten million people."

We spent about an hour together. The last thing I told him was that when he walked out from behind the curtain he should shake hands with me. "I'm the announcer, I'm not the boss, I'm the next guy down. A lot of people identify with me. If you ignore me, they think you're ignoring them. When Barry Goldwater was on the show, he didn't bother to shake my hand. Now Barry Goldwater is a nice man, and he certainly didn't mean to slight me, but people noticed and they didn't like it."

The first thing he did on the show was walk straight over to me and shake my hand firmly. When Johnny asked him the question to which everyone wanted the answer—was he going to make another run for the presidency—he replied, "Actually, I think you ought to run for president. Let me tell you a few things. I'm an expert on how to run for president. Not how to win, but how to run . . . First let me tell you your assets. You're young . . . you come over on television like gangbusters. And boy, I'm an expert on how important that is."

"You're not gonna lend me your makeup man, are you?" Johnny asked.

"No," Nixon replied, "I'm going to lend him to Lyndon Johnson." In fact, Nixon hired *The Tonight Show*'s makeup man to work with him during the 1968 campaign. And when he won the election, I was asked to produce the inaugural gala. The inaugural gala was very different in 1968 than it is today. It was much smaller, much less important. I don't believe it was even televised nationally. But I agreed to do it—I mean, this was a request from the president-elect of the United States—and I put together a wonderful show.

I'll also never forget the night that the Reverend Martin Luther King appeared on the show, just a few months before he was assassinated. Because he was such a charismatic world leader, it was sometimes easy to forget that he was also a human being. The *Tonight Show* format allowed people to show a side of their personality not usually seen in public. Dr. King explained that he had flown home to the United States from Russia that afternoon. "And as soon as we started out, they notified us that the plane had mechanical difficulties and that kept us on the ground . . . Well, finally we took off and landed, and whenever I land after mechanical difficulties, I'm always very happy. Now, I don't want to give you the impression that as a Baptist preacher I don't have faith in God in the air; it's simply that I've had more experience with him on the ground."

Just about the only movie star who refused every invitation to be on the show was Cary Grant, who told Freddy de Cordova that he wanted to be remembered for his performances. But for many other film stars, just like politicians, the show was an opportunity to reveal aspects of their personality rarely seen by their fans. Burt Reynolds, for instance, claims his appearances on *The Tonight Show* turned him into a big star by allowing him to show his irreverent, self-deprecating side, which he then displayed in films like *The Longest Yard.* The movie star whose appearances I most enjoyed was James Stewart. One of the reasons we got along so well was that we both were military pilots who had stayed in the reserves after the wars. I'm sure we must have talked about flying, although I don't really remember that. Everybody knew James Stewart as a brilliant actor, but few people knew that he wrote poetry until he started reading his poems on the show. I mean, these poems were not classic literature; instead they were warm, sometimes funny, and always heartfelt. One of the very few times I saw tears in Johnny's eyes was the night James Stewart read a poem about his dog who had died. Stewart eventually published a collection of his poems, which became a big best-seller. One night, he explained that he and his wife, Gloria, had just returned from a trip to Africa, the one place in the world Johnny had always wanted to visit, and he had written a poem about it. "Lake Berengo is a body of water," he read, "its surface smooth as glass. But getting to Lake Berengo is a genuine pain in the ass."

I also saw tears in Johnny's eyes the night Michael Landon, who was dying of cancer, made his last appearance on the show. That was a tough, tough night. Michael Landon was a wonderful person and he and Johnny had become very good friends. We all knew he was dying, but on the show that night he displayed extraordinary strength and courage. He insisted that he was going to beat the disease; who knows if he really believed that or not. Maybe he was in denial, maybe it was his way of bolstering his confidence, or maybe it was just his way of coping.

Several years later I saw the same kind of courage displayed by my son Michael in the weeks before his death.

One night I will certainly never forget was the night I got nervous. Now, I never got nervous. Maybe I got a little nervous when I was selling pots and pans and a young woman wearing only her robe sat down on the bed next to me and the robe opened a little bit. And maybe I got a little nervous when the North Koreans were aiming at me, but I never got nervous on *The Tonight Show*. That show was at its best when things went wrong, when the jokes weren't funny or the sketches fell apart, so what was there for me to be nervous about? That the jokes would be funny? That Johnny and I would follow the script? So I never got nervous on the show. Except this one night. I sang on the show once, just before I opened my nightclub act, and I wasn't particularly comfortable that night. But that wasn't the night I was nervous. The only time I got nervous was the night I appeared on the show as a guest. My movie, *Fun with Dick and Jane,* had been released and I had gotten very nice reviews. One reviewer said I was so good in the picture that he didn't even realize it was me. Now how about that for a good review! But that night Johnny said, "We have a movie star in our midst," and he interviewed me about the picture. Actors got nervous when they came on the show because they had to be themselves, they couldn't hide inside a character. I was always myself on the show; this time I had to be an actor. Johnny was terrific; he treated me very seriously. But you know how nervous I was?

Yeah, yeah, I know. If anybody knows the line that goes here, it's me.

I was so nervous that when we showed a brief clip from the movie, the palms of my hands were sweating. I was so nervous that I could feel beads of perspiration rolling down my spine. I was so nervous that when my good friend Johnny Carson, who was treating this very seriously, stood up at the end of my interview to say good-bye, I didn't even notice that he wasn't wearing any pants. I didn't even notice that my good friend Johnny Carson who was treating my film debut very seriously was wearing boxer shorts with little hearts on them. I didn't even know it until someone commented on it after the show. That's how nervous I was.

Anyone would have loved to be there the nights we had the legendary stars on the show, performers like Hope, Groucho, Dean Martin, George Burns, Red Skelton, Sinatra, Ethel Merman, Pearl Bailey—I'll never forget the night Pearl Bailey practically dragged Johnny out of his chair and they improvised a song and dance number—Jack Benny, John Wayne, Lucille Ball . . . We had so many great stars on the show that at times I understood completely what George Gobel meant the night he came out following Hope and Martin and said, "Did you ever get the feeling the world was a tuxedo and you were a pair of brown shoes?"

But the nights I remember much more than these appearances were the nights when stars were born. Particularly the young comedians.

Bill Cosby had been turned down three times before he made his first appearance on the show. He was so good that right after the show I called my manager and told him that we'd had this kid on that night who was going to be a big star, and suggested he find out if he had a manager. When he was on again two days later, Sheldon Leonard saw him and the following morning offered him the starring role in *I Spy*.

Joan Rivers had been turned down six times before she made her debut on the show. The next day she was overwhelmed with offers.

Rodney Dangerfield wasn't young, Rodney was always old for his age, and he had been around for a while before he came on the show. "If it wasn't for pickpockets," he said, "I'd have no sex life at all." I loved those nights when someone like Rodney, who had been working at it for a long time, finally made it into the major leagues.

When I heard Steven Wright wonder, "If you were in a vehicle traveling at the speed of light, and then you turned your lights on, would they do anything?" there was no question in my mind that he was going to make it.

Leno, Letterman, Garry Shandling, Seinfeld—*The Tonight Show* gave so many of the great comedians the stamp of approval. It was thrilling for me to be there to see this young talent come of age. I remember the night Bill Maher explained that his mother was Jewish and his father was Catholic, so when he went into confession he would bring a lawyer with him. "Bless me, Father, for I have sinned. I think you know Mr. Cohen."

No one who was there the night Dr. Heimlich demonstrated his maneuver on Loni Anderson will ever forget it. Or the night Carson threw Rickles into a tub of water, or the night actor Oliver Reed was pontificating about the role of women and Shelley Winters came from backstage and poured a glass of water over his head. But I also enjoyed the eccentrics we had on the show, maybe because they were precisely the same people who would have been contestants on *Who Do You Trust?* decades earlier. In a world becoming more and more homogeneous, it's comforting to know there are still people out there who collect sheep manure. One night, I remember, a lovely woman who found faces and designs in potato chips brought her collection on the show. "Don't they break?" Johnny asked her.

Of course they broke; they were potato chips. "Oh yes," she admitted. "Look at this one. It's Yogi Bear. I broke his neck." She glued this potato chip back together.

As I picked up a chip, I said, "Look at this one."

As she turned toward me, Johnny reached down under his desk, grabbed a potato chip, and chomped down as loudly as he could. There is no mistaking the sound of a potato chip being eaten. A look of complete horror crossed the woman's face. She was stunned. Johnny just sat there smiling, once again the innocent young man from Nebraska.

Now, I suspect the nut lady knew exactly what she was saying. A lovely elderly woman, she was curator of a nut museum in Florida. After reminding the audience how many streets in America are named after nuts, Walnut, for example, she pointed out that we often refer to nuts in conversation; or, as she said so endearingly, "You'll find that during intercourse, they are valuable."

Now that was the kind of line that only sweet elderly women and comedians named Carson from Nebraska can get away with. "Probably play a major role," Johnny agreed.

She then confessed, "I guess you know by now that I'm a spokeswoman for nuts."

"Well," Johnny replied knowingly, "you're certainly right about that."

Only once while working on the show was I ever really scared, and that is certainly a night I'll never forget. It wasn't really on the show. For the first ten years we did the show from New York, but we usually went out to California for several weeks each year. We were there in early February 1971. At one minute of six in the morning I was asleep in my room on the seventeenth floor of our hotel in Universal City when I was suddenly awakened by a herd of elephants trying to break into the room. At least that's what it felt like. After I became conscious I realized it was an earthquake. The entire hotel was swaying. I ran into the living room, which had floor-to-ceiling glass windows. From those windows I could see the power transformers at Universal Studios falling off their concrete moorings; they were exploding and shooting sparks into the air. For a split second I thought we were under attack; that's what it looked like.

I had no idea what to do. I know this may be hard to believe, especially from a pilot capable of doing loops in an open-cockpit biplane, but the fact is I'm afraid of heights. I have no idea why, but I have a very difficult time even going near the windows when I'm in a tall building. Even when I start thinking about it, I can feel it in my legs. But not that night. That night I didn't have time to be afraid of heights. Besides, it looked like the ground was getting much closer. At one point the building swayed so much I didn't think it could make it back again, I thought it would tumble over, and I actually considered jumping. I wondered, if I landed in a tree could I survive? Finally, about fifty years later, the quake ended and the building settled down.

All the power in the building was gone. I didn't know how badly it had been damaged, but it seemed to me the smart thing to do was get to a lower floor. A much, much lower floor. People were gathering in the corridors, many of them were crying. I just took charge. We didn't have a flashlight, so I made torches out of newspapers and started down the emergency stairs. As we reached each floor, we opened the door and shouted that we were walking down to the lobby if people wanted to come with us. Eventually the group swelled to about sixty people. Finally we reached the safety of the lobby.

For the first time I realized how silly I looked. I was wearing pajamas and socks with big holes in them. But as I got to the lobby one of the first people I saw was Doc, and he was dressed exactly the same way—except he was carrying his trumpet. At that moment I realized there was only one thing to do. I asked the concierge what time the bar opened. "Eleven o'clock," he said.

"Wanna bet?" I asked. That bar opened early that day, really early.

About two hours later I went back up to my room. I insisted on moving to a lower floor, and as I was packing my bags the phone rang. It was the hotel operator. "Mr. McMahon," she said, "this is your wake-up call."

"I'm up," I told her. I don't think it was possible for anyone to be more up than I was at that moment.

Bob Newhart was on the show that night. Obviously we were all very tense. In the middle of the show, the world started shaking again. Every earthquake, whether it's a big one or a small one, sounds the same at the beginning. The first thing you hear is that sound, a low rumble—to me it sounds like freight trains approaching—and the vibration follows. During the show, Johnny and Newhart were talking about something when the aftershock started. First the rumble, then the heavy overhead lights started banging together. The sound moved from the top of the studio toward us like a wave. There is no more helpless feeling than being caught in the middle of an earthquake—on national television. The cameras were taping this, so I think we all tried to look as calm as possible. I can't speak for Carson or Newhart, but my heart was pounding. We had a studio full of people there and a lot of heavy equipment hanging from the ceiling. I'll tell you, that was frightening. Johnny and Bob and I were getting ready to leave the set when the aftershock stopped just as suddenly as it had started. Johnny was terrific, he immediately tried to settle everybody down. "Okay," he said, "it's all right, it's an aftershock, there's nothing to worry about." Then he turned to Newhart and said, "Anyway, Bob, you were saying . . ."

Newhart looked at him for a moment, then said, "Johnny, there is no point in finishing that story. Nobody is paying any attention to what we're saying."

Never in my life have I been happier to leave a studio than I was that night.

One show I did not remember until I saw the tape was the night the actor Jay Silverheels, who played the Lone Ranger's faithful Indian companion, Tonto, was a guest. But as I listened to him describe his relationship with the Lone Ranger, I couldn't help but think about how much we had in common. "I work thirty years as faithful sidekick for Kemosabe," he began. "Hunt, fish, make food, sew clothes, sweep up, stay awake all night listen for enemies of Kemosabe. Risk life for Kemosabe. Thirty lousy years . . ."

I'd better make that thirty great years!

Hi-yoooo, Silver!

6

More than any other, the night that I will never forget was May 22, 1992. Our final show. I had been just as surprised as everyone else when Johnny announced almost a year earlier that he was leaving. I had no warning. I don't think he told anyone except his wife, Alex, that he had decided to quit. There had been so many times in the past when it looked as though he might leave that long ago I had stopped thinking about it. In 1979, when after considerable deliberation Johnny decided to continue doing the show, NBC President Fred Silverman took the news calmly. "I got down from the chair," he explained, "and put the rope back in the closet." I don't know why Johnny finally decided that this was the right time, but it was. Johnny Carson has always been a master of timing.

NBC asked me to continue with the show for six months after Johnny left, but there had never been any question in my mind that I would leave with him. It was time for me too. Years earlier I had given him a statue of Don Quixote with his faithful Sancho Panza, on which I'd had inscribed, "I follow ever in your footsteps, O Master. But you told me it would only be for ten years."

That last show was incredibly emotional, incredibly. In addition to the show ending, Johnny and I were ending a thirty-four-year professional relationship. We'd been together more than half our lives. "Ed has been a rock for thirty years," he said on that show, "sitting over here next to me . . . We have been friends for thirty-four years. A lot of people who work together on television don't necessarily like each other. This hasn't been true. We've known each other thirty-four years, we have dinner together, we're good friends, you cannot fake that on television. Some of the best things we've done on the show have just been, you start something, I'll start something . . . I got a letter from a guy. It said, 'Now you're gonna find out if Ed McMahon really thinks you're funny.' "

I responded to those kind words with the nicest gesture I could think of at that moment. I invited him to appear on *Star Search*. I mean, the guy needed a job. And with his experience he had a real shot at the one-hundred-thousand-dollar first prize.

It took me a long time to get used to the fact that the show had ended. At one point my assistant had made an appointment for me on a Thursday afternoon. A Thursday afternoon? "I can't do that Thursday," I started to explain. "I have to . . ." And then I realized I didn't have to do anything at all. I called Johnny and asked him if the same thing was happening to him.

"Every morning when I'm reading the newspaper," he said, "I start writing jokes for the monologue in the margin. And then I realize, who's gonna hear these jokes? The fish?"

On that final show, Johnny said that when he found something he wanted to do, he would be back. As it has turned out, that was his last professional appearance. He's spent the years since then enjoying his life. I've seen him or spoken to him infrequently; occasionally we've had lunch.

But I'm not really surprised by his retirement. Nothing Johnny did surprised me. In a 1967 interview, I told *Time,* "Johnny is not overly outgoing or affectionate. He doesn't give friendship easily or need it. He packs a tight suitcase."

About ten years later, after we had been through so much together, Johnny asked me one day, "What did you mean, I pack a tight suitcase?" Ten years later. It had been on his mind for ten years. What I meant by that, I told him, is that he was not a man of great excesses. He takes with him only those things he needs. And that applied to every part of his life. Johnny always traveled light, he carried his own bag, he never had an entourage, no makeup man, no hairdresser. He lived life with a minimum of fuss.

Johnny Carson was a paradox. He was far more comfortable in front of millions of people than he ever was with a small group. Even he admitted he didn't particularly enjoy small social gatherings. If he had to be at a party, I'd look over and see him standing in the corner entertaining a small group of people with sleight of hand, card tricks, or coin tricks. He knew that people thought he was cold and aloof but he really didn't care very much what others thought about him. After spending time with Johnny, my daughter Claudia decided, "It was an amazing thing to see. Everybody wanted a little piece of him, they wanted to show him something or ask him something. The only way he could have possibly handled that was to shut down. No one has the time or energy to deal with that pressure and still put on a live TV show every day, the only way to do that is to withdraw. Other people might think he was detached, but I thought that was necessary for survival."

I understood what Claudia was saying. I couldn't even guess how many times I was with him when a woman told him, "I undress in front of you every night, and my husband doesn't mind," or a man said to him, "You're ruining my sex life." By nature Johnny is very shy, he's a loner; I've always been very gregarious, but I will tell you Johnny always tried to be polite. He used to suggest to those men, "Why don't you put on a better show than I do?" but I know how wearing it was on him. He could be tough, particularly with people who did not do their jobs. There was tremendous pressure on him. When you're responsible for getting a show on the air every night, as he was, you depend on a lot of other people to do their jobs. If the show failed, no one blamed the lighting technician. So Johnny had a short fuse for ineffectual, inefficient people. But the fact is that most members of our technical staff stayed with the show for many years, even when their seniority qualified them for more lucrative jobs, because they were the best people in their fields and *The Tonight Show* was a wonderful place to work.

As far as being aloof, when Johnny met someone whose work he respected, he was completely open, and he'd end up telling the most engaging stories. And he is an incredibly loyal friend. After Burt Reynolds's career went into a steep decline, Reynolds became seriously ill. There were all kinds of rumors about his illness and many people with whom he was once close disappeared. As he said, "I found I could save a lot of money on Christmas cards. But not Johnny. Johnny called me every week."

I have been asked so often what Johnny Carson is really like. There is no easy answer to that question. The best answer is that he is like no one else I've ever known. He's as funny and charming in private life as he was on the air. He didn't turn that wit on and off for the camera. We were sitting at Jilly's bar late one night, well past midnight, when Frank Sinatra walked in. This was still pretty early in *The Tonight Show*'s run, so although Johnny was hot, he certainly wasn't the star he would become. And Frank Sinatra... well, he was the biggest and most powerful person in show business, and Jilly's was his hangout. People went there just because they might see him. So when he walked in, the entire restaurant quieted. Everybody was watching him. The king was in his palace. Believe me, if God had walked in at that moment, the only way He would have gotten any attention was if He had said He was with Mr. Sinatra. No one dared say hello to him until he said something to them first. Until he walked past the bar. As he did, Johnny said loudly, in a voice dripping with irritation, "Frank, I told you 11:30!"

Once, I remember, we were in California and we wanted Ethel Merman to come on the show. She'd recently ended her very brief marriage to actor Ernest Borgnine and I think she was a little embarrassed about it. So she was reluctant to do the show. Talent coordinator Shelly Schultz set up a dinner for us, hoping Johnny could make her comfortable. When she sat down at the table Johnny looked at her, smiled, and said, "You know, I had a headache that lasted longer than your last marriage."

"I'll have something to drink," she said, laughing. Fortunately. She made a great guest.

One of Johnny's few passions is astronomy. It wasn't just a little hobby; he had a powerful telescope and was extremely knowledgeable about outer space. Sometimes during commercial breaks he'd tell me about the things he'd been able to find in the previous night's sky. In fact, when the show ended I thought he might do humorous PBS specials about space. Johnny and I went with Bill Rosenthal of D'Arcy McManus, Budweiser's advertising agency, to the Kennedy Space Center, as it was then known, to watch the launch of Neil Armstrong's flight to the moon. We were seated only a row behind former president Lyndon Johnson and dignitaries from around the world. When the rocket was launched, a shock wave just rolled over us. It was awesome, more than any of us expected, and Carson said softly, "Jesus Christ."

With that, the representative of the Vatican, who was sitting directly in front of him, turned and said, "Name-dropper."

Afterward astronaut Gene Cernan took us on a private tour. We had to walk across one building on a metal cat-walk about ten stories high. I took one step, stopped, and froze. With my fear of heights, there was absolutely no way I could cross that walkway. Johnny, of course, was very sympathetic. In fact, I was worried about him. He was laughing so hard I thought he might fall off. I guess I was one of the few people who could get him to loosen up. On occasion, when both of us were single, we'd go to Ft. Lauderdale for what we called our "Raise Hell" weekends. It was our way of escaping the pressure of the show. Many nights in Florida and later at the great restaurant Sneaky Pete's in California we'd end the evening up on the band-stand. I'd be singing my ad-lib blues, making up lyrics about everybody in the place, and Johnny would be back-ing me up on the drums. For a while, when *The Tonight Show* was not yet the phenomenon it was to become, we were as tight as brothers.

Johnny even spent several weekends with my family in Gulph Mills. Only later did Claudia tell me that she had a big crush on him, or as she admits, he was the first older man she didn't look at and think "Ugh." It was at that house that I threw a big surprise birthday party for him. I think I was more surprised by the fact that I was able to success-fully surprise him than he was by the actual surprise. How do you surprise Johnny Carson? Very carefully.

The offices of *TV Guide* were not far from this house. We convinced Johnny that *TV Guide* wanted to put us on the cover but that they wanted to shoot the cover photo at their headquarters. He didn't want to do it—being on the cover of *TV Guide* was not particularly important to him—but his manager convinced him to do it. We agreed that he would pick me up on his way. When he got to the house, one of the kids told him I was out back by the pool. He walked outside to find seventy friends, relatives, and business associates waiting for him. He was shocked, and touched.

On the last *Tonight Show* Johnny introduced the members of his family who were in the audience that night, telling them, "I realize that being the offspring of somebody who is constantly in the public eye is not easy . . . I want you to know that I love you and I hope your old man hasn't caused you too much discomfort . . ."

Those words struck my home. They were the same words I might have used. For thirty years *The Tonight Show* dominated my life. My personal life was lived around the demands of my career. If someone invited me to an event or a dinner a year in advance, I would have to look in my book to see if we were doing a live show or a repeat that night before I could accept it.

I missed my daughter Linda's birth because I was in Korea, but I missed my son Jeff's birth because I was between shows. Jeff was born while I was doing *Who Do You Trust?* We did two shows on Friday, between shows Johnny and I went to Sardi's. While I was there someone came over to me and said, "Congratulations, you've just had a son."

I can't even begin to estimate the impact of the show on my family. Certainly it dominated all of our lives. An actor creates a character on the stage or screen that has nothing to do with real life, but on a free-flowing television program like *The Tonight Show* real life is the central theme. People who'd never met me thought they knew me. I remember I had an audition with Goodson and Todman for a game show very early one morning. I was standing on the traffic island in the middle of Park Avenue when a cab driver leaned out the window. "Hey Ed," he shouted, "it's eight o'clock in the morning. You sober?"

"Yes," I said.

"Good boy," he said, then drove off. I understood that. That was his frame of reference, that's what he knew about me. I accepted this kind of kidding in the manner in which it was intended. When Alyce and I returned from our honeymoon, I had seventy-five cents in my pocket. *The Tonight Show* made possible the kind of financial success we had never even dreamed about. It enabled me to provide my family with a very comfortable lifestyle, even though I often couldn't be there to enjoy it.

The Tonight Show certainly contributed to the end of my first marriage. Alyce raised our children while I was out building my career. She did all the things that a mother and father were supposed to do. For years I commuted to New York every day because Alyce and the kids were comfortable in Philadelphia. And some nights I'd end up staying in New York for meetings. There was no such thing in our home as a family dinner. When it became obvious after the first few years that *The Tonight Show* was going to be on the air for a long time, Alyce finally agreed to move to the lovely community of Bronxville, about a half hour outside New York.

We rented a gigantic house in Bronxville; I think it had twelve bedrooms. After we left, it became the Icelandic Embassy. But by the time I got home at night the kids were in bed and Alyce was upstairs. I'd end up making myself a greasy cheeseburger, opening a bottle of wine, and listening to the radio. That's when our marriage really started falling apart.

Eventually we bought our own home in Bronxville and tried to become part of the community. The kids went to school there, we joined the clubs, but that didn't make things any better. Usually the taping of the show ended about eight o'clock and a lot of nights I had business meetings after that. The truth is, I was leading a very exciting life and I was enjoying it. I felt very guilty that I wasn't doing more to save my marriage but I didn't know what to do. Eventually I asked Alyce for a separation. I never planned to get divorced because I never planned to get married again.

When the show went to Hollywood in 1972, Alyce stayed in Bronxville. Being forced to move to Los Angeles was the breaking point for our marriage. I was going—there was never any doubt in my mind about that. Finally, she moved to Los Angeles with the family and we made an attempt to reconcile, but it was much too late. When we were married in 1945 neither one of us could have anticipated the opportunities that would be available to me, and I took advantage of them. My career didn't break up my marriage, but it made it easier to end it.

At times my career was rough on my kids. Being the child of any celebrity is difficult, but the fact that I was on television all the time and so much was publicly known about my private life made it much harder on them. My daughter Linda once admitted to me that she secretly wished I'd been a plumber, like my grandfather and my uncles had been, because her life would have been more normal.

The kids were constantly being reminded that Ed McMahon was their father. It must have seemed to them that every time they turned around, there I was. My presence was inescapable. Except at home. Once, when Linda was in elementary school, they allowed her class to watch the broadcast of a space flight. But when they cut to a commercial, there I was, Linda's father. When Claudia was at Syracuse University, Budweiser distributed life-size cardboard displays in which I was holding a six-pack to retailers all over the country. Many students knew that Claudia was my daughter, and she couldn't stroll across the campus without strangers telling her, "Pick a pair of Bud" or "This Bud's for you."

My kids were embarrassed about all the attention they

received for things over which they had no control. My celebrity made it difficult for them to establish their own identities. Apparently, for example, it was considered extremely important at Bronxville High School to appear in candid photos in the yearbook. Only a very few people from each class made it. When Linda was a freshman they ran two pictures of her; the caption under one of them read, "Heeeeere's Linda," and under the second picture, in which she was holding a soft drink, "Bud Makes Me Wiser." She was horrified. Crushed. Maybe it seems like a small thing, but Linda knew it had nothing to do with anything that she herself had accomplished except being my daughter. "Where am I in all this?" she wondered. She was so upset that she insisted on transferring to another school.

After spending years doing social work with children, Claudia decided to go into show business. I was doing *Star Search* and I was able to get her a job with the production company. Obviously she got the job because she was my daughter, but what parent wouldn't help his child? Particularly a person like Claudia who had spent so many years working with underprivileged kids or in poverty programs. And the trade-off for getting the job was that she had to deal with a lot of animosity from a few people who resented her being there. To compensate for that, she made sure she was the first one there in the morning and the last one to leave at night. As "the child of," she knew, she had to work harder than most people to prove she was capable of doing the job.

And my son Michael . . . my oldest son, Michael, was never able to find his own place in life. He struggled with my celebrity his entire life, resenting it, fighting it, sometimes using it, but never successfully dealing with it. Of all my children, Michael was the one who suffered the most because of my work.

Jeff, my youngest son, just accepted it. When Jeff was a

child he didn't quite understand exactly what it was that his father did, except that every time he turned on the TV his father seemed to be talking to him. Eventually he figured it out, but it didn't make any difference. Very early one Sunday morning he was in Dallas driving to a golf course with a friend, he turned on the car radio—and there I was, promoting one of my projects. "It's eight o'clock Sunday morning and I'm in Dallas, Texas," he told his golfing partner, "and there he is."

One of the consequences of my fame was that all of the kids were more sensitive to their mother's feelings. Often when Alyce and I were out together people would approach me and ignore her. I'd always introduce her, but I know that was unpleasant for her. That wasn't the kind of life she wanted. The kids saw that happening and they didn't like it. They had to put up with it too. We'd be out somewhere and people would ask me for an autograph; I tried to be nice, but the kids wanted to get wherever it was we were going. And as they got older, people would tell them, "Please say hello to your Dad," to which they would often respond, "I have a mother too."

Only Claudia was old enough to really remember what life was like before I started doing *The Tonight Show*. Claudia remembers the day she had to wait with her mother until I earned enough cash by pitching a holiday toy for us to celebrate Christmas. My other children grew up with *The Tonight Show*. To them it was nothing special; it was their father's job, part of their life, something they just had to put up with. I used to have a summer home in Avalon, on the New Jersey shore. It was a wonderful community, and Johnny would often make jokes about it. Everybody knew where our house was, and too often late at night teenagers would pull into our driveway, honking the horn and screaming, "Where's Johnny?" "Heeeeere's Ed." This was the kind of stuff, and much of it was well meaning,

188

that the kids had to put up with their whole lives. That was tough for them. When someone was nice to them, they never knew if it was because of who they were, or because they were Ed McMahon's children. As a result they became very close. They knew they could trust each other. Throughout their childhood they were each other's best friends.

They didn't often watch the show on television, but they enjoyed coming to the studio, especially if someone they wanted to meet was going to be on that night. They knew everybody on the crew—Linda even took guitar lessons from band member Bucky Pizzeralli. They were allowed to watch the show from backstage and even go into the green room where some guests were waiting. Most of the time it was exciting for them. Most of the time. Jennifer O'Neill was on the show one night, I remember, and during a commercial break Claudia came out and told me, "She's so beautiful, I wish I could ask if I could borrow her face for one night." Well, I made the mistake of telling that to Johnny, and when we went back on the air, Johnny said, "We're always hearing how jealous women are of each other and how quick they are to criticize each other, but Ed's daughter Claudia just said the nicest thing . . ." And then he proceeded to repeat it to ten million viewers. Claudia was so embarrassed as only a high school girl can be. I thought she might never speak to me again. Or at least until the next time we had Cher or the Jackson Five on the show.

My children and Johnny's kids and Doc's kids all got to know each other. Our families never socialized very much—maybe that was because of all the divorces—but the kids certainly had an unusual bond. In some way, all of their lives revolved around *The Tonight Show*. They knew that the show was responsible for so many of the wonderful things in their lives, as well as the difficult ones.

I tried to include the kids in as many things as I possibly

could. It was one way of spending more time with them. In Philadelphia, for example, Claudia and Michael appeared in commercials with me. For several years Jeff pushed the red button to light the Rockefeller Center Christmas tree, and he even got to play a junior astronaut on a record album I did titled *What Do You Want to Be When You Grow Up?* And Linda would go with me when I hosted America's Junior Miss pageant.

They also got to meet a lot of tremendously interesting people because of *The Tonight Show.* I mean, how many kids get to have Jonathan Winters spend a weekend at their home? For two days the kids just followed him around the house in Gulph Mills. All I heard that weekend was the sound of laughter, interrupted only occasionally by someone saying things like, "I don't think we're supposed to walk on that table," "Boy, Dad never lets us touch that," and "What do you think'll happen if we open this one up?" If you can imagine what it would be like to have Robin Williams on fast-forward in your house, that's a hint of what it was like to have Jonathan Winters as a houseguest. Let me put it this way, by the end of the weekend it was the kids who were exhausted.

One Thanksgiving I took Jeff to dinner with me and my second wife, Victoria, at Frank Sinatra's house in Beverly Hills. Jeff was in college at this time. As we walked in, Frank was playing with his dogs, and Sammy Davis Jr. was standing at the bar. I loved and respected Sammy Davis. Jeff had met him several years earlier, but hadn't seen him in a long time, and went over to him to say hello. He said politely, "Hi, Mr. Davis, I'm Jeff McMahon, I'm sure you don't remember . . ."

Sammy stopped him. "Babe," he said, "you kidding? I remember you when you were only as tall as I am."

David Steinberg was a frequent guest on the show and he and Linda became good friends. When he was dating

Carly Simon he'd take Linda to her concerts, and they would often have dinner together. But he completely shocked Linda one day when he told her, "I love your Dad. He's cool."

That was perhaps the last thing she ever expected to hear from him. "You think my father is cool?" She couldn't believe it. "My father? You think my father is cool?" Of all the things I had ever been in her life, cool was not one of them. As anyone who has played the role knows, "cool" is the antonym of "father."

My children were in the audience when we taped the final *Tonight Show*. And when Johnny told his kids that he hoped the discomfort they had suffered because of the show had been worth it, my children looked at each other . . . and shrugged. That's an equation to which none of them knew the answer.

One thing my kids really disliked about the show was the fact that I was portrayed as a big drinker. That was an important aspect of the character Johnny created for me. Let me admit at this point that this was not a difficult role for me to play. I didn't even have to draw on my acting lessons; in this case I was more of a method actor. And my method was, sure, I'll have another one.

Until recently, until society began to look at alcoholism as a serious problem, there was a tradition of happy, friendly drunks, good-time guys, heavy-drinking characters in show business. It has been used as a comic device throughout the entire history of show business. I was one of a long line of people—admittedly it was a long wavy line—that started in vaudeville and minstrel shows. On Jack Benny's radio show, for example, Phil Harris was the resident carouser. Dean Martin claimed he was once stopped by the Los Angeles highway patrol; when they told him to stand on one leg he stood on one leg, and when they told him to close his eyes and touch his nose with his forefinger he closed his eyes and touched his nose with his forefinger, but when they told him to walk a straight line he objected. He looked right at them and said, "Not without a goddamn net I won't!"

In my nightclub act I quoted the great W. C. Fields, certainly the most famous inebriate in show business history, who said, "A man must believe in something, and I believe I'll have another drink." George Gobel once claimed, "I have never in my life been drunk. Frequently, however, I have been overserved." Jackie Gleason played a wonderful drunken character, Crazy Guggenheim, and Foster Brooks did a hysterical drunk act even though privately he didn't drink.

It's a character who has served as the basis for endless jokes. Actually, maybe "served" isn't really the proper word here. But the guy who likes to have a good time, who enjoys a good drink, or even a bad drink, has always been a good target for a joke. It was a role that fit me well. I mean, I'm a big tall Irish guy, I'm gregarious, and for a long time I enjoyed it. For example, when Jay Leno was hosting the show, he said to me, "Now you seem like the kind of guy, perhaps one night . . . ," and with that he pretended to lift a glass to his lips.

Naturally, I objected to that. "What does this mean?" I asked, repeating his gesture. "One night?" I continued, perhaps even a bit insulted. "How about every night? I mean, why only one night? Is there a drought?"

I got the joke. Fortunately, I usually got the drink too. Johnny created my character on *Who Do You Trust?* After doing the show Johnny and I would often go to Sardi's or Danny's Hideaway and end up at Jilly's and we'd have a wonderful time. Johnny would actually have a more wonderful time than I did, but on the show the next day Johnny would tell stories about my behavior. "Ed and I were out last night, and I asked him why he drank so much," was the kind of thing Johnny would have said, "and he said he drank to forget. So I asked him, 'To forget what?' and he said, 'What was that question again?'"

Now the truth is, as Johnny has often admitted, he was the one who did not hold his liquor very well. Three drinks and he was broadcasting from a distant network. But by the time we got *The Tonight Show* my character was well established. It worked very well for us. And it was based on fact. I drank. Sometimes I drank a lot. I'm a big man and I could hold a lot of alcohol. And I did. I was never an alcoholic—I never needed alcohol to get through the day—and I never drank when there was work to be done, but when it was time to play, I played. I don't know when or why I started drinking. No one in my family was a serious drinker. My father usually had a couple of beers when he came home from work, occasionally he had a glass of scotch or maybe he'd have sherry with dinner, but I don't think I ever saw him have a martini. Nor did any of my uncles drink excessively. I don't remember ever seeing a McMahon get drunk.

I guess I started drinking when I was working in the carnivals. I was young and I was one of the few people with the show going to college and for me that was a way of proving I belonged. There's a lot of alcohol around a carnival. A lot of people walked around with a half-pint of whiskey in their back pocket. I didn't get into that so much as having a few beers at the end of the day. For me, drinking has always been a reward, payment for a good day's work. You finish your work, you're entitled to a couple of drinks.

I started taking my drinking seriously in the marines. At the end of the day the pilots would get together for happy hour, perhaps the longest hour in history, and talk flying. When I was in Korea not only were we working very hard under difficult conditions, people were trying to kill us. About the only place to go to relax was the officers' club that

I'd built. One night, I remember, we'd been drinking and we were walking to the mess hall in a downpour, the whole camp was one big mud bowl, and this buddy of mine whose nickname was Herkimer kept slipping into foxholes. After he did that a couple of times I stood on the edge of the fox-hole, looked down at him lying in the mud, I mean he looked as miserable as we all felt, and said, "Herkimer, I told you the last time you did that it wasn't funny. It wasn't funny then and it isn't funny now. So the next time you fall in a foxhole, no one's gonna laugh. But this time, Herkimer, we will laugh."

When I got back to the States I started commuting to New York to try to get voice-over work in commercials. I'd get there early in the morning and try to schedule inter-views and auditions, but most of the time was spent wait-ing, waiting for a return phone call, waiting for a meeting, waiting for an audition. I'd have an interview at 10 A.M. and my next appointment wouldn't be until 2 P.M. If waiting had been a profession, I would have been a star. Michael's Pub on East Forty-eighth Street became my office. Michael's Pub was the hangout for people in this line of wait . . . work. Everybody would gather there between appointments. It was at Michael's Pub that I met the best voice-over people in the business, people like Pat Hernon, who later became a weath-erman, the great Bill Wendell, Bob Delaney, who broadcast the Boston Red Sox games, the great Fred Collins, known for his cigarette tag line, "*and* . . . they are mild," as well as the line "More people watch ABC than any other news orga-nization." Believe me, when Fred Collins told you they were mild, you believed they were mild. And when Pat Hernon told you it was raining outside, you could look outside and tell how much he'd had to drink.

During the hours we spent waiting at Michael's Pub many of us became close friends. Now, most of us would drink only coffee during the day, we wouldn't even have a beer before going to an audition for a beer commercial, but after that last audition or when the phone didn't ring again, well, we did a little drinking. A little drinking? Let me be a little more precise about this: this group was to drinking what Charles Eiffel was to erector sets.

Both the best and the worst thing about drinking excessively is that you really can't remember exactly what you did when you were drinking. I can state unequivocally, however, that there is absolutely no truth to the story about Pat Hernon and me climbing the Rockefeller Center Christmas tree. Now, there may well have been a discussion about the possibility of climbing that tree, there might even have been some wagers placed on our ability to climb that tree, but we did not climb the tree. Oh sure, maybe we did attempt to climb that tree, but as my close friend Charlie Cullen will attest, the guards never let us close enough.

On another occasion, I remember, Bobby Quinn, the director of *The Tonight Show*, Mort Rosen, who owned Sneaky Pete's, our hangout in Los Angeles, and I flew to Las Vegas to surprise Johnny when he did his nightclub act. We stayed the whole weekend, the whole, long weekend, and we drank to the New Year. I think by the time we finished, the New Year we were drinking to was 2146. Our flight back to New York was not direct, and apparently when we stopped in Los Angeles Mort Rosen got off the plane. Now, he didn't tell me he was getting off, so I still believe it was his fault that I thought he was sitting next to me the entire flight. I don't know who it was that I was speaking to during that trip, but he must have thought he was Mort Rosen because he never corrected me.

The most embarrassing thing that ever happened to me while I was drinking took place years later, when I was the spokesperson for Budweiser. The wonderful people at Anheuser-Busch had a party at a club in St. Louis. This combined two of my favorite activities, business and drinking. As the evening was coming to an end, a terrific man named Jimmy Orthwein, the chairman of the board of D'Arcy McManus, the brewery's advertising agency, invited several people back to his house to continue the party. Hey, more party? That sounded like a good idea to me. He gave me directions to his home and I told my driver how to get there. We drove down this long, very private road, past several beautiful homes, until I told the driver where to turn. I was the first one to arrive, but fortunately the front door was open. So I went in and decided to get everything ready for the others.

It was a beautiful home. I puttered around, I set up the glasses on the bar, I went into the kitchen and filled two ice buckets, I put some soft music on the stereo and turned on just enough lighting to create the proper atmosphere, I poured myself a drink, and just as I was about to light the fire, I turned around and saw a woman in her nightgown standing on the stairway with two children. "What are you doing in my house?" she asked.

What was I doing in her house? That seemed like a good question. "Isn't this the Orthwein home?" I asked, feeling quite certain I knew the answer.

"No," she said, "this is the Griesedieck home."

I knew that name. The Griesedieck family owned Falstaff brewery, one of Anheuser-Busch's competitors. So not only did I walk into someone's home early in the morning, turn on the stereo, and pour myself a drink, probably scaring them to death, but I'd invaded the home of a big rival of the company for whom I was the spokesperson. Now, had I really been thinking clearly at that moment, I might have said, "I guess you've never seen my program, *Bloopers and Practical Jokes?*" or, "Remember that notice you got from American Family Publishers that said you may have already won ten million dollars?" Instead, I said, "I'm really sorry." I started cleaning up the house. "Let me just turn off the stereo and put these glasses away. I'll just be a minute, let me turn off the lights, and I'll go out the same door I came in."

Now, for just one minute, put yourself in this woman's place. There she was, asleep, happy, when suddenly she was awakened by the sound of music coming from downstairs. The lights were on, someone was in the kitchen. She walked slowly downstairs, and there, in her living room, Ed McMahon was standing by himself having a drink. Now, I really don't know what was going on in her mind at that moment, my guess is that she didn't think Ed McMahon had broken into her house just to have a drink, but whatever it was, I've always hoped she thought she was dreaming rather than having a nightmare.

"Ed isn't drinking anymore," Johnny announced one night, ". . . of course, he isn't drinking any less either." Or, "The first time Ed saw Niagara Falls he asked, 'Does that come with scotch?' " The truth is, I drank, sometimes I drank a lot, but I didn't drink as much or as often as people believed. If I had, I wouldn't have been able to function as well as I did. I considered myself a drinking man, but physically I'm a big man and my system could absorb a great deal of alcohol. I could drink a lot. Besides, I used little tricks when I was drinking. For example, I always had a sip of water between sips of drinks. A sip of wine, a sip of water. A sip of a martini, a sip of ice water. Maybe that diluted the alcohol; whatever it did, it enabled me to drink a little more than most teams.

One night I think I remember I spent in the St. Louis home of the great Gussie Busch, who could party with the best of me. Gussie used to have a little test. At the end of a meal I went with him into the smoking room in which he served his famous Pick Me Up Charlies. This was a drink served in a glass with a narrow top; it looked like a cordial

197

glass. A Pick Me Up Charlie consisted of Courvoisier, a cognac, topped by a slice of lemon and a single sugar cube. You drank it by chewing the lemon slice and sugar cube until they became a sweet and sour pulp, and then drank the Courvoisier through this filter. It was a very potent drink. Most people had two or three, and all of a sudden it was Wednesday.

Please don't tell anyone, but I set the all-time record. Seventeen. At least that's what I was told later. Much later. But please, keep that to yourself.

I never objected to Johnny's jokes about my drinking or the creation of this image. Object to it? I encouraged it. And I used it. People believed that I was their kind of man, the kind of regular guy who lived next door or with whom they could sit down and have a friendly drink. My reputation as a drinking man helped put me on a first-name basis with America. Everybody knew me as Ed, Big Ed. This image was certainly part of the reason I was hired by Anheuser-Busch as the spokesperson for Budweiser. I even wrote a slim book, *Ed McMahon's Barside Companion*, which was filled with bar games, jokes, bets, and tricks, such as how to make a needle float on a glass of water, how to make up your own "Tom Swifties," like "'I had trouble with my power saw,' he said offhandedly," and how to answer questions like "Can a man marry his widow's sister in the United States?" The answer to that question is no; in order to marry his widow's sister he would have to be dead.

Because of my reputation, whenever I was in a restaurant or a club people would send drinks to my table. Naturally I didn't want to hurt their feelings. Once, though, that created a little problem. I spent the evening with my good friend Jimmy Breslin, who was making the rounds of New York taverns in search of his column for the next day. We wound up at the bar of a well-known midtown restaurant, sitting next to a ruddy-faced man wearing a hat. This man turned to me and said, "I know you. I'm gonna buy you a drink."

When someone I don't know speaks to me, I try to relate to them as an individual, I try to kid with them, make them feel I'm paying attention to them, not just giving them some sort of celebrity response. "That's very kind of you, sir," I said to this man, but then I jokingly added, "However, I never drink with a man who wears a hat at a bar." Breslin was just staring at me. I could tell from the lack of expression on his face I'd done something wrong. The whole place quieted. What I did not know was that this man was the head of a mob family running Newark or Trenton.

"You know what?" the man said, hitting me in the shoulder. "You're absolutely right." He removed his hat and we had several drinks together. Later Breslin told me, "That's the kind of guy who would have shot off your kneecap just for laughs." Well, I thought, there's an unusual sense of humor.

I went through several different periods in my drinking days and nights. There was my martini period, a scotch and soda period, scotch and water and vodka and water, scotch without vodka and water, and red and white wines. I did love those martinis before dinner. The question I have been asked most often about my drinking was what I did for a hangover. Now this was the most amazing thing of all: I've never had a hangover in my life. Never. There were many days when I'd wake up on what I assumed to be the next morning and I wasn't very sharp. It took me a while to focus. But I never experienced the traditional hangover, complete with headache, nausea, and spinning room. I know how bad they can be, though. One man who knew how to drink was my friend John Wayne. Duke was one of the great men of this world and a good friend. When Budweiser was repeating a television show we'd done together, they asked us to do several radio spots to promote it. Duke volunteered to do these commercials on the *Tonight Show* set. They set up a little recording area for us. I expected him hours after we'd finished taping the show, but to my surprise, when I walked backstage after the show he was standing there, waiting for me. "McMahon," he yelled in his booming voice, "I quit drinking!"

I was surprised. "Really, Duke?" I asked.

"Absolutely," he said firmly, and then added, "well, except tequila."

And later that night, after we'd finished taping the spots, we went to Chasen's and drank tequila. And then we drank a little more tequila. And then a . . .

In my barside companion I quoted a college study that stated that it takes from twelve to thirty-six hours for the body to return to normal following a night of drinking, and suggested that the best thing to do is just sleep it off. Well, if that's true, my body will get back to normal just after my 181st birthday. For me, the key to preventing a hangover is to always have something to eat before going to bed. That way the alcohol works on the food. But the best hangover remedy I know about is the hair of the dog, a Bloody Mary with tomato juice. Apparently whiskey depletes the vitamin B in your body and a Bloody Mary replenishes it. A good cold Budweiser with a few drops of Worcestershire sauce will do pretty much the same thing, because there are a lot of B-complex vitamins in the yeast.

Among the lessons I learned from drinking was that I had to watch out for parked cars. As I stepped out of a cab after an evening of celebration with Charlie Cullen, I slipped and fell heavily into a parked car, spraining my ankle. They had to put it in a cast. On the show the next day, when Johnny asked, "Well, what happened to you?" I had to tell him the truth. With a sigh I admitted, "You probably won't believe this, but I got hit by a parked car."

Anheuser-Busch once commissioned an eighteen-month study by the Wharton School of management research to find out why people drink. The study identified four types of drinkers. Indulgents, an incredibly small percentage of people, use alcohol to escape reality. Social drinkers use alcohol to sublimate their inhibitions; a drink helps them feel more comfortable at a party. A third group of people use alcohol to control others; at parties they'll tell the bartender to pour doubles to get everybody loose. But the largest group were the reparatives, those people who work hard and like to relax at the end of the day with a drink. I was in that last group; I was a reparative. No matter how much I drank the night before, I was never late for an appointment, I never missed a day of work, and I never showed up unprepared to do my job. In the thirty years I did *The Tonight Show* I probably missed six shows, five of them because of illness and the sixth was the night I took off because Claudia was leaving for Europe on her college graduation trip and I wanted to see her off. Listen, some days it was tough, I'd come home very late, Alyce would be asleep, and I'd write on the bathroom mirror in toothpaste, "Please wake me at 8." And at eight o'clock the next morning I'd be up and getting ready for work.

Only once did I ever appear on *The Tonight Show* slightly . . . considerably . . . less than sober. That afternoon, while I was having lunch with some friends, among them the great songwriter Paul Williams, I got word that two lawsuits in which I was involved had both been settled in my favor. Normally I wouldn't drink during lunch if I were doing the show that day. But this news was so good I had to celebrate. I wasn't really drunk, although I certainly had a nice buzz on. Maybe I shouldn't have done the show that night, but my strong sense of responsibility—and several martinis—outweighed my good judgment. I guess the problem started when Johnny introduced Joan Embry, the wonderful representative of the San Diego Zoo. "We've had this lady on the show very often in the past, I guess, seven or eight years," he began.

I tried to help him out. "Nine years," I said firmly.

"Nine years, yeah," he agreed. "Several plus several'd be about nine." He was just beginning to sense that something might be wrong.

"You said seven or eight, then . . ."

"I didn't say seven or eight," he insisted. "I said several . . ."

There are few people more insistent than someone who has been drinking and is convinced he's correct. "Then you said, 'seven or eight,' and I said, 'It's nine.' The animals you had as babies are now . . . ," I had to pause to figure this out, "ten years old."

"That'd be about right," he agreed. He still wasn't sure how to handle me. I suspect he felt if he left me alone no one would notice.

The worst thing you can do when you have too much to drink is pretend that you're sober. And that is what I tried to do. "Remember those animals that . . . did something funny on your tie? Those little baby lions were one year old. Now they're treacherous and ferocious ten-year-old animals."

Johnny patted me on the arm. "Okay." Then he tried to save me. "Joan Embry's here tonight . . ."

That was not going to be possible. "She's now thirty-two," I interrupted.

"That's right. Joan is an animal handler and a trainer and . . ." Johnny couldn't resist any longer. He started laughing as he looked at me and said, "You really think you're fooling everybody, don't you?"

"No, no, no, no. I'm just doing my best to help."

"I know that," Johnny continued, but not easily, ". . . and she does her three horse shows a day, did you know that? At the animal park?"

What I didn't know was how to be quiet. "Boy, is that an exciting idea."

Now Johnny was getting into it. "Would you like an army cot or something maybe? Time to catch up on a little nappy-poo or something, maybe?"

See, my feelings were hurt. I was trying to make a point, even if I had no idea what it was, and my friend Johnny Carson was making fun of me. "I love Joan. I'm the only one who went to see her," I said defensively. "Doc has never seen her, you've never seen her. I went to the wild animal farm . . ."

"It's all right, it's all right . . ."

"But you're upsetting me."

"No, no, I don't want to upset you."

Now I was insistent, "I went down, Joan and I . . ."

Johnny was trying to calm me down, saying solicitously, "I know you did. It's all right."

"Don't say . . . I know Joan. I went down there." Then I added proudly, "I held a baby gorilla."

Johnny finally realized he had to save me. "I couldn't go with you that week. You held a baby gorilla. And let's get her out here real quick . . ." And Joan came out to end that conversation.

Did I mention that I went down to the San Diego Zoo?

Although I never had a problem with my reputation, my kids did. They didn't think it was funny at all; they never laughed at Johnny's jokes about it. There's a good reason for that; not only did they have to put up with all types of remarks from both friends and strangers, they also had to live with the reality of my drinking at home. And at home it wasn't very funny. It's accurate to say that alcohol played an important part in the failure of my first two marriages. It didn't cause them to break up, but it exacerbated the problems that already existed.

Alcohol led to a lot of arguments. Things that otherwise would have had little meaning suddenly became important, and words that wouldn't have been said and probably weren't even meant were said. The more unpleasant it got, the easier it became for me to stay out at Michael's Pub or Jilly's drinking with Hernon and Jonathan Winters and sometimes Carson. The kids knew the part that alcohol played in the end of my marriage to their mother, and they didn't like the jokes.

It was because of the impact on my children that I sued one of the tabloid newspapers. Look, I understand that the trade-off for success in the entertainment industry is the loss of much of my private life. I accept that. During my career there have been many things printed about my private life that I didn't like, things that were very embarrassing to me, but I knew these papers had the right to print them. But when one of these publications printed made-up stories that were hurtful to my children, I had to take legal action.

Now, my taking action against a publication for writing that I had too much to drink may seem a bit like our first spokesmodel on *Star Search,* Sharon Stone, complaining that someone wrote she was too beautiful. I'd been telling my own jokes about my drinking for years. But in this case they went too far. They reported that I had consumed an entire bottle of scotch during a flight to London and had gotten so drunk and obnoxious that I caused a disturbance and then barely managed to stagger down the gangway at Heathrow. Every part of that story was fabricated. I wasn't on that airplane, I hadn't been to London in five years, I did not cause a disturbance, and I no longer drink scotch. Even then I might have just ignored the story had my daughter Katherine not come home from school crying. I don't know if her classmates teased her about it or she heard it on the news, but it affected her. People were saying that her daddy had done some bad things. I don't have much of a temper. Just about the only time I get angry is when someone is bothering my family. And then I get very angry. One night, for example, I was with my daughter Linda in P. J. Clarke's in New York. A man standing next to her started bothering her, repeatedly trying to put his arm around her.

I poked him in the chest so hard I knocked him to the floor. I remember exactly what I said to him, "It will not be necessary for you to touch me or any member of my family for the rest of your life. Do I make myself clear?"

I think I was probably just as angry about this tabloid story. In a sense, this paper was touching my daughter. I couldn't poke it in the masthead, so I sued for libel.

It was very easy to prove that the story was wrong. I simply produced my passport. That was evidence that I had not been to England. The source of the story, we discovered, was a friend of the writer, who had overheard a conversation in which someone said a person who looked like Ed McMahon had been drunk and disorderly on that flight. They assumed that if it looked like me, and he was drinking, it had to be me. They had no defense.

Winning damages was much more difficult. Libel means that a story damaged your reputation. Even though the story was a complete fabrication, how could I prove I had been damaged by being identified as a drinker when so much of my reputation was based on the fact that I liked to drink? In fact, the paper's lawyers actually claimed that this story improved my image.

In their defense presentation they showed the tape of that night I was a bit tipsy on the show. But the fact is that this story could have damaged my reputation. No matter how much I've had to drink, I've never bothered anyone and I've always been conscientious about my work. Only a lawyer for one of these publications would think that being drunk and unruly could improve someone's reputation. Just prior to the publication of this story I was discussing a show with a major studio. After the story was printed they lost interest in the show. Was that because of the story? Impossible to prove, but certainly the possibility existed. And as my lawyers, Neil Papiano and Barbara Derkowitz, wondered, how many nameless people were considering inviting me to a function or hiring me to host a show and didn't when they read that I was so drunk I practically fell down the gangway? Eventually we settled, and let me say I was happy with the settlement, but more important, I was able to show my daughter that the story was wrong.

My reputation made me an easy target for the tabloids. As part of the resolution of a lawsuit I had filed, one of the major tabloids had to inform me before they ran any story about me. That didn't mean I could stop it, but they had to at least attempt to check the facts with me. One evening I was at dinner with Charlie Cullen and the lawyer Paul Tobin. A Los Angeles sportscaster I knew came in with his date and we greeted each other. That was the extent of my interaction with the sports reporter. As I drove home that night, less than two hours later, the phone in my car rang. A reporter from the tabloid was calling to check out a story that I had been at this restaurant with two beautiful women, had been drunk, and had gotten into a brawl with this sportscaster over his date. I've known Charlie Cullen for more than forty years, and not only isn't he a woman, he certainly isn't beautiful. Oh, maybe in the right light he's nice-looking . . . The only way someone could have believed that I was with two beautiful women was if they had been drinking very seriously. And even with all the drinking I've done, I still don't know of any alcoholic beverage strong enough to turn Charlie Cullen into a beautiful woman.

I now have a new ending for Johnny's old joke "Ed isn't drinking anymore . . ." It's "Good." See, it's not a joke anymore. I gave up drinking for a beautiful woman—no, not Charlie Cullen—my wife, Pam McMahon. Before we married she told me, "I'd like to have you around for a long time, and that isn't going to happen if you keep drinking." Since I'd like to be around her for a long time, that made a great deal of sense to me, so I've cut down to a few glasses of red wine at the end of the day. And even that wine is for medicinal purposes—I'd feel awful if I couldn't have it.

I don't miss my drinking days. No matter how much I'd had to drink, I always believed I was perfectly in control. But I wasn't. The only regret I have is that when I was drinking I wasn't quite as sharp as I could have been. I think my edges were dulled. I may have accepted a little less from myself than I otherwise would have. And sometimes I wonder how much more I might have accomplished had I been completely in control for the last thirty years.

Years ago, I might have celebrated the fact that I had stopped drinking by lifting my glass and declaring, "I'll drink to that." But with all the problems caused by drinking excessively, I don't use that line anymore. My Christmas tree–climbing days are over.

Although the memory does linger on. My great friend Tony Amendola, the former president of D'Arcy McManus Advertising in St. Louis, has had two heart transplants. After the first one, I sent him a telegram reading, "Glad you're well. If I had known your heart was in such sad shape, I would have given you mine." To which Tony responded, "Your heart yes, your liver no."

7

One night we had a five-year-old spelling champion on *The Tonight Show* and Johnny was showing him some simple sleight of hand. He made a quarter disappear, then produced it from the little boy's ear. The young man tried to do it himself, then asked Johnny, "How do you make it really disappear?"

Without hesitation, Johnny told him, "You get married."

Our personal lives were always topics of discussion on the show, particularly our marriages and divorces. One night, for example, Doc complained, "I was out Christmas shopping for Johnny today. It's hard to buy for him because what can you buy for a man whose ex-wives have everything?"

One of the classic moments on the show took place the night before Thanksgiving, when Johnny asked Doc if he was going to help his wife stuff their turkey. "Noooo," Doc told him, "there is no Mrs. Severinsen."

"Oh, that's right," Johnny said. "I didn't mean to do that."

"The fact that I never helped her stuff her bird was one of our big problems," Doc explained.

"I thought that was your problem," Johnny laughed, then admitted, "You know, I forget all about that. We've been together so long that I forget sometimes where we are . . ."

"She's still stuffing the turkey," Doc added a little bit later, "but now it's with money."

"Well, it's nice to know you have no bitterness . . ."

There were many times when I wished my personal life wasn't so publicly known. It wasn't fun having my personal failures exposed on national TV. But Johnny and Doc and I knew that every person in our audience had problems of their own; they were watching us to be entertained, maybe to forget their problems, so whatever we were feeling inside, there was nothing we could do about it except bite the bullet and keep smiling. It was a lot easier to joke about these things than it was to live through them.

During the time we did the show I went through two very painful and very public divorces. Those were the kinds of things that made the newspapers, so we couldn't avoid talking about them, we couldn't pretend they didn't happen. At times my life was very glamorous—I did get to go to wonderful places and among my friends are some of the most talented people in the world. I know how fortunate I am, but no matter how exciting my life might have seemed to viewers, most of the time the things that concerned me on a daily basis were the same things that they were dealing with: trying to make my marriages work, raising my four kids—including my son Michael, who was very troubled—and earning enough money to pay the rent and make alimony payments.

As W. C. Fields might have said, "Ahh yes, my good friends, I believe very strongly in the sanctity of marriage." In fact, I believe in it so strongly that I got married three times! That was certainly never my intention. When I married Alyce Ferrell, I was twenty-two years old and I thought I was marrying her for better or worse, but definitely forever. I was raised a Catholic, for a long time I was a daily communicant, and I believed that you married for life. My parents did not have a good marriage, they separated several times; that had been tough on me. I didn't want my kids to have to live through that.

Alyce was a lovely person and a very attractive woman. She was petite, charming, very innocent, I thought, and vibrant. She had a lovely southern accent and traditional southern values. For a long time we were very good together: she made a beautiful home for our family, my friends loved her, and she was a wonderful mother to our children.

We started with nothing. For a time we lived on whatever I made that week on the boardwalk or in my dry-cleaning business. One of my proudest moments was when I was finally able to buy her a car for her birthday. I had it well planned. I had cut footprints out of paper and when she was sleeping I laid a path from the bed to the window. I had covered the window with paper and written HAPPY BIRTHDAY on it, but I had cut a hole out for the dot over the *i*. When Alyce followed the footprints to the window and looked through that hole, there was her car parked in the street. It had taken me days to get that parking spot. The car was used, it was all I could afford, but we were both thrilled.

The first house we owned was in Hialeah, Florida. I was on my way to Korea, she was pregnant with our third child, and I didn't want to leave her in an apartment, so we bought a house for eleven thousand dollars in Hialeah. Since my Marine Corps pay was only nine thousand dollars a year, that was a lot of money. When I came home we returned to Philadelphia, and eventually moved from the Drexelbrook apartments to a beautiful house in the suburb of Gulph Mills. Days after we moved in I got the call from Dick Clark's producer telling me to come to New York to audition for *Who Do You Trust?*, and my life changed forever.

I commuted to New York every day for eight years.

When it looked as though *The Tonight Show* was going to last, we moved to Bronxville, just outside the city, into a larger house. We lived there until we separated and I moved with *The Tonight Show* to California.

I was much more a qualitative father than a quantitative one. There were a lot of nights, a lot of family dinners I missed. I don't just mean that I wasn't there; I mean that I really missed being there.

I tried to make up for it as much as I could by making the time we spent together special. When I was with my kids I tried to make life as much of a party as possible. A long time ago I started something I called "the sky's the limit." That meant when we were out for dinner they could order absolutely anything they wanted and as much of it as they wanted. To the kids it meant they could have the chocolate cake—and the ice cream sundae, or six ice cream cones—if that's what they wanted. I mean, you would die before you could eat all that, but just knowing for that one time in your life you could have as much of anything as you wanted made it special. You could have your cake and eat it too, and then have another cake if you wanted it. I did it with my four children with Alyce, I do it with my grandchildren, and now I'm doing it again with my beautiful adopted daughter, Katherine Mary.

We had several family traditions. On Christmas, for example, all their presents would be spread out around the living room—except their big present. That would be in another room. I was big on spoiling my kids. I tried to get them whatever it was they wanted, a bicycle or skis or a classical guitar; the sky was the limit on presents too. Once, I remember, more than anything else Linda wanted to get her ears pierced and Alyce didn't think it was a good idea. Linda wanted it so badly, she would buy pierced earrings, break off the stems, and glue them to her ears. Well, I talked Alyce into it and one Christmas her big present was in a tiny box. It was a pair of pierced earrings. I told her that the next day I was going to take her to have her ears pierced. So the next day we went to the doctor's office and as I was waiting outside she started screaming. I couldn't resist. "Sorry, Linda," I yelled to her, "but that's the price one must pay for beauty."

One of the best of our family traditions was spending the summers at our house in Avalon on the Jersey shore. A lot of our friends from Philadelphia bought property there, so it was like one large family gathering. At night we'd take long walks on the rickety old boardwalk or go to the ancient movie theater—I think we saw *The Dirty Dozen* a dozen times—and once each summer all the men would pile the kids and their friends into three big station wagons and the whole raucous mob would go to the amusement park in Wildwood. That was a big event; the kids would start talking about it in June. It seems to me that the main object that night was to see exactly how much junk food—popcorn, candy, ice cream, pizza—we could eat while going on every ride that turned your stomach in a new direction. Let me pause here to say one thing: if I never again, not even once more, ride on the Hell Hole, a ride that spins so fast that gravity pins you against the wall and reminds you never to combine ice cream and popcorn, that will be too soon. Sure, I sometimes missed events in the kids' lives, but we'll always have the Hell Hole.

The biggest tradition was our Fourth of July weekend gala. Our wedding anniversary was July 5, so to celebrate that we staged a big horseshoe tournament on the beach right in front of our house, pitting the bayers, the people who lived on the bay, against the beachers, the fine, upstanding human beings, the wonderfully giving, generous people who lived on the beach. We were beachers. We'd close off the block for the day, kids would get dressed in costume, people would mount floats on cars, I'd serve hot dogs, and my son Jeff would be the bartender. And the next day we'd hang a banner on our house announcing the winning team.

Another of the great Avalon traditions was my having problems with my boat. I like to think of myself as a skilled yachtsman. I like to think of myself that way, even if it isn't true. I always had a boat and at least once each season there would be some sort of minor boating disaster. I'd run aground, I'd run out of gas, I'd crash into something small. The truth is, as anyone who has ever owned a boat will tell you, it wasn't always my fault. One summer, for example, I got a beautiful Donzi, one of the greatest speedboats ever built, and my friend Bob Gillin and I were going to drive it from a New York yacht club to Avalon. We had a big party at the yacht club—Carson, Skitch Henderson, a lot of people from the show were there—and they piped us aboard my new boat and we were ready to cast off. Then Gillin had the audacity to ask me, "You did remember to get the charts, didn't you, Ed?"

Of course I did. I was prepared. I'd stopped at the local Gulf station and gotten their best road maps. I don't know what Gillin was complaining about that day; if that boat had gotten lost on any highway in New York state we would have been able to get back safely. And there was certainly a lot of water pictured on them.

At night, water looks pretty much the same. One evening Alyce and I and the Gillins took my boat to a waterside restaurant. We were all nicely dressed. During dinner the Gillins had an emergency at their home, and someone offered to drive them. Alyce went with them and I took the boat by myself. When I hadn't returned by two in the morning everybody got scared. They thought I had gotten lost and taken the boat out into the ocean. In the middle of the night several of my friends got into their boats and started searching for me. At sunrise they alerted the Wildwood police. Now there was a full-scale search going on for me.

Meanwhile, the mosquitoes had found me. I had taken a wrong turn somewhere and had gotten lost, then I'd run aground. There was nothing I could do but go to sleep until the morning and then hail a passing boat for help. At seven o'clock an elderly couple in a small boat were puttering by when I stood up in my boat and asked for assistance. Now, imagine this nice elderly couple just out for a nice morning on the water, when suddenly Ed McMahon stands up in a boat and asks for help. I guess it could have been worse; they could have found me standing in their living room.

So as half of Avalon and the Wildwood Police Department searched for me, I was towed into the bay by this lovely couple in their tiny boat.

So much for tradition.

There were many nights when the kids were asleep by the time I got home. I often left messages for them to find in the morning. I had this little label maker; I would press letters into a plastic strip with an adhesive back and stick it to their mirror. So Michael would walk into his bathroom and see my reminder, SHAPE UP OR SHIP OUT, and Claudia, who used to stoop, would find my message telling her, KEEP YOUR SHOULDERS BACK, and Linda, who spoke like a baby when she wanted attention, would find DON'T TALK BABY-TALK on her mirror.

But more than big presents or trips or ice cream, what I tried to give to my kids was a reasonable set of values. I tried to teach them to respect other people. I've always believed that we're here on earth for a purpose, and that is to do as much as we can with what we're given. It's my modification of the biblical credo, where much is given, much is expected. To me that means both working hard in whatever it is that brings you financial support as well as using whatever you have to benefit the people around you as much as possible.

It means being thoughtful and courteous, being supportive of other people, caring for them when they need it, and giving back to others as much as possible. I'm so fortunate to have had a talent with which I've been able to make a fine living, but I also always felt I had an obligation to use my success to help other people. I know that sounds altruistic and I don't mean it that way. I mean it as I said it: it's an obligation and I don't think you really have a choice in the matter.

I didn't try to tell these things to my children as much as try to set an example for them. I've always tried to be courteous and respectful to everyone, whether it's a waiter in a restaurant or the CEO of a big corporation. I've been active in hundreds of charities, especially the Muscular Dystrophy Association, the Horatio Alger Association, which offers support to deserving young people who need help with college payments, and St. Jude's Ranch for Children, which provides a loving environment for kids who have been mistreated. And as a person who remembers seeing those despicable signs—IRISH NEED NOT APPLY—I've always fought bigotry when confronted with it. My kids had to listen to all my stories about growing up with Japanese kids and then having to defend them in many heated discussions during World War II. They've always seen me with friends of absolutely every race and color. Years ago we belonged to a country club in Westchester County. One weekend Claudia came home from college with her roommate, who was Chinese. This country club refused to let them in. Well, I liked that club, and many people who belonged to it were nice people, but my family didn't belong there. I went over there that day and resigned. I may have even raised my voice while doing so. Believe me, no McMahon ever set foot in that club again.

Alyce and I also tried to teach our children the value of money. That can be a difficult thing to do when kids are raised in an affluent environment like Bronxville. But we tried. The kids all had chores and responsibilities around the house and they worked in the summers. In Avalon Michael worked at a gas station, Linda worked at a bakery, and Claudia was a waitress. When we were in the car, driving from New York to Bronxville, for example, I'd intentionally drive through some of the worst neighborhoods. I wanted my kids to see how less-fortunate people lived, I wanted them to see the drug addicts nodding out on the street, I didn't want them to be blind to real life.

If the kids needed something, Alyce and I would get it for them. But if they wanted something, we often made them work for it. One year Claudia became enamored of figure skating. It became her passion and she wanted to go to a skating camp in Hershey, Pennsylvania. When we said no, she decided to earn enough money to pay for it herself. So she put a box in her closet with a Hershey bar wrapped in it to remind her of her goal and started saving her money. She saved her lunch money, her milk money; she charged me fifteen cents to iron my shirts, which was a bargain compared to the ten cents she charged for handkerchiefs. She worked so hard and saved so much money that eventually she had saved enough to convince Alyce and me to help her pay for it.

The kids also spent time with Alyce's family in Lacoochee, Florida. Alyce didn't like to fly, so they would take a sleeper train down to another world. For two weeks they lived on the farm with their grandparents and cousins. They got to ride horses down the main street in town, they had chores, they experienced a lifestyle that didn't revolve around money, clothes, and cars. Believe me, no one in Bronxville kept pigs in their backyard. At their grandparents', they were exposed to things that they would never have to deal with in New York. For example, the only chickens Jeffrey had ever seen in Bronxville were on his plate. So for him, the animals on the farm—the pigs, horses, and chickens—were pets. Jeffrey didn't believe his grandfather when he told him he was going to slaughter the chickens for food. And he was devastated when his grandfather did just that.

Bronxville was so small and exclusive that at times it was easy to forget that there was a big and sometimes rough world outside. The time the kids spent in Lacoochee reminded them that most people didn't live in big houses in fancy communities.

We raised the kids in the Catholic religion. In fact, when we were living in Bronxville, Alyce took lessons from Monsignor Kaneely, a wonderful man and teacher, and was eventually baptized herself. The kids always went to early Mass on Sundays, even if on occasion Alyce and I didn't get there until much later, since early Sunday morning always followed late Saturday night. I've always believed that an understanding and appreciation of religion, any religion, is very important for children. A religious education teaches children to appreciate so many of the things that will really matter in their lives. And I have been fortunate enough to meet some extraordinary people in the Church. But when the kids were growing up, parochial schools enforced discipline much more harshly than today. And sometimes, I felt, the things done to my children had to be addressed.

When Claudia was in second grade, for example, rehearsing for her confirmation, a nun put a wreath on her head and said, "You have such beautiful hair. Where did you get it?"

"The sun," Claudia told her.

The nun slapped her in the face. "No you didn't," she corrected her. "You got it from God."

When Claudia told me that story at dinner, I threw down my napkin, got up, and went to the convent. I don't believe hitting a child is an effective teaching tool.

And when Claudia was in sixth grade she got caught reading a comic book during a break in an exam. The nun warned Claudia that the next time she got caught reading a comic book, she was going to have to stay after class. And when it was pitch black, the nun was going to make her walk down the hallway and then press a button that would cause the floor to open up and drop Claudia into an alligator pit, and then the nun would close the floor and leave her there.

That's not education, that's terrorism.

I wanted my children to learn how to think for themselves. I wanted them to feel free to ask questions and find their own answers. The last thing I wanted them to do was accept any stereotype without at least examining the issue. So dinners at our house were very important; we'd sit at the table for a long time talking and often arguing about things. In my professional career I've always tried to keep my personal politics private. People guessed, but nobody ever knew how I voted or how I felt about national issues. For example, as a proud marine, I supported the troops fighting in Vietnam, but in fact I did not support the war itself. For several years my kids and I all wore POW bracelets to remind us that Americans were suffering in North Vietnamese prisons, and I helped raise a lot of money for this campaign, but in 1972 I think I might have been the only person in Bronxville who voted for George McGovern.

Being the oldest, Claudia, I think, was a lot like me. Of all the kids, she was the most rebellious. Unlike most of the other young women in Bronxville, she had absolutely no interest in being a debutante, although her mother would have liked it. She refused to participate in the traditional "coming out" activities, she wouldn't even join a sorority. At the end of her sophomore year, when everyone else was sunning at the pool, she went with a friend to Berkeley, where she painted apartments for eight dollars an hour, took courses at the university, and spent time with the Black Panthers. It was obvious even then that she just was not the kind of person who was going to get married right away, have children, and settle down. That wasn't Claudia.

When she graduated from Syracuse University we gave her a round-trip ticket to Greece with an open return and a Eurailpass and let her go. She was very nervous about going to Europe by herself—she didn't know anybody—and we agreed that if she wanted to, she would come home in a few weeks. I asked her to do one thing for me. I have always been fascinated by the golden age of Greece; I had dreamed about seeing the Parthenon and the Acropolis and had never been able to do so. "I want you to go there for me," I said. "I just want you to stand there and tell me everything you see."

Claudia was the first of my kids to leave the house and I was probably more nervous about this trip than she was. You really never know how successful you are as a parent until your kids go off on their own. I took the night off from *The Tonight Show* to watch her go. I actually missed a night of work, so you can imagine how important this was to me. None of us really knew what to expect, most of all Claudia. She really did think she'd be back in a few weeks.

Thirteen months later she came home. From Greece she went to Afghanistan and Turkey, then India, England, Ireland, and Scotland. India was not quite as spiritual as she had anticipated—when she woke up her first morning, the owner of the hostel in which she was staying was trying to sell her to one of his friends. She went hiking for several days, ending up in a small Tibetan village, where she met the Dalai Lama standing outside a temple, and he invited her in for tea. This was the daughter I was so worried about. I think this trip might have been the first time in her life when being my daughter had absolutely no value. As Claudia pointed out, the Dalai Lama was one of the few people in her life who didn't say, "How 'bout that Budweiser commercial?" I'm quite sure the Dalai Lama had never seen *The Tonight Show*. Although you have to wonder how he might have interpreted Tiny Tim.

Like me, Claudia had been inspired by President Kennedy. She had intended to join the Peace Corps when she returned, but after spending a year traveling around Europe—in which she earned almost all of the money she needed working as an English tutor or a housekeeper—she decided that there was very little a twenty-two-year-old woman could teach people in a Third World country. So she joined the Vista program and worked with black families in a tiny town in Kentucky. There, for the first time, she was exposed to racial hatred; crosses were burned on her front lawn. She lived with five other girls in a house with no hot water and a coal stove, trying to establish a food co-op for the poor people in that town. Not only did they fail, they had to leave when grocery store owners who were over-charging these people threatened them.

At the time she didn't tell me about these things. I think we had reached the delicate stage in our lives where the child has to protect the parent. But if she had, I think I would have handled it well. I would have gotten right up off the floor where I'd collapsed, and handled it well. After Vista Claudia worked with emotionally disturbed children for eleven years, then became a social worker in Philadelphia. She worked in a last-chance program for kids who had drug and alcohol problems, or who were abused by their parents. These were all high school dropouts ordered by the courts to participate in this program or live in a juvenile detention center. Ironi-cally, she worked in some of the same buildings I had pointed out years earlier when I wanted my children to see that not everybody was as fortunate as we were. Her office was in a condemned building with no heat, and she would begin just about every day by taking guns away from these kids.

Finally, when funding for that program ran out, she decided it was time to earn a real living for herself. After sleeping on her sister's couch for several weeks, she got a job at *Star Search* through her family connections. Although initially she did have to deal with resentment from a few people who thought her talent consisted of being my daughter, she eventually became a senior talent coordinator—where she discovered Rosie O'Donnell, Drew Carey, and Martin Lawrence for the show. After *Star Search* went off the air, she moved into the news division at ABC, where I have no pull, and she has become a senior producer.

When the kids were growing up I was never much of a disciplinarian. I was a much better threatener. When I got really angry at one of them I would tell one of the others, "Go upstairs and get the black belt." I assure you, no one ever got hit with that belt. And chances are that a half hour after I'd lost my temper I would be knocking on the door of their room apologizing.

So most of the punishment was left up to Alyce. When she got mad she'd use southern threats; she'd warn the kids that she was going to go outside to the tree and get a switch. She did that just about as often as I used my belt. Most punishments consisted of their being confined to their room or not being allowed to watch their favorite TV shows.

That worked fine with Claudia, Linda, and Jeffrey, but not with Michael. My son Michael was difficult. I think my celebrity affected him much more than his brothers and sisters. Being the son or daughter of a celebrity can be the toughest thing in the world. How do you find your own identity when your name is Frank Sinatra Jr. or Jean Paul Getty III? Or when your father is on TV every night? We named him Michael Edward McMahon—I wanted him to have a name all his own—but if he ever wanted to be Ed McMahon he had that option. But he was definitely a Michael McMahon, a big, handsome, charming Irish kid.

He was the only one of my children who ever made me lose my temper. That's one of the things at which he was very good. From the time he was a little boy he was always getting into trouble. Always. There was an embankment behind our house in Philadelphia, and just about every night when I came home from the studio I'd have to climb down that steep embankment in the dark to retrieve toys and bicycles he had thrown down there, return them to our neighbors' children, and apologize for him. When we got a new gray couch, it was Michael who spilled an entire bottle of Mercurochrome over it.

I loved to work with my hands and I built a beautiful bar out of Philippine mahogany, equipped it with a complete set of professional bar glasses, brandy snifters, beer glasses, martini glasses, and Alyce placed philodendrons growing out of bottles filled with colored water on either side. I was proud of my carpentry work. Linda was christened the day after it was finally finished, and we had invited all of our friends to come back to the house for a party. While we were gone, Michael climbed up on a stool and pulled over the entire bar. Every glass broke, the colored water spilled out and destroyed the carpet, liquor bottles broke. When we got home, my first reaction was fear—I was afraid he had killed himself. But when I saw he was all right, my second reaction was also fear—I was afraid I was going to kill him.

As he got older he didn't change at all. I once gave him a pellet gun and we'd go out in back of the house and shoot cans. The next thing I knew the police were at the house reporting that he was shooting out the back windows of passing cars. I bought him a motorcycle and he drove it across the neighbors' lawns and almost drove through the plate-glass window of a car dealership. No matter how much Alyce and I tried, we couldn't seem to get through to him.

He didn't respond to discipline. He spent a lot of his childhood restricted to his bedroom. Or so we thought. He had an extension ladder hidden in his room and he'd sneak out when we were asleep. I found out when someone told me they had seen him downtown in Bronxville when I had personally locked him in his room. As I discovered, he had been sneaking out that way for years. He always danced to his own music. Once, I remember, we left him to baby-sit Jeffrey. Now that was our mistake. He took seven-year-old Jeffrey to a big party where they both had a good time.

He was such a charming kid that it was hard to stay mad at him for very long, but he helped me. This was the most frustrating thing I've ever had to deal with. He was my oldest son, I loved him about as much as was possible, and yet I couldn't get through to him. I didn't know what to do. After he died someone gave me a videotape of him doing wonderful impersonations. Now, I knew he did those imitations, I'd heard that he did a very funny Carson, Sammy Davis, Howard Cosell, Steve Martin, . . . and particularly me, but he would never do any of them for me. I don't know why; maybe he was worried I would be disappointed in him.

He was strong and handsome. All the girls in the neighborhood were crazy about him. When he was in eighth grade a senior at Sarah Lawrence College in Bronxville gave him the key to her dorm room. Claudia and Linda were just crazy about him. To Linda he was the big brother every girl should have; her only problem with him was that she never knew if her friends were nice to her because they liked her or because they wanted to be around Michael. The girls were always covering for him, always protecting him. Once, I remember, he was on restriction, confined to his room, and he slipped out and ran away. He enlisted Linda to "find" his note a few hours after he'd left and give it to us, and he went up to Syracuse to stay with Claudia. We were on the phone with Claudia, who was in the infirmary with strep throat, telling her Michael had run away again and might be on his way to see her, when he walked into the infirmary with his big smile. As she looked right at him, Claudia told us, "He isn't here, but if he does show up I'll call right away."

There was one night I completely lost control. My children had heard all my stories about being a marine, but they had never seen me really lose my temper. With them I had always been a pushover, "mush," as Linda described me. But when Claudia turned eighteen we bought her a sports car for Christmas. A little MG. We were going to give it to her when she came home from school, so we put it in the garage and wrapped a big ribbon around it. Michael and his friends went into the garage and took it out for a drive. They were drinking and they had an accident. I don't know what happened, but Michael smashed in the side of the car. I was away when Alyce realized Michael and the car were gone. She was petrified something had happened to him. About one o'clock in the morning she was standing on the sunporch, which overlooked a long driveway, when suddenly Michael and his friends appeared, pushing this dented car up the hill, backward, the long celebratory ribbon dragging behind.

I don't know what I would have done to him if I had been home at that moment. As it was, when I found out, Alyce had to hold me back. All the anger, frustration, and, I guess, disappointment I had felt for years finally exploded. It was a terrible night, a terrible moment.

And yet, at times he was such a wonderful person and I was so proud of him. There was one day, one Saturday afternoon, that I will never forget. Michael was never a great student—when I look back on it now I think it's possible he had a learning disability—but he excelled on the football field. His senior year he made the all-county team. In his life, that was one place where being Ed McMahon's son was of absolutely no consequence. He was a running back and in the biggest game of the year, against Bronxville's archrival, Tuckahoe, Bronxville was losing by a touchdown. They scored to tie the game. Under the rules of football, when a team kicks off to the other team following a touchdown, either team can recover the ball after it goes ten yards. It's called an onside kick, and it very rarely works in the kicking team's favor. But with only minutes left in the game, Michael kicked the ball the required ten yards, then recovered it himself. On the very next play he broke through the line and ran for the winning touchdown. I think that might have been the happiest day of his life. I can just close my eyes and see him that day, the big smile on his face, so proud of himself.

I was the commencement speaker at Michael's high school graduation. "I would like to properly introduce myself," I said. "In these quarters I'm known as Michael McMahon's father . . . Michael's success on the football field has made me known around here, and that's nice . . ."

And it was nice for me—but especially for Michael.

It's amazing how a man and a woman can have four children, raise them in the same environment, and have them turn out so differently. Linda was my little angel. She was the typical teenage girl, very much into boys and her music. Of all the presents I ever gave her, the one she valued most was a used bedsheet. Not just any used bedsheet of course; this was a sheet from the Warwick Hotel in New York City, a sheet that one of the Beatles had slept on! She still has it, neatly folded in her linen closet and never used again.

I almost had a problem with Linda in school too. Her class was being taught the religious version of the story of creation, starring Adam and Eve, and Linda raised her hand and repeated the scientific version of evolution as I had told it to her. The sister apparently got very angry with Linda and told her that the story of evolution was heresy, to which Linda replied defiantly, "I know it's true because my father told it to me!"

When my daughter told me this story, I asked her the same question I occasionally find myself asking my young daughter, Katherine Mary, today: "What color would you like that Porsche to be?"

Linda has three children of her own now. She was the first of my kids to get married. She had a beautiful wedding, she looked radiant, she was marrying a wonderful man named Peter Schmerge, everything was absolutely perfect—except that when I was making my toast I mispronounced her new last name.

Is there a Dr. Freud in the house?

When Alyce and I separated, Jeffrey was the only one of our children still living at home. Our marriage ended in so many ways long before it was over. Maybe if I had been satisfied to stay in Philadelphia our marriage would have survived. But I wasn't. When I was offered opportunities I took them, and that meant leaving Philadelphia and, eventually, leaving New York. Besides *The Tonight Show* I was doing commercials and quiz shows, hosting events, and trying to run several different side businesses—I had a stationery company and a game company. Often after working all day, then doing the show, I'd have to meet with my business partners or investors, or Johnny Carson would want me to have dinner with him, or I simply wanted to go out with friends for a night on the town. I don't think I was overwhelmed by my success, but I wanted to enjoy it. And there was a time when being married became a burden. I just wasn't being married very well. I wasn't running around, I wasn't having affairs, but it seemed as though I was always traveling or always busy. I began to feel guilty. Very guilty. After a while I felt so guilty that our marriage wasn't working and that I wasn't helping it work that I asked Alyce for a separation.

That was some night. What I remember about it was that she said to me, "Go up and tell your son." Jeffrey was twelve years old at that time. And I think with his brother and sisters gone, the house must have felt empty to him. On those nights when I came home after the show he'd be waiting for me behind the front door. We'd watch television together for an hour while I ate my dinner. The night I told Alyce I wanted a separation I asked her if she wanted me to stay the night or leave, and she asked Jeff that same question. "If he's gonna leave," Jeff said, "he should go."

What made a painful situation even more difficult were some of the nasty and untrue stories written by a columnist named Jack O'Brien. O'Brien wrote that when *The Tonight Show* moved to California I went with my whole family in a limousine to the airport, got out of the car, held up one ticket, and said, "I'm going to California and you're not." Of course, there wasn't one shred of truth to that story, but it was printed.

The separation and eventual divorce were very difficult for Alyce and me and the older kids, but it was most difficult for Jeff. He was the child whose life was changed most drastically. I tried to be there for him as much as I could; on several occasions, after doing the show on Friday night I got on the red-eye, the late-night flight from Los Angeles to New York, to be there Saturday morning for a football or basketball game or other event, and on occasion he'd go with me on trips. I was always trying to find ways to compensate. When I was involved in a real estate development, for example, I had a lovely house in Florida right next to a lake. Well, a Florida development kind of lake. An if-you-left-the-water-running-for-the-weekend kind of lake. But it did have an alligator that would come up on shore at night and the fishing was good. One day I brought Jeff out back to show him the sign I'd made naming this great body of water Lake Jeffrey, making him the only kid in his class with a lake named after him. When I couldn't be there physically I always made my presence known with a telegram or phone calls or some sort of contact, but for a time I was out of his life.

In fact, for a time I was out of all my children's lives. They were so angry that they refused to have any contact with me. They were supportive of their mother. If you've ever wondered when it was hard to do *The Tonight Show* and appear to be just old happy Ed with the booming laugh, that was the time. That was the time when professionalism counted. At some time in their life, every performer has to work when their personal life is falling apart. I knew that—I saw Johnny Carson go through some rough times in his personal life without letting it affect his performance—but knowing it didn't make it easier to do. As it turned out, though, it was good practice for what was eventually going to happen.

At times like this Johnny Carson and I actually became closer. We had become close friends on *Who Do You Trust?* because we liked going out together to party and drink, but we became better friends on *The Tonight Show* because we commiserated with each other. Each of us knew when the other one had personal difficulties he was trying to work through.

Finally Bob and Marti Gillin took it upon themselves to arrange for me and the kids to meet with a counselor. Talk about caring friends; I've been blessed with a multitude of them. I flew in from California. It took several sessions, and eventually we started speaking again. Several years earlier I had read a story about the Kennedy family on a rafting trip and I had decided that someday I wanted to do that with my family. I couldn't imagine there would ever be a better someday.

Claudia couldn't go, but Michael, Linda, Jeffrey, and I sailed on a raft down the Colorado River. It was a healing trip for all of us. We camped under the stars, had water fights all day long, drank the pristine waters of the river. We sailed past the cabin where Butch Cassidy and the Sundance Kid had hidden from the Pinkertons, past caves where Indians had lived before the birth of Christ; we sailed right past our problems.

At the end of the trip we flew directly from Lake Powell to Las Vegas and checked into Caesar's Palace. The difference between the peace along the Colorado River and the glitz of Las Vegas could not have been more pronounced, but after sleeping on the sand for five days, we all appreciated the satin sheets of the hotel. Sammy Davis Jr. was performing and we all went to see him, we gambled, and when we left, the rift between us had been healed. Things weren't perfect; a twenty-six-year marriage had broken up—and the pieces would never be put back together. I accepted the fact that some of the feelings could never be resolved, but my kids and I had found a way to communicate.

I had always thought that divorce was something that happened to other people, so I wasn't prepared for all the emotional and the financial complications. For a young couple who had started out with seventy-five cents, Alyce and I had done very well. How do you split up the assets of twenty-six years? Legally. Lawyers do it. And unfortunately in our case, publicly. A lot of things were written about me that weren't true. In that situation, I learned, there wasn't too much I could do except show up on time ready to work and laugh at Johnny's jokes. Boy, laughter helps.

After our divorce was final Alyce moved out to California so Jeff would be closer to me. Alyce was devoted to all of her children. We did make a brief attempt at a reconciliation, but it was too late, too much damage had been done. It was time for all of us to move on with our lives.

While Claudia, Linda, and Jeffrey moved forward in the world, Michael floundered. He was often "between engagements," as he described it. He tried a lot of different things: he had a handyman business, a private car business; I helped him get jobs at ESPN and Anheuser-Busch; he was always planning the next business—he was going to open a cheese store and a landscaping business—but he just was never able to find a place to be content. And I think every time he failed, he thought he had failed in my eyes, which made it even more difficult for him.

For a time he moved out to California and shared an apartment with my assistant, Corrine Madden. Like just about everybody else who spent time with him, she adored him. Michael always had a twinkle in his eye. And maybe a little like his grandfather and his father, he had just a bit of the fanciful in him. Corrine told me a story that was just typical of Michael. One afternoon she came back to the apartment after work and the sink was filled with Michael's dishes. She washed them and put them away, but the next day, and the day after that, the same thing happened. Finally, she said, "You know, Michael, when I come home from work I've been finding your dirty dishes in the sink and you're here all day . . ."

Michael calmly explained that he was intentionally allowing his dirty dishes to pile up in the sink because by cleaning all of them at one time he was saving soap and water. That was so typically Michael. Corrine told me that story at Michael's funeral.

The ironic thing about Michael's death is that it came just after he'd spent a year working with abused children at St. Jude's Ranch, which may have been the most satisfying time of his life. I started working with St. Jude's in the late 1960s. One night I was doing my nightclub act at the Tropicana Hotel in Las Vegas when Charlie Vanda, one of the first people to give me an opportunity in Philadelphia, introduced me to an Episcopal priest named Father Herbert Ward. As I quickly learned, Father Ward was small of stature but very large of heart. He'd started a ranch for abused children in Boulder City, Nevada, near Lake Mead, and Charlie and Shirley Vanda wanted me to see it. On Saturday morning, as we drove out there, Father Ward told me about St. Jude's.

This was long before people realized that many American kids were being brutalized by their parents. Almost no one had even heard the term "child abuse." But Father Ward had created St. Jude's to be a safe place for badly abused children, children who had been taken away from their parents by the county or state. These were kids who had been slammed repeatedly against a wall until bones were broken, or kids who had been burned with cigarettes or scalded with boiling water, or had their clothes set on fire. I couldn't believe the stories he was telling me. His plan was to create a supportive environment in which small groups of children could live together safely with volunteer "parents." By the time we got out to Boulder City, Father Ward had me hooked—and then I saw St. Jude's Ranch.

It consisted of a few little shacks. It didn't look as if it could last the summer. But Father Ward is some terrific salesman—the man could have sold boardwalk meat slicers to a chef—and with the help of a lot of people he built St. Jude's into a modern forty-acre facility overlooking Lake Mead. He's changed the lives of hundreds and hundreds of kids. Of all the charities for which I've done work, St. Jude's has my heart. Maybe because it's so small that every little thing you do really does make a difference, maybe because it saves lives on a daily basis, and maybe just because I love seeing these children safe and smiling, I serve on the board of directors and have long been active in fund-raising. In fact, right on the campus there is a beautiful building known as the Ed McMahon Child Care Center.

Father Ward and I have become so close that when I remarried he performed the ceremony. Twice. But the one thing I never expected was that St. Jude's would be so valuable to one of my own children. When Michael finally ran out of options I suggested he try living on the ranch. Father Ward was glad to have him, and Michael seemed to blossom there. Children had always taken easily to Michael and he worked well with them. He used sports to help them regain confidence in themselves. Maybe because he got so deeply involved with their problems he didn't have time to concentrate on his own, and for the first time in so many years he appeared to be happy. But after a year he got restless again, he needed some time for himself, and went to Florida.

It was while he was in Florida that he first started feeling ill. I told him to see a doctor; he refused. Instead he drove to his mother's house in Philadelphia. He was so weak that for two days he could barely get out of bed. He complained of stomach pains. Alyce took him to her doctor, who diagnosed Michael's problem as a peptic ulcer. Minor. Treatable. We didn't think much about it. I mean, Michael was forty-four years old, big and healthy; there was no reason to believe anything was seriously wrong with him.

He drove across country to St. Jude's. Father Ward called me the day he got there. "Something's wrong with him," he said. "He really looks very bad." I insisted Michael fly to Los Angeles. The moment I saw him I knew that he was very sick. My doctor, Dr. Phil Levine, took a complete set of X rays. As Michael waited outside, the doctor held them up to the window. I could see right away that too much sunlight was blocked by big black spots on those pictures.

"Michael has cancer of the colon," he told me. Cancer? My son? That just didn't seem possible. He was only forty-four years old. "I'm going to start him on chemotherapy, radiation right away . . ."

"Will that cure it?" I asked.

He shook his head. "This isn't something that can be cured. But it'll prolong his life."

And then I asked a question that no father should ever have to ask about his son. "How long do you think he'll live?"

"Maybe six months."

I had to fly that afternoon to Washington, D.C., for the annual meeting of the Horatio Alger Association. As a member of the board it was important that I be there, but I didn't know what else to do. At times you just keep going because you don't know how to stop. We met in the chambers of the United States Supreme Court—Clarence Thomas is a member of Horatio Alger. It was the first time I'd been in that room. To be standing a few feet away from the long

233

bench where so much history has been made, and to be not guilty of anything, inspires a feeling of tremendous awe. For a few minutes it helped me forget the horror of that day.

Michael refused to believe that he had cancer. At one point I suggested to his oncologist, Dr. Larry Heifetz, that we just tell Michael the truth, and then Michael and I would go to Las Vegas for a few days and just raise hell. "No," Dr. Heifetz said, "you can't tell him. He knows I know the answer, and when he's ready to ask the question, he'll ask me. He won't ask you, his mother, his sisters, he'll ask me, 'How much time have I got? Am I gonna get out of this?' That's when he'll be ready to know."

Just a few years earlier I had seen the same spirit in Michael Landon. The last time he appeared on the show everyone knew he was dying, but he just wasn't going to admit it. His attitude was, I'm fighting this thing to the end and I'm going to win. Whether he was kidding himself, trying to live the lie that he was going to make it, or just clinging to the last bit of hope, it didn't matter. And I saw this once again in my son.

Finally, there came a day when Michael was ready to know. He asked Dr. Heifetz how much longer he had to live. "It's hard to know," the doctor explained, and then tiptoed around the answer as gracefully as possible. The number of days didn't really matter; it meant that Michael was ready to deal with it. At home we tried to be positive, we all tried to pretend that this was an illness from which he would eventually recover. We did the best we could, and we waited.

By this time I was married to the former Pam Hurn, an extraordinary woman in so many different ways, and Michael came to die in our house. We turned one room into a hospital room and Claudia came out from New York to take care of her brother. Claudia was there for Michael every minute of his last few months, every minute. It was the most beautiful expression of love imaginable. She became his nurse, she took him to the hospital for chemo and radiation, she went with him to the nutritionist and made sure he ate only what he was supposed to, she administered morphine to kill the pain, she changed the electrodes attached to his back to diffuse pain when scheduled, she gave him his pills, and when necessary, she changed his diapers. At night she slept on the floor at the base of his bed in case he should need something.

Linda was there as much as possible. She'd fly out for several days, fly back to see her children, then come right back. She hated leaving to go back because none of us knew what to expect, and she wanted to be there at the end. And Jeffrey was there whenever he could get away from work. It had been a long time since we had all been together in one place, and there was something comforting about that. I didn't know what to do. It's rare that I'm at a loss for the right words or the proper actions, but nothing in my life had ever prepared me for this.

For a long time Michael had not been on good terms with his sisters. If he wasn't mad at Claudia, he was mad at Linda. There was no reason for it—they'd never fought—but he found reason to be angry with both of them. Even when Claudia was doing everything possible for him he would lash out at her. But in the last weeks, the kids fell back into their childhood patterns, when the girls had idolized their brother. Claudia and Linda competed to see who could please him the most. Linda would carefully fold his dinner napkins into triangles and Claudia would respond by bringing him an extra piece of chocolate, then Michael would grade them. He'd award them points for being attentive but deduct points for things like forgetting to bring a fork. Michael said he thought Linda had the edge because she was used to being a mother. It was heartwarming to see them end up as close as they had been as children, loving each other.

Michael never stopping fighting. One afternoon we went out for lunch. By this point he had shriveled down to nothing, he was gaunt and had little energy, and without actually saying it, I implied how important it was that he enjoyed whatever time he had. And Michael responded, "Oh come on, Dad, it's not as bad as that."

I left the next day for New York, then I was going to Washington to appear with a symphony orchestra and a chorus, reading two pieces at the dedication of the Korean War Memorial. I called Claudia from New York to ask about her brother. When she answered the phone, she started crying. She told us to come home as quickly as possible. While I was in New York I started planning Michael's funeral.

We all gathered in the house. Alyce came from Philadelphia several times. She usually stayed in a nearby hotel, but when he started failing she stayed with us. Pam tried to make her as comfortable as possible. It was a strange situation, seeing Alyce with Pam, but so many years had passed since our divorce, and Alyce had also remarried, so although awkward, it wasn't difficult.

Michael was in a coma and there was nothing anyone could do but wait. During the night we took turns staying in the room with him. About midnight, Linda and my stepson, Pam's son Lex, were in Michael's room and his breathing became difficult. We all gathered in his room and were with him when he died. We bowed our heads and said a prayer.

Three or four hours later I did a car commercial. People might not understand that, but my family did. I needed to be busy, I needed to be occupied, I certainly wasn't going to be able to sleep, and I had made this commitment. All of the people involved had flown out from New York. This had been scheduled for months. Besides, I hoped that losing myself in work might make the terrible pain go away for a few seconds. I told the director, "I don't want people to know this, but I lost my son a few hours ago and anything we can do to make this go as fast as possible, I'd really appreciate." Sometimes you just keep going . . . We did it in one take, and then I went home to finish making the necessary arrangements.

Just about the first phone call I got was from Johnny Carson. Johnny had lost his son Ricky, who was just a great, loving kid, in a car accident, so he knew exactly what I was going through. The words said at a time like this aren't really that important, but the emotional support is enormous. Steve Lawrence, who also had lost his son, called and we talked and it all helped. Once the phones started ringing, they didn't stop for days. We all tried to keep busy, keep moving.

It seemed as if it had been just hours earlier that I had spoken at Michael's high school graduation and now I was speaking at his funeral. My hands were shaking but somehow I got through it. Alyce came back to the house with us, and I think she was as surprised as I was about how natural it all felt. When we came back from the memorial service Alyce and I and our three kids spent just a little time together in one of the bedrooms discussing some things that had to be discussed. I was lying on the bed, wearing a comfortable old pair of socks—they had big holes in them, as I've worn just about forever. And all of a sudden Alyce leaned over, grabbed one of the socks, and said, "I can't believe it. The same socks!"

Never, never in my life have I so enjoyed the sound of laughter.

We all wanted to memorialize Michael in some way that would help other people but be a place that said Michael in some permanent way. So, inscribed into a stone monument at the top of a hill at St. Jude's that overlooks the football field there is an etching of him with his name and the name of the facility, the Michael McMahon Memorial Sports Complex. The message on the plaque reads: "Michael Edward McMahon—April 12, 1951–July 28, 1995—ACCEPT GOD IN YOUR HEART AND HE WILL HELP GUIDE YOU IN THE GAME OF LIFE.

I'm so proud of my children. Claudia is senior news producer at the Fox network, Linda and Peter Schmerge are the parents of three of my grandchildren, while Jeff, an executive at the National Football League, and his wife, Martha, are the parents of my fourth and youngest grandchild, Maggie McMahon.

I wasn't there as often as I wanted to be when they were growing up, but I know that I did the best job I could. And sometimes, when I wonder how anyone ever finds the proper balance between raising a family and sustaining a career, I think back to one night in Ohio. The kids were young and I was working in summer stock; I was doing a musical on the Kenley circuit somewhere in Ohio. It was opening night and we had a full house, five thousand people. At the end of the show, as part of our contracts, the performers were required to meet the audience and sign autographs. After that we had the opening-night party.

Alyce and the children were arriving by train late that night. As the train began pulling into the station about one o'clock in the morning, Claudia told her mother, "Don't worry if Dad isn't here. It's opening night and you know he has to sign autographs and go to the party. Somebody'll be here to pick us up and he'll be at the hotel . . ."

Claudia was worried that her mother would be hurt if I wasn't there and was making all kinds of excuses for me. And when she finished, Alyce said matter-of-factly, "Your father will be waiting for us at the train station."

Alyce knew me. When the train arrived I was the only person waiting on the platform. Always, I did my best to be there.

8

The beautiful starlets who appeared on *The Tonight Show* were rarely shy about showing off their charms. One night, when Eddie Murphy was a guest, a well-endowed young woman admitted that her figure had "opened a lot of doors for me."

"Uh yeah," Johnny agreed, "I would think so."

"I think that once you get in the door, though," she continued, "there are nine thousand other busty blonds who also got in the door."

At that point Eddie Murphy interrupted to ask, "Where's that door at?"

I'm very good at a lot of things, but being alone isn't one of them. I guess you might say that I'm only good at being alone when there are a lot of other people around. I had gotten married when I was twenty-two years old and had been married twenty-six years; I was almost fifty years old when Alyce and I separated and, for the first time in my adult life, I was single.

I didn't know anything about dating. Fortunately, I was a fast learner. Dating, I discovered, was like riding a bicycle: you just had to keep everything in balance. Look, it wasn't very difficult for me to get dates. Instead of taking a girl dancing to Frank Sinatra's records as I'd once done, now I could take my dates to dinner with Frank and Barbara Sinatra. I also discovered an amazing fact about women: although I had aged almost thirty years since I'd last dated, most of the women with whom I was going out were still in their twenties!

As with just about everything else in our lives, the fact that I was dating young girls became a topic of humor on the show. "Ed was a little late getting here tonight," Johnny would explain. "His date's baby-sitter didn't show up." Or, "You know, Ed was telling me just before the show about a new restaurant he'd taken his date to, and, uh, I have to admit, I was surprised. I didn't know Gerber's even had a restaurant."

Uh-ooooooo!

If there ever was a perfect time to be single, it was in Los Angeles in the 1970s. It was sort of the command post for the sexual revolution. People were always trying to fix me up with their friends or relatives, but I really preferred to meet people myself. I met a wide range of interesting women and encountered problems that in my wildest dreams I could never have anticipated. One lovely woman I was dating posed for *Playboy,* and during the shooting accidentally sat on an anthill. This was not a good thing. It was also not an area in which I had any expertise. Ask me about going down the embankment to retrieve toys, but don't ask me what to do when a naked woman sits on an anthill.

There was no prohibition against dating people who appeared on *The Tonight Show,* and at times members of the staff did date guests. I wasn't really comfortable about doing it myself—until the night we had a lovely woman who had been an equestrian in the circus on the show. She was working as an actress at that time and had just made her first movie. As she moved down the couch closer to me I became more and more attracted to her. Two guests later she was sitting next to me, and I invited her to see my nightclub act later that evening. That was my first romance after my divorce. Both of us loved the circus, and although she was the first bareback rider I'd ever gone out with, I'm sure I wasn't the first clown she'd ever dated. Our relationship lasted several months, and she was the only guest on the show I ever asked out.

I did not intend to remarry. I wasn't against it; I just never thought about it. Marriage seemed like something that was part of my past. I'd raised my family. In fact, Alyce and I were just legally separated, not divorced. And I kept thinking that way until I met Victoria Valentine in 1974, when I flew to Houston to host a party for Budweiser. She was a VIP hostess for National Airlines and met the plane when we landed. As we waited for my luggage we started talking. Looking back, if my luggage had been on time, my life would have been so different. Her name, Victoria Valentine, fascinated me; what a nice name. We discovered very quickly that her best friend was Scotty Sanders, then the wife of golfer Doug Sanders and one of the wonderful women of the world. I called Victoria the next day on the pretext that I needed help with travel arrangements and managed to get around to asking her out. Actually, "out" probably isn't accurate. I invited her to come to New Orleans, where I was doing my nightclub act at the Roosevelt Hotel.

Scotty Sanders convinced her to go. We had our first real date after my performance, just Victoria and me and two hundred other people, including Al Hirt and Pete Fountain. After that we were on the phone every day. Four weeks later, on Valentine's Day, I told her, "You are the valentine of my life." A year later I proposed. I gave her an engagement ring and a little note that read, "Will you marry me a year from the day in a city to be announced?" You know, with my schedule I never knew where I was going to be. The night I gave her the ring we had dinner with John Wayne. As women do, she was showing it to everyone. Duke took one look at it, looked at me, then shook his head, and said, "Conservative, aren't you?"

We were married in San Francisco by Father Ward on my fifty-third birthday, March 6, 1976. The party started that night and continued for several years. Like me, Victoria knew how to enjoy herself and we lived the Hollywood life. We went to all the parties, restaurants, and openings; wherever it was fashionable to be, that's where we would be, whether it was Swifty Lazar's Oscar night party, Chasen's, Ma Maison, or weekends at Frank and Barbara Sinatra's home in Palm Springs. It was easy to get caught up in that whirlwind and I did.

When we were first married we built our dream house in Beverly Hills. This house was designed by my friend the great architect Carson Wright. It had four bedrooms, six bars, in which the only beer served was Budweiser, living rooms and dens, a formal dining room, a recreation room and media room, a custom-built two-hundred-bottle wine cooler with a separate temperature control for each rack, a brook stocked with beautiful Japanese koi, which ran right under the patio decking and surrounded the outdoor Jacuzzi.

Now, I love planning surprises and I wanted to do something special for our anniversary—so I decided to have an intimate dinner with Victoria in the house. At that time the "house" had just been framed; it consisted of a foundation and a lot of two-by-fours nailed together. There were no walls, no doors, no windows, just a lot of two-by-fours. I had borrowed everything I needed from the great restaurant Ma Maison: a table with two chairs, dishes, silverware and crystal, the wine cooler, flowers—I'd even taken pictures off the walls of Ma Maison and hung them on the two-by-fours.

When Victoria and I arrived she was stunned. We dined by candlelight—we had to because there was no electricity in the frame. As a portable radio played classical music in the background, Pepe, the legendary bartender from Chasen's, the creator of the world-famous flaming martini favored by W. C. Fields, served martinis and wine. My friend Patrick Terrier, owner of Ma Maison, served caviar and veal prepared on a Coleman stove. It was an incredibly romantic evening.

The night was marred only by the occasional squeal of car brakes, as people driving by would glance over and see waiters in tuxedos serving dinner in the frame of this house, then stop and back up to get a better look.

It was a wonderful house, but when we adopted Katherine Mary we needed a lot more space, so I bought a house that had been built by David O. Selznick, the legendary producer of *Gone with the Wind,* among many other classic movies. The house was four levels, eleven thousand square feet, and some of the great parties of Hollywood history had taken place there. It was thrilling for me to sit at the bar and realize that I was sitting right where W. C. Fields, Ronald Colman, and Errol Flynn had sat. Charlie Chaplin's house was directly across the street. It was a lifetime away from an apartment near the boardwalk in Atlantic City.

For several years Victoria and I had a wonderful time together. We did everything possible to please each other. She dressed to please me, she made my life as comfortable as she knew how. And I did things that had never previously interested me. Victoria loved horseback riding, for example, so I bought her a horse. When she wanted me to learn how to ride I bought myself a beautiful black horse. Then I remembered—I didn't like riding horses. If God had wanted me to learn how to ride a horse He wouldn't have invented limousines. Maybe I got up on that horse once or twice, but I would always find some excuse not to ride. I was a lot better at making excuses for not riding than I ever was at riding.

Victoria loved to ski so I took skiing lessons. We used to go to Sun Valley and I just fell in love with that place. I wasn't a very good skier, my legs weren't strong enough—I should have used that excuse for not riding. To me the best thing about skiing was that it was followed quickly by après-skiing. Eventually I figured out that if I didn't go up the mountain in the first place I didn't have to ski down the mountain to get to where I already was. So I gave my skis away and concentrated on perfecting my après-skiing style.

It was a good marriage for a long time, but we always had some problems. When we first got together, I explained to her, "The most important thing in my life are my friends and friends need nurturing. All you have in life is an accumulation of friends. I mean, you can have eighteen cars, but you can drive only one. You can have fifty pairs of shoes, but you can wear only one. But friends, you can have as many of those as you can handle." And during that marriage I don't think we nurtured some of my oldest friendships as much as we might have. I found myself seeing people I'd known and loved for many years less and less. Listen, I accepted it. It was my responsibility as much as hers.

By far the most important thing to come out of our marriage was our little girl, Katherine Mary. For almost ten years we never even thought about having a child. It just wasn't part of our marriage. Victoria seemed very happy. And me? I already had four grown children and two grandchildren. To be honest, the prospect of starting all over again with a baby was not something that seemed appealing to me at all.

After being me all those years, I was amazed how wrong I could be about myself.

The whole thing started when my daughter Linda allowed Victoria and me to baby-sit for my eight-month-old granddaughter Alexandra for two weeks. Victoria and I picked up Alex in New York and brought her back to Beverly Hills. I'd long ago forgotten whatever I'd once known about taking care of a baby, but somehow we managed without any help. We did everything ourselves. We took her everywhere with us. I remember sitting on the floor in Aaron Spelling's wife's lovely gift shop changing Alex's diaper one night. We did such a good job that Linda let us do it a second time. That was all we needed; we fell so madly in love with Alex that whatever parental urges were stirring in both of us came right to the surface and we decided to try to adopt a child of our own.

I wanted a little Irish Catholic girl, that was my dream, but the truth is we would have settled happily for any kind of baby. We just got lucky. We found an attorney in another city who made all the arrangements for us and then we waited. And we waited a little longer. We waited about a year. That was actually a good thing, because it allowed us to experience all the anticipation of a pregnancy. I think so many of the feelings that come with a natural birth are caused by the waiting. We told no one that we were doing this, not even Victoria's mother, because if we couldn't find a child we didn't want people to feel disappointed. And maybe we didn't want to jinx it.

Katherine Mary was five days old when she arrived in our lives. The night before we picked her up I didn't sleep, I reread Dr. Spock from cover to cover. She was dressed all in white when I first saw her, with a little crocheted white hat covering her head. She was a beautiful baby. We named her after my grandmother, Katie, and Victoria's mother, Mary. And I got exactly what I wanted, an Irish lass, complete with the requisite Irish temper. When she wanted something, she bellowed. When she wanted her bottle, she let us know loudly.

Everyone was shocked when we told them. I think it was

more disbelief than surprise. My children especially didn't know how to deal with the fact that after all these years they had a new sibling. Jeffrey sighed when we told him and said, "Thank God, I'm not the youngest anymore." Linda's children, who were older than Katherine, had a difficult time understanding their relationship to her. Linda tried to explain all about the divorce and that Katherine was her new sister, just like Claudia was her sister, and that made Katherine their aunt. So when Alex met her Aunt Katherine for the first time, I said to her, "This is your Aunt Katie."

She looked at me, sighed, and said, "Granddaddy, it's not normal to have a baby aunt."

I discovered immediately that one of the biggest differences between having a child naturally and adopting one is the paperwork. It makes no difference in the way you love that child. It never even occurred to me that I might love her in a different way than my other kids. I don't have a control valve on love. I took one look at my little girl and I think she smiled at me and that was it. One smile and we were bonded forever. Maybe the thing that surprised me most was how many people I had known for a long time, people I thought I knew well, told me that their child or children were adopted. We got hundreds of lovely letters and cards from people all over the country. During one of the first trips we made with Katherine, a woman came up to us and said, "I'm so happy for you. I was adopted and I've had a wonderful life, thanks to two loving parents."

A friend of ours sent us a lovely poem that begins, "Not flesh of my flesh or bone of my bone, but desired of my heart . . ." and closes with the beautiful lines, "And never forget, for one single minute, you didn't grow under my heart, but in it." We framed it and hung it on her wall.

I was able to spend more time with Katherine than I had with my other kids. I mean, I changed her diapers, I got up and fed her at all hours of the night, I took her everywhere with me. By the time she was six months old she'd been to lunch at the Polo Lounge in the Beverly Hills Hotel several times, although she brought her own. When I served as grand marshal of a St. Patrick's Day parade, she rode on my lap in the car, and when I visited Ireland for the first time in my life, I took her with me. Sometimes during meetings I'd keep her on my lap and feed her. I went with Victoria for every visit to the doctor. It wasn't just that I was starting a second family, it was almost as if I were starting my own second childhood.

I wasn't used to getting up in the middle of the night, and it was tiring, but it was a pleasant sort of exhaustion. Satisfying.

Katherine was born just before Christmas and received more presents than we could count. She had more teddy bears than FAO Schwarz; she even had two stars in the heavens named after her, one a gift from our doctor, the other from a wonderful stranger. The first time Johnny Carson saw her he picked her up and she cooed and gurgled. Of course, as I reminded him, many women have done that with Johnny. One night we were talking about my baby on the show and he admitted, "I don't know what to buy a young girl."

I suggested, "Well, stocks and bonds are always nice."

Instead he sent her a gorgeous silver frame engraved with her name. He knew that was much more romantic than stocks and bonds.

By the time she was three years old she knew that Johnny was my boss. I remember one morning I was leaving for work and I gave her a big hug and a kiss and she asked, "Where are you going, Daddy?"

"I'm going to work," I told her. "I've got to make a living."

She considered that for a moment, then told me, "Well, have a nice day, and say hello to Mr. Carson." Three years old and she knew how to butter up the boss.

At first Victoria and I were worried about what this

would do to our marriage. We'd had a great relationship for nine years, we knew it was going to change, we just didn't know how or how much. What happened is that we became closer—at least for a time.

If I hadn't expected to get divorced a first time, the prospect that my marriage to Victoria would not last seemed even more improbable. As far as I was concerned, we were married for life, and adopting Katherine seemed to make us even better together.

So I guess it's accurate to say I was stunned when I found out that Victoria was having an affair. Stunned? I don't think that even begins to describe how I felt. That was about the last thing I would have thought possible. Now, in retrospect, I've been extremely fortunate. As a result of the end of my marriage to Victoria, I had the great good fortune to meet Pam and fall in love and marry her and experience a kind of love so deep and true that my life has been turned in a new direction. But at the time of my divorce from Victoria I was deeply hurt.

It's hard for me to write about it. Some of the people who worked for me knew about it before I did and didn't know what to do. They were in a difficult situation. But after a while it was obvious even to me that something was going on. Our relationship had changed. At one point I confronted her and she denied it. But something was wrong and I had to find out for myself what it was, so I hired a private investigator. Imagine, me, hiring a private investigator to follow my wife. I wanted to be wrong.

I had no experience with this kind of situation, I didn't know what to do. Fortunately, I was surrounded by people who cared about me, and they were incredibly supportive and helpful. They were there when I needed people to be there. The whole thing seemed like a terrible dream to me; this was the kind of thing that happened to other people, certainly not to me.

My assistant, Madeline Kelly, was in contact with the investigator. He compiled irrefutable evidence that Victoria was having an extramarital affair with a Beverly Hills police officer. Madeline and the investigator sat down with me and showed me the evidence. The range of feelings I experienced was unbelievable: pain, betrayal, embarrassment, anger, and great sadness. I decided immediately that we would get a divorce, but my biggest concern was Katherine. Victoria and I had taken on the great responsibility of raising a child and my heart was committed to her in every way. I didn't want to do that casually, I didn't want to be a part-time father, not again, not at this time in my life. So when I filed for a divorce, I also filed for custody of our daughter.

For Katherine's sake we tried to make the end of our marriage as civil as possible; we even went to the opening of our friend Marvin Davis's new restaurant together the day I signed the divorce papers. I just went to work every day and did my job as best I could. But everyone was surprised when I filed for divorce. Even *Tonight Show* producer Freddy de Cordova, whom I saw every day of the week, admitted that he was shocked when he heard the news.

And it was news. For a time it seemed like I couldn't open a newspaper without reading about my life in one of the columns. These stories were most often exaggerated or inaccurate, but they were always hurtful. Reporters were calling all the time asking me to make a statement. My picture was on the cover of all of the tabloids. As someone who has spent my life talking, even I knew that sometimes the best possible thing to say is nothing. The most I said to anyone was, "Look, I'm a marine, and marines hang in there." It was one of those times when you wish some major news event would take place to occupy everybody's attention.

The only thing I could do was put on my game face and continue going about my life as best as possible. When you're going through a situation like that in public you think that every person on every corner knows all about it. Every time I noticed someone looking at me I just knew that they were thinking about this. I remember a story Doc Severinsen once told me. He was in a hotel room having an argument with his wife, and right in the middle of it he heard this fluttering sound. He looked and saw a piece of paper being slid under the door. It was a note from several people asking for his autograph. So Doc and Emily stopped the fight, opened the door, signed some autographs, and had a nice chat, then closed the door and started screaming and yelling all over again. That's how I felt, as if the world was watching my life. Doing *The Tonight Show* was not that difficult; Johnny Carson always knew just how far he could go on the show about all of our personal lives, his own included, and he knew this was not a topic for humor.

I hired a lawyer. Paul Tobin, a fellow marine, explained to me that in California, once the personal animosities are removed, a divorce is no more than a business deal. It's the breakup of a partnership. The only good thing about the entire divorce agreement was that I didn't have to ride that horse anymore.

To me, the money was secondary. It was important, obviously—I had worked very hard all my life—but still secondary. I knew I could always make more money. People are always going to need a good metric slicer. But Katherine . . . she mattered to me. Eventually we settled for joint custody and Katherine spends substantial time with both of us. And, I think, because we both cared so much about her, the divorce was about as amicable as possible given the circumstances.

My friends and my older children were very supportive. Claudia was living in San Francisco so I flew up there to be with her and Linda joined us. As a symbol that a period of my life was ending, they decided that we should throw away my one pair of white Gucci loafers. They just never thought that their father really belonged in white Gucci loafers. That was much too Hollywood for them. To them, I was a torn-socks kind of guy. But these loafers turned out to be the shoes that wouldn't go away. These were the loafers from *The Twilight Zone*. Three different times we tried to throw them away, but each time they returned. The first time we held a family ceremony around a wastebasket. "Okay," I announced, "I'm ready to let go of them," and dropped them in the basket. But when we came back from lunch, they were sitting neatly in my closet, cleaned and polished. That night we left them outside the room; the next day they were back in the closet. We tried the wastebasket again, again they returned.

Changing my life wasn't going to be as easy as it appeared.

This was so silly, but it was just what I needed. The three of us just laughed and had fun. Finally, Linda disposed of them. Being with Katherine, being reminded of the best part of that marriage, was also important to me. One afternoon when Katherine was about five years old we were on my boat and I was playing a lovely album on the stereo system, Natalie Cole I believe it was, and there was a line in one song, "Every day's a beautiful day . . ." When Katherine heard that, she put her arms around me and added her own line, "Especially if it's a day with Daddy."

"Honey," I responded once again, "what color do you want that Porsche?"

Once again, I was single. Being single is my second choice. For me, it isn't as enjoyable as being married to a woman I love, but there are a lot of very beautiful things about it. And I met several of them. This time, as soon as Victoria and I separated, I began getting hundreds of letters from women. After having suffered a terrible blow to my ego, this was very flattering. Some of these women were just offering advice: "What you need, Ed, is an older woman who can cook for you," "What you really need is a nice down-home type woman." Some of them made offers:

"You've had enough of these Hollywood types, I've got a trailer you can move right into," and "I'm the kind of woman who knows how to pamper a man," and some of them sent photographs.

I was better at being single this time than I had been in the past. Well, I had more practice. And this time, this time I was certain I wasn't going to get married again. I had my career, I had my two families, I had so many wonderful friends, and I had several attractive women in my life. Although some of the women I dated were beautiful, it was obvious they weren't right for me, and I knew that immediately after the first seven or eight dates.

Whee-yoooo!

There just was no need for me to marry again. But at Milton Berle's eighty-third birthday party, Lillian Crane, a former Ziegfeld showgirl married to the great comedy writer Harry Crane, whispered in my ear, "I have the perfect woman for you. She's beautiful on the outside and the inside."

Since Lillian is a woman of great style, taste, and good humor, I knew I wanted to meet this person. I called Pam Hurn and we made a blind date, lunch at the Polo Lounge at the Beverly Hills Hotel. For years I've had lunch in the same booth at the Polo Lounge; people knew they could often find me there sitting right behind a full plate.

When Pam walked in the door, I was instantly attracted to her. Pam is tall and elegant, but it was the warmth of her smile that lit up my heart. I took one look at her and thought, if Lillian is right, if this woman really is as beautiful on the inside as I see she is on the outside, then this could be something serious. From our first moment together she was so easy to be with. Three hours passed in minutes. It was obvious we were going to see each other again. I didn't tell her I'd decided never to marry again. In fact, I completely forgot that I'd decided that.

Pam later told me she'd decided that day that we should be together. Well, as they say, the groom is the last to know. We met on a Tuesday afternoon. That night I invited her to a small birthday party I was throwing for my housekeeper. On Thursday we went to see Frank Sinatra performing at the Greek Theatre, and during intermission we went backstage to have a drink with him. On Friday we had dinner on my boat, where I had been living since the divorce. On Saturday we went to Tony Bennett's concert, then went backstage to spend time with him. That was some first week, and by Sunday I was convinced that she was as special as Lillian Crane had promised.

The better I got to know her, the more attractive she became to me. Pam had a son, Lex, by an earlier marriage, whom she'd raised by herself. He was then serving in the Marine Corps. Maybe I had Sinatra and Bennett and a large boat to impress her, but on her side she had the United States Marine Corps. No contest. And the fact is that although she enjoyed all the things we did together, she was not the type of person who was impressed by celebrities or glitz. She was one of the most down-to-earth, sweetest people I'd ever met. As my daughter Linda would later say, it was as if the skies opened up and she dropped out of heaven just for me. Pam was working in advertising when we met, but by passion she was a dress designer. She'd had her own company, she'd designed and manufactured ready-to-wear hand-painted fashions. For a while it was a successful company; she had showrooms in New York, Dallas, Atlanta, and sales representatives all across the country. Major department stores and upscale boutiques carried her clothes. When the 1980s recession hit, these shops couldn't pay their bills. She had to abandon her dream. She was working as an advertising executive.

Everything I learned about her was impressive. She had been active in everything from the rock music industry to her church, a mostly black church in south central Los Angeles ministered by Dr. Frederick Price. Years ago Dr. Price had founded a day-care center for single mothers living in that area that had grown into a school. He had added a grade each successive year until in 1996 he graduated his first six high school students, each of whom was accepted by a major university. The school now occupies thirty acres no more than a well-placed nine-iron shot from the spot where the recent riots started and has 310 students. Pam donates 10 percent of all the profits from our company to this school, and after we were married I produced a concert for the Price School Scholarship Fund that raised almost one hundred thousand dollars. We had the brilliant songwriter David Foster, Kenny G, Shanice, Billy Porter, a two-hundred-voice choir, and a full orchestra.

Our relationship progressed with all the subtlety of two locomotives racing toward each other on the same track. From the day we'd met, everything seemed so right. It was as if we were destined to be together. Several weeks after we'd started dating, my son Jeffrey came to California for the weekend with his lovely girlfriend, Martha. The fact that Jeff had brought Martha out to spend time with me meant that he was serious about her. The three of us took my boat to Catalina. Pam was working and couldn't go with us. Jeff and Martha were so obviously in love that I pointed out, "As captain of this ship, once we're three miles off land-mass, I can marry you. That's one of the oldest traditions of the sea. It won't last a lifetime, but it will certainly tide you over for the weekend."

I missed Pam terribly. Since meeting we'd spent so much time together that I hadn't had the opportunity to feel what my life was like without her. Well, it didn't feel good at all. So I spent most of that weekend on beautiful Catalina island standing at the pay phone just outside the ladies' room in the Black Buffalo Nickel Cafe telling Pam how much I cared for her. "I'm in love with you," I told her, "and if you're feeling the same way I am, you know where it's going to lead."

"I was just waiting for you to catch up with me," she said.

Those are the moments about which love songs are written. Not particularly the fact that I was standing outside the ladies' room, but that instant when you realize and accept that this is the person with whom you'll be sharing a future. Seven months after we'd met, we eloped. I wanted to be married by Father Ward in the chapel at St. Jude's Ranch. Father Ward and the judge who would perform the legal service were the only people we told. Our plan was to fly to Las Vegas with Katherine and my assistant, Toni Holliday, after *The Tonight Show* and drive out to St. Jude's the following morning to be married.

At 5 A.M. Pam and I walked into the Las Vegas marriage license bureau. The woman typing our papers looked up and recognized me. "You!" she said. "Are you doing what I think you're doing?"

Now, since we were in the marriage license bureau at five o'clock in the morning getting a license, there was not a lot of room for denial.

Later that morning, as Pam drove us to Boulder City, I turned around and showed Katherine and Toni two small ring boxes, a blue one and a black one. "Okay," I said, "I'll tell you what's going on. Pam and I are getting married. Toni, you're going to be the maid of honor. Katherine, you're going to be the ring girl and the best man. The blue box is the prettiest, so that's for the lady, the black box is for the man. When the priest asks you for the rings to bless them, you'll hand them to him . . ."

Because this took place during Lent we couldn't be married in the chapel, so we were legally married in the Ed McMahon Child Care Center at St. Jude's. What do you do the night of your marriage when your best man is your five-year-old daughter? It's automatic; you go to Excalibur, the medieval jousting spectacle, where you eat your wedding dinner with your fingers. Our team was the White Knights and they won, which we agreed was a fine symbol. Back at the beautiful Golden Nugget Hotel we had our wedding cake, although in this case it was our wedding key lime pie.

On Monday I appeared on *Live with Regis and Kathy Lee* and announced that I'd gotten married over the weekend.

Since then Pam and I have done even better than live happily every after; we've lived healthily ever after. I believe Pam saved my life. When we got serious she told me, "I love you and I want us to be together for a long time, but the only way that's going to happen is if you change your habits. You're going to have to learn how to eat healthy."

All those years I hadn't been eating just for myself, I was eating for the starving kids all over the world my grandmother Katie had told me about. My weight had always been a big topic for Johnny's jokes, and over the years it had gotten bigger and bigger. To me it seemed as if I was either always on a diet or always about to go on a diet. I was always going to start the strictest diet known to man—next Monday morning. Through the years I'd tried probably fifty different diets, everything that came along, the Stillman diet, the grapefruit diet, the hard-boiled-egg diet, Dr. Atkins's diet, the Scarsdale diet. One I particularly loved was the martinis and whipped cream diet; now there was a diet that was right for me. It was based on the theory that if you kept your carbohydrate intake to less than sixty grams a day you would lose weight and could still eat steak, drink martinis—but you couldn't eat watermelon because it contained too many carbs. I tried fasting—that's when I learned that the slowest thing in the world is a fast. They all worked for a short time.

I wasn't just eating too much; I was also eating too much of the wrong things. My favorite breakfast, for example, consisted of a bagel with the bread scooped out, filled with tomato, and covered with melted American cheese and spices. By not eating all of the bagel, I figured, I was cutting down on starch. Pam changed all that. She taught me about nutrition. She figured out how to cook everything I love, but with low-fat ingredients. You can't taste the difference, but your body knows.

Now, I had cut down considerably on my drinking before I'd met Pam. But Pam insisted I drink. One glass of red wine a day, with my meal, which is very good for the heart. The truth is that sometimes I cheat a little: it's still one glass, but I fill it twice.

I married Pam for better and for worse, but I don't remember anyone saying anything about exercise. My response when I was asked to do some exercise on *The Tonight Show*—"I have a man who does that for me"—was true. Except for that part about there being a man. Earlier in my life I had been a good athlete and in Marine Corps condition, but later in life my exercise had been limited primarily to climbing in and out of limousines. As I'd gotten more successful, in fact, my shape actually began to resemble a dollar sign—I had a round bulge in the front and a round bulge in the back. Pam put both of us on an exercise program. We have dueling treadmills—two treadmills that face each other. And if we don't get outside for a fast walk in the morning, we use those treadmills. Now I can go nowhere faster than ever before. I also started lifting weights. I'd always wondered why the weights were called dumbbells when I was the one picking them up over and over and putting them right back. But as I've learned, moderate weight training is an excellent way of keeping muscles trim and flexible.

The result has been that I'm in the best condition of my adult life. The one place I resisted Pam's attempts was when it came to alternative medicine. The closest I'd ever gotten to alternative medicine was taking a multivitamin. But Pam asked me to go with her to see her doctor, Soram Singh Khalsa, M.D., who uses a combination of Western and Eastern medicines. I agreed to go with her, but I made it clear that I had no intention of getting involved myself. When I walked into the office, all the doctors were wearing turbans. I felt as if I were walking into a Tibetan monastery. The last person I had seen wearing a turban was Carnac.

I told Dr. Khalsa, "I hold in my hand the final . . ." Well, actually I told him I was there to be a supportive husband, that Pam was his patient. And I told him that as he examined me and showed me a simple diagnostic technique called applied kinesiology. And I told him that as he prescribed a program of herbs and nutritional supplements. And I continue to tell him that twice a month during our regularly scheduled appointments. And I'm firm about it too!

And that doesn't even include acupuncture. I try to be a positive person, and one thing about which I've always been positive is that I don't like needles. I could land an airplane on an aircraft carrier at night or fly over enemy lines while people were shooting at me, but the idea of getting a needle or having my blood taken frightened me. Needles hurt. So it was difficult for me to accept the concept that being stuck with needles took pain away. But when I started having back problems, Dr. Khalsa claimed that acupuncture might bring relief. Yeah, sure, I thought, I know how that works. The needles hurt so much they make you forget all about the pain in your back. But I agreed to try it. I really do dislike needles so this wasn't easy for me.

The biggest problem with acupuncture, I discovered, is that it gives medicine a bad name. Who wants to get a treatment called "puncture"? It sounds painful. It sounds like "root canal." But it worked for me, my back pains were greatly diminished. And to my surprise, it was about as painful as a mosquito bite. So what acupuncture really needs is a new name, something like "spot therapy," or "pleasure points." I just call it relief.

Before I met Pam the chances that I would completely change my lifestyle, that I'd limit my drinking to a glass or two of red wine, follow a diet of nutritious low-fat foods, take an array of vitamins and herbs, exercise every day, and let people wearing turbans stick needles in me were probably about the same as that of Aunt Blabby modeling in *Sports Illustrated*'s swimsuit edition. Maybe even a little worse. You know, with the right lighting, on a beach, Aunt Blabby wasn't so . . .

But I had no choice, I had to do all these things. Once again I need all the energy I can muster because I'm about to go into battle one more time: my daughter Katherine is now a teenager. If Doc were doing the music for this book, this would be the page for really terrifying music. Thus far I've learned one thing about raising a child in this rapidly changing world: the fact that I've already raised four children is absolutely no preparation for raising Katherine. I realized that when she was just a baby. Instead of the traditional Dr. Dentons and sailor suits, the baby stores sold everything from baby flapper outfits to astronaut suits. Everything in her life had to have a theme, she couldn't just be a pretty baby girl. Her bedroom, for example, was done in Miss Piggy; everything from lamps to drawers featured the divine Miss P.

Very few of the lessons I'd learned about child raising applied. Personal computers didn't exist when my older kids were growing up, so they never surfed the Internet; not only didn't they have their MTV, television consisted of only about six channels; there were no such things as Sega or Nintendo, serious sports for girls, body piercing, or even rap music; they had very little exposure to drugs; they didn't have to worry about AIDS; and they knew very little about sex.

Things are so different now. Katherine was as sophisticated at eleven years old as my older daughters were when they were sixteen. When she was five years old we took her to Spago, one of the most popular restaurants in Los Angeles, and she ordered an artichoke. An artichoke? I didn't even know what an artichoke was until I was thirty-eight. She asked for asparagus. It is a known fact that not a single child in the 1950s or 1960s ever asked for asparagus.

Children today have access to so much more information than children of any other era in history that the old methods of raising children no longer apply. They have a hundred TV channels and they're taught about drugs in school and they know about sex. Know about it? When Katherine was twelve we told her Aunt Martha was going to the hospital and that Maggie would be born that day, and Katherine replied, "Oh, you mean she's having a c-section?"

Kids have so much more knowledge about the world. It's impossible to restrict their access to it; the best thing to do is try to channel it in a positive direction. "Channel" really is the right word. I refer to television as "the sorcerer." It can be magical, it can be an extraordinarily effective teaching tool, but if parents aren't careful it can take control of their children's minds. Katherine does not have a TV set in her bedroom, and we try to monitor the shows she watches; but like kids of any time, the shows she wants most to watch are the shows we don't want her watching. And even if she doesn't see them, her friends at school do, and the next day they're talking about them.

Katherine does have her radio, her boom box, in her room. Long ago radio stopped being a medium limited to playing the top forty love songs. Now kids listen to *Love Lines*, where young people frankly discuss their sex problems, shock jocks who talk about anything, and instead of love, the songs are about suicide and self-mutilation. If I were trying to create my own radio show today in Katie's parlor, instead of introducing Enoch Light and his Light

Brigade and reading cigarette ads from *Time,* in order to be realistic I'd be interviewing a topless dancer and reading condom ads from *Spin*.

Even if we wanted to, it's impossible to shield kids from these things. There are so many external influences. Drugs just weren't a part of my older kids' childhood. But Katherine started learning about them in second grade. Pam and I made a deal with her: we agreed that if she doesn't smoke, drink, or use drugs by her sixteenth birthday we will take her on a trip anywhere in the world. She decided the one place she wants to go, of any place in the entire world, is New England. Maybe she heard me talking about Lowell, but much more likely she saw something about it on TV that impressed her.

She learned about things like the dangers of smoking and AIDS in her Catholic elementary school. I hosted a benefit the school produced to raise money for pediatric AIDS. Kids know how AIDS is spread, they are much more sexually aware than any previous generation. I'm the one who has had to learn how to deal with a whole new set of problems. One day I drove home with Katherine and her friend, and as we got out of the car, she said, "Daddy, we forgot to stop at the department store. I have to get a training bra."

I can't imagine Claudia or Linda even saying the word "bra" to their father. When I'm faced with a situation I don't know how to handle, I try to be the thoroughly modern parent. "Oh," I said, not knowing what to say. "Let's go inside and let Pam handle that. That's for the Pammy department."

Faced with this barrage of information, kids grow up very fast. Katherine did get her training bra, and one Saturday afternoon several months later Pam and Martha were going shopping with her. Katherine wasn't ready and finally Pam gave her two minutes. Eleven-year-old Katherine came out to the car out of breath. "I couldn't find my bra," she explained, and added sadly, "and now I'm sagging." And after a pause she concluded, "Everyone'll know I'm not wearing a bra."

When I was raising my kids in the 1960s I was the authority figure. I set the rules and the kids lived by those rules. The magic words, after "please" and "thank you," of course, were "because I said so." Why can't I do that? Because I said so. How can you do that to me? Because I said so.

That would never work with Katherine. As I've had to learn, everything is negotiation. "What do you think about this plan?" "If you do this today, we'll do that tomorrow." And when you reach an agreement, you'd better follow through with your end of it.

One thing hasn't changed, though. The best form of punishment is depriving a child of something he or she wants to do. When Katherine misbehaves she is confined to her room—and we take the boom box out. As she gets older, of course, I'll have to start looking for a collapsible ladder. I remember the afternoon we were going to UCLA for a full day of activities with celebrities to raise money for multiple sclerosis. Pam's son, Lex, was bringing thirty members of his college fraternity to work as coaches, timers, and ushers, and Katherine was in heaven. She adores Lex, and the chance to spend time with him and his friends was important to her. But she was less than charming several times and finally, as we were driving to the campus, she said something very rude to me. Pam turned the car around and we confined Katherine to her room, where she had to write a one-hundred-word essay on the topic "Why I must have a good attitude."

When Pam and I came home that afternoon she had finished. After listing several reasons, she closed the essay by admitting "It's important to have a good attitude, otherwise your room will become your best friend."

I am trying to correct the worst mistake I made with my

older kids by spending much more time with Katherine than I did with them. I go to her school functions and outside activities and whenever possible she travels with Pam and me. When we went to Detroit to host a benefit for an animal shelter she came with us. On the plane I explained to her that there would be many dogs at this event and under no circumstances could we bring home another dog. Between our dogs and Lex's dog we almost qualified to be a kennel. So this time, no way, no more pets. Under no circumstances. Katherine understood.

We named our new dog Lucky. I managed to hold out about five minutes. There are some things that just never change.

Katherine is turning out to be a lovely Irish lass, exactly what I'd hoped for. She's independent, opinionated, and smart, and she knows every route directly into my heart. When she was six years old we were at a luncheon and she came over and said to me, "Daddy, let's go up and do the Daddy and Katherine Show."

There's a request that is impossible to resist. See, ever since Katherine has been old enough to deliver a punch line I've been teaching her the great vaudeville jokes. What good is a straight man without someone to deliver the punch line? Although I guess it would be more accurate to say I was playing straight *person* to my daughter. So, in front of the audience, she told me, "Oh, Daddy, it was Lincoln's birthday and I didn't even send him a card."

"Why send him a card?" I asked. "Lincoln is dead."

"Dead?" she said with surprise. "I didn't even know he was sick!"

People often ask if it's hard raising a young child at my age. I suppose the best answer to that question would be, at exactly what age is raising a child easy? What makes raising Katherine a joy is that she is part of a large and very modern extended family. Pam and Katherine have formed their own wonderful relationship. One Halloween, for example, Pam turned the house into a fair. We took out all the furniture and put in carnival games and booths and served ice cream and cotton candy to more than one hundred kids. Pam and I and our friends Kenneth and Josie Castleberry dressed as clowns and entertained. We had a hot dog man and someone to paint the kids' faces. In the backyard we had a haunted house. We had glass eyeballs and frozen ice hands floating in the punch bowl. At Christmas we tented the backyard and had fresh-baked cookies for the kids to decorate, and then we donated the cakes and cookies to the needy.

Katherine also has her older brothers and sisters and their children—my grandchildren, her nieces and nephews. And she has her stepbrother, Lex. When it became obvious to Pam that our relationship was going to be serious, she called Lex, who was in marine boot camp, and told him she was going out with Ed McMahon.

Apparently Lex was very impressed. Not that I was a television personality, not that I was the spokesperson for the largest-selling beer in the country. "Ed McMahon," Lex said. "Mom, he's a colonel in the Marine Corps!" Now *that* impressed him. He always referred to me as "the Colonel": "Mom, tell the Colonel they had me doing this . . . ," or whatever. Often Pam didn't understand what he was talking about, so she'd ask him to explain it.

"Mom," he'd tell her, "don't sweat it. Just tell the Colonel, he'll understand. It's a marine thing." It's a marine thing. So how could Lex and I not get along?

The first day I met him I was working aboard my boat when I was suddenly blinded by the sun glaring off his shoes. I looked up and saw this handsome young man with a friend. "Good to see you, marine," I said.

"Good to see you, Colonel," he responded. "Permission to come aboard, sir?" Marines talk to each other like that, like police officers talking to suspects on badly written TV shows. Lex and I had the Marine Corps in common, which meant we spoke the same language, so we got along very well right from our first meeting. Growing up, Lex had no father—he doesn't even get a Christmas card from his natural father—so I've happily taken on that role. Although he'd never been much of a student, getting by mostly on charm and football, when he left the Marine Corps he went on to graduate from the University of California, Santa Barbara, and is presently in law school.

I often express my feelings through little poems. On our fifth anniversary, I wrote a poem for Pam. It reads, partially, "Oh, I've been lucky in my life, once or twice. But lucky in love, that's a roll of the dice. Well, luck turned to love, and a wonderful life, and brought me a lover, a friend, and a wife." Now, Coleridge it's not, and it only begins to explain the way I feel about Pam. There is one more way in which Pam has changed my life. She has gone back into the fashion business, creating a couture line creatively named "Pam McMahon." Her gorgeous dresses are carried by Neiman Marcus, Saks, many of the top boutiques. When we got together, we agreed that we would really be together. So when she is doing truck shows, meaning showing her new line, if I'm not working I go with her and our partner, Greg Mills. I carry the dresses and maybe sell a little. So Pam has turned me into something I've never been before: besides everything else, I am now a proud *schmatta schlepper.*

Life with Pam is full of surprises. I knew she was planning something for my sixty-ninth birthday, for example, because my best friend Charlie Cullen had explicit instructions to take me out of the house early in the morning and make sure I didn't return until evening. I guessed she was having a nice dinner for about twenty people. But as I returned home after taping *The Tonight Show,* I was surprised to be greeted by a Marine Corps honor guard standing on the front steps of the house. The first thing I noticed was that Lex was in the middle of the honor guard. On the side a photographer kept snapping pictures. It took me a moment to realize that the photographer was my son Michael. I walked into the house and it was filled with people from my life. Friends from different parts of my life from all over the country. Pam had turned the house into Ed's Jazz Joint. The backyard had been tented, the furniture had been replaced by round tables with dripping candles, there was a band in the corner.

"When Ed met Pam," I once wrote, "so the story goes; There wasn't much twinkle in those traveled toes. A life that was full had taken its toll; And the joie de vivre had left that merry old soul. But a blind lunch meeting had changed all that. And a beautiful brunette showed him where it was at. She was witty and honest, direct and wise; And you can see the sparkle in his weary eyes . . ."

I was so lucky to meet her.

9

One of the important things I learned from Johnny Carson was the danger of overexposure. That was something I was always careful to avoid when, in addition to appearing nightly on *The Tonight Show*, I hosted daily quiz shows like *Snap Judgment*, *Missing Links*, and *Whodunnit?* as well as numerous parades, appeared on countless television specials, made records, did my nightclub act, acted in motion pictures and both on and off Broadway, sold items on the cable shopping channels, produced and served as master of ceremonies at events like Nixon's inaugural gala, the bicentennial celebration, and many fund-raisers, and hosted successful programs like *Star Search* and *Bloopers and Practical Jokes*.

I couldn't even begin to estimate the number of parades in which I've marched, ridden, or broadcast, from Macy's spectacular Thanksgiving Day parade to Virginia's Apple Blossom Festival. I've been the King of the Rice Festival in Louisiana and the King of the Winter Carnival in Lake Placid, New York. You get three people standing on a corner waiting for the light to change, I'll describe it to you. For me, hosting a parade requires good assistants, people who provide correct information when you need it, and warm socks. Generally, when you broadcast a parade you stay in the same spot for several hours. Invariably your feet get cold. Very, very cold. One of the greatest presents I ever got was a pair of electric socks. Battery-operated socks. I put a triple-A battery in each sock and they warmed right up. People would laugh at my beloved electric socks, and they kept laughing until right about that moment when their toes began to turn blue.

When I served as King of Bacchus in New Orleans's Mardi Gras parade I had to ride on a float for seven hours. Now, there are no bathrooms on a float, and parades do not make rest stops. So the other device that proved invaluable to me is called "the policeman's friend." It's a little pipe that runs down your leg and enables the Budweiser that comes in to go out without the whole parade having to stop and wait for you. That just worked for me; the year before the king of Bacchus had gotten a bit tanked and had fallen off the float. Now, on occasion I may have fallen off the wagon, but I was determined not to fall off the float. I guess you might say, thanks to my "policeman's friend," I stayed afloat.

Ooooooooo.

I did, however, fall off the roller-skating elephant. I've ridden on just about every type of conveyance in parades, from the Clydesdale horses in New York's Puerto Rican Day parade to the back of a convertible at the Indianapolis 500. But one Thanksgiving, producer Dick Schneider came to me with an unusual idea. Heading the parade that year was an elephant on roller skates, and Dick thought it would be just great if I opened the parade by riding in on that elephant. I don't even like to ride horses, and an elephant is as big as . . . as an elephant. I didn't particularly like this idea, but because Dick wanted me to do it, I agreed to. So at the proper time they got a stepladder and the elephant leaned down and I climbed up on his neck. Now, if you've ever noticed, when girls ride elephants in a circus they hold onto its ears and they lean way back. Apparently that is proper elephant-riding technique. But it's a little more difficult to do that when you're holding onto a microphone and leading a parade.

"Well, here we are friends," I said when we went on the air. "This is the biggest parade you'll ever see, and I just had to arrive on the biggest animal you've ever seen . . ." And that was just about the time the elephant decided to get rid of whatever was on his neck. He flipped his head and I went flying off. I was caught in midair by several policemen. Which is why I consider myself one of the policeman's friends.

Now, broadcasting a parade is not particularly difficult as long as everything proceeds as planned. The prepared copy provided all the information I needed to describe the great high school marching band, the floats, the balloons, and the dancers. Here they come, there they go, weren't they marvelous . . . But things rarely go as planned. One Thanksgiving, for example, I was just beginning my introduction for the Snoopy balloon. "Coming down Broadway next is my favorite character. This is the part of the parade I look forward to every year . . ."

And as I was describing Snoopy, I suddenly heard Dick Schneider screaming into my earpiece, "Don't mention Snoopy. Snoopy just blew up!"

How do you tell all the little children watching the parade and waiting for Snoopy that he's exploded? How many nightmares will that cause? Listen, I knew it wasn't the *Hindenburg*. It was Snoopy. "But that will be coming a little later in the show," I continued, without a pause, "so right now let's look at the beautiful costumes on the . . ."

Although I've participated in numerous parades, there are some things that even I can't adequately describe.

Macy's parade always ended with Santa Claus, which announced the beginning of the Christmas season. One year, as he climbed down off his sleigh a little girl handed him a bunch of balloons. He held the balloons in one hand, took the little girl's hand with his other hand, and together they started walking into the store. And as he did, on national television, his pants fell down to his ankles. As I watched, Santa Claus started waddling into the store in his long johns. "And so, ladies and gentlemen," I said as quickly as I thought of it, "if you want to know what to get Santa for Christmas, get him a belt."

For most performers, it's their success on the stage or screen that gets them invited to appear on talk shows. It was just the opposite with me. Nobody really knew if I could act, but producers believed viewers would buy tickets to see me in a different role. I wasn't a classically trained actor, but I had performed in several plays at Catholic University and I was familiar with basic stage terminology, words like "stage" and "script." I started my acting career working in off-Broadway theaters. Way, way off-Broadway. Several states off-Broadway. Ohio.

During my vacations from *The Tonight Show,* I did theater-in-the-round in big tents for Lee Guber, who was later married to Barbara Walters, in Valley Forge, Pennsylvania. I played Rusty Charlie in *Guys and Dolls,* I played Buffalo Bill in *Annie Get Your Gun,* and I got to sing the magnificent song "There's No Business Like Show Business." I believed every word of that song. And to get to sing it every night, that was thrilling.

Robert Ludlum, who eventually became one of the best-selling writers in America, owned a theater in a mall in Paramus, New Jersey. I did *Anniversary Waltz* for him. The moment *The Tonight Show* finished, I'd get in a car and race to New Jersey for the performance. On matinee days, I'd do the show, drive into New York to tape *The Tonight Show,* then turn right around and make it back just in time for the opening curtain.

I starred with singer Carmel Quinn in *Wildcat* in summer stock for a great producer named John Kenley. On closing night the cast did everything they could to try to upset me. In one scene, for example, I dropped a coin into a wishing well. Unbeknownst to me, that last performance a crew member was hiding in the well. I gently dropped my coin, and in response a bucketful of water came splashing out of the well all over me. In another scene I had to enter a jail cell through a door. The crew installed the set upside down, so that while saying my lines I had to climb up and over the transom into the cell. See, these are the kind of professional problems an actor has to learn to overcome on his way to the Broadway stage.

I made my Broadway debut in 1966. My friend Alan King was appearing on Broadway in the comedy *The Impossible Years*. When he had to leave the show for two weeks to fulfill a nightclub commitment, he asked me to substitute for him. Actually, I'd worked on Broadway before. I'd sold Morris metric slicers and toy gyroscopes out of a Broadway storefront with great success. Obviously this was very different, this time the audience paid *before* they saw my performance.

I rehearsed for several weeks in the afternoons, and by the time I opened I was well prepared. Not only did I know my lines, I knew everybody else's lines, I knew the stage manager's cues, I knew the ushers' names, I even knew the guy who stood in the front of the theater at intermission asking for money. One of the sweetest sounds I've ever heard was my first laugh on opening night. Believe me, the first laugh is always the toughest. Until that moment I was nervous, uncomfortable. After that, I just sailed through my performance. You know, when an audience doesn't have expectations, it's very easy to fulfill them. Nobody really knew what to expect when they saw me onstage, and I like to think that I surprised them. The theater critics were very nice about my performance, but perhaps my favorite review came from a friend of mine, who said, "You know, you didn't remind me of you at all."

The worst review I've ever received—for anything I've ever done—was *Women's Wear Daily's* review of my nightclub act. I had never really considered doing a nightclub act. I mean, what was I going to do—sell slicers? But as I became known, people wanted me to host luncheons and banquets and affairs. I'd put on my tux and do the regular hello, how are you, did you hear the one about, let's hear it for our honored guest, thank you for coming. With four kids to put through college, the added income was welcome. And I enjoyed myself, I enjoyed meeting people, I enjoyed good food. While doing this I became friendly with a man named Frank Banks, who was running the St. Regis Hotel. He began urging me to put together a nightclub act and play the Maisonette Room at the St. Regis. Finally, he pinned me down to a date. It was almost a year in the future, so far away it didn't seem it would ever actually arrive.

But the more I thought about it, the more I liked the idea. Both Johnny and Doc would often do weekend concerts and nightclub dates and earned considerably more in one night than I received for a month of dinners. I decided to put together an act. With my talents, I had absolutely no idea what to do. I hired writers, I took singing lessons, and I put together an act unlike anything previously seen in New York. My set consisted of a theatrical trunk covered by a piece of black velvet. I walked out onstage and removed the velvet to reveal . . . a Morris metric slicer! "Ladies and gentlemen," I began, "let me introduce to you the famous Morris metric slicer. Now forget about the two dollars they were made to sell for . . . that's all right, madam, I was astonished to hear myself say that too . . ." I did the whole pitch,

I showed how to cut a potato in a curlicue so that it popped right back. When I threw in the plastic juicer, I drained several gallons of water from a grapefruit—then showed the audience how I filled it in a bucket of water "for the next generation." And I closed that pitch with the line that always got the biggest laugh on the boardwalk—and I prayed to God that it would work in a sophisticated club— "with this slicer you can slice a tomato so thin you can read a newspaper through it. That's right, I know a lady in Bayonne, New Jersey, who had one tomato last her all summer long . . ."

It worked. The audience laughed. Oh, maybe I didn't sell any slicers, but it got my act off to a great start.

Then I sang several songs. I'd always been able to carry a tune, just not too far. Once, I remember, I sang with Count Basie's band at the Riverboat in the Empire State Building. On the show, I'd sung a little when we played Stump the Band, although the way I sang some of those strange songs, it was more like Confuse the Band. But in preparation for my nightclub act I took singing lessons with a vocal coach. In the act, I sang the pitchman's anthem, "Trouble" from *The Music Man*, I did a medley of rainy day songs, a medley of songs about New York, and some Cy Coleman songs.

And finally I did a whole bit about the "Drinkers' Hall of Fame." For this I needed no coach. I'd conclude this with a tribute to W. C. Fields. I did an impersonation of him; as I sang a final song, I'd slowly put on his gloves and his hat and his bulbous nose and finish as Fields. It was a nice act.

Overall, my reviews were very good. The *New York Times* wrote that I proved a "genial second banana also can be a genial top banana . . . he has the ability to handle complicated lyrics . . . altogether the results are likable." Count Basie said, "His act is a bitch!" In fact, the only negative review came from *Women's Wear Daily*, whose critic wrote, "This is the worst act I've ever seen!"

273

Compared to what, I wondered. Armed with that review, I took the entire back page of *Variety* and printed almost all of the reviews—and right in the middle of it included that terrible review. That might be the worst review ever used in an advertisement.

While getting ready to do my act I was terrified. I didn't know how people would respond to me. But once I did it, and got good reviews and a wonderful response from the audience, I decided to take my act to Las Vegas. All the hotels had great shows. I knew I wasn't ready to play Vegas. My act was about an hour long; in Vegas an opening act was always less than a half hour—the hotels want their guests back in the casinos as quickly as possible—so I decided to tour with my act until I had refined it to twenty-eight killer minutes.

For two years I performed in the smallest and strangest places you can imagine. I played a restaurant in Westchester County, New York; after dinner they pushed the tables out of the way and brought in a small stage. I played Great Falls, Montana; Moscow, Idaho; Akron, Ohio; Chicago, Houston, Lake George. In one small town I performed at the county fair; I showed up at the fairgrounds wearing my tuxedo and the guard didn't want to let me in—he wanted proof I was the entertainment. I mean, I was wearing my tuxedo. I don't know what kind of town this was, but I sort of assumed most people did not put on their tuxedo to go to the fair. In the middle of my performance one of the band members sitting behind me started eating a meal from Burger King. In one small town in Illinois, my business manager, Lester Blank, didn't trust the men running the fair, so he told my assistant, Corrine Madden, not to leave the grounds without our check. At the end of the show, Corrine went to get the check and Lester and I waited in the limousine with the motor running. She leaped into the car with the check and screamed, "Okay, let's go!" We handed her a glass of wine and took off.

Not fast enough, as it turned out. The check bounced.

Now, it's well known that music groups make demands when they sign a contract. They want certain beverages in the dressing room, they want bowls of M&M's with the blue ones removed, they insist on all types of perks. Well, I had some pretty specific demands written into my contracts too: I insisted that they supply half a head of cabbage! And not only that, I also demanded a tomato, a potato, and a grapefruit. I mean, when I arrived in a town I didn't have time to go grocery shopping for my act.

After two years of preparation I knew I was ready to play Las Vegas. I was the opening act at the New Tropicana Stage for Ann-Margret. She had a colossal show, set changes, backup singers, lavish costumes, even motorcycles. I had my Morris metric slicer. Opening night in Las Vegas was one of the very few times I've ever been nervous before a show. So many of my good friends had successfully played Vegas, the audience was filled with people I knew. But as soon as I got that first laugh I relaxed. I was well rehearsed and I knew from two years of experience that my act worked.

My backup "group" was Corrine Madden. At one point in the act I began talking about Budweiser beer and that was her cue to stick a can of Bud through the curtain. Supposedly I didn't know it was there. That can of Bud always got a big cheer. But as time passed, Corrine's hand got stagestruck. Instead of simply holding up the can, she'd stick it through the curtain, then when I turned around, she'd draw it back, or she'd wave it back and forth. This might be one of the few times in show business history that the performer was upstaged by the can.

I played Las Vegas for five years. I was the opening act for top names like Steve Lawrence, Eydie Gorme, Shirley MacLaine, and Mac Davis. I worked every big stage: the Tropicana, the MGM Grand, the Frontier, Caesar's Palace.

For a long time I would finish *The Tonight Show* in Los Angeles and race to the Burbank airport, where a private plane was waiting for me with its engines running. I'd change into my tuxedo on the plane, a car would meet the plane in Las Vegas, and by four minutes of eight I'd be tying my bow tie as I walked toward the stage. I'd do two shows, have dinner, and go to bed, then take a commercial flight back in the morning.

Although I had a wonderful time performing, I never made any money. I was paid twenty-five thousand dollars a week, which was tremendous for an opening act, but the private plane would cost me fifteen thousand dollars, and after I finished paying everybody else and tipping the waiters, I barely broke even. I did, however, get to keep all the cabbages I could carry.

Most people don't think of me as a movie star. Probably because I'm not. But I've made several movies, playing everything from a ruthless mob boss to the father of a teenage werewolf. Martin Sheen, Donna Mills, Beau Bridges, and I all made our film debuts in the same 1967 movie, *The Incident*. The story is about a group of people terrorized by two hoods on a New York City subway car. I played Mr. Don't Get Involved, who eventually provokes the incident by defending my daughter. Now, acting is one of the few professions in which the key to success is defined as "don't be yourself," and I think director Larry Peerce was concerned I'd play too much Ed McMahon. He didn't want an Ed McMahon character, which is why I got the part. So in order to evoke real emotion from me for my big scene, Sheen and Tony Musante staged a fake fight in rehearsal. I knew they were faking it, but I acted as if I believed it was real. No one knew I was acting, which is the goal of all actors. And so when I was successfully not myself in the scene, everyone believed it was because I believed the fight was real. Acting can be very complicated sometimes.

In *Slaughter's Big Rip-Off* I played a mob boss out to kill Jimmy Brown. Naturally, I get killed at the end. It was great fun for me to play a nasty, mean, downright dirty character. At the end I got shot. Several of the reviews complimented my death scene.

Fun with Dick and Jane, starring George Segal and Jane Fonda, was the best movie in which I appeared. It's the story of an upwardly mobile Los Angeles couple trying to cope after he loses his job. At first Jane suggests they economize by not using the swimming pool heater, but when their landscaper literally rolls up their front lawn and carts it away because he wasn't paid, they turn to a life of crime. I played the executive who got drunk and fired George Segal. I got very friendly with both Jane Fonda and George Segal. Jane was the kind of person nice enough to come to work at four in the morning for hair and makeup so we could get my work done early enough for me to get to *The Tonight Show.* I'll never forget the director, Ted Kotcheff, telling this million-dollar cast, "Okay guys, we've gotta get this one done because Ed has to leave." Imagine telling Jane Fonda to hurry up because I had to get to NBC.

Not only did I get excellent reviews—the *New York Times* wrote, "The members of the supporting cast, headed by Ed McMahon as Dick's alternately smarmy and sozzled former employer, are excellent"—but Columbia Pictures campaigned for a Best Supporting Actor nomination for me. Although I wasn't nominated, I was invited to the Academy Award ceremony that year. Apparently I was quite proficient at playing "sozzled."

Unlike many actors, I've never been worried about being typecast. Please, typecast me. In *Love Affair,* with Warren Beatty and Annette Bening, for example, I played the role of a commercial spokesman named Ed. I like to claim I'm a method actor—in this case my method was just showing up. I was a natural in the role.

277

Most people loved Steve Martin's *Father of the Bride*. The worst picture I've ever made could have been titled *Father of the Werewolf*. Instead it was called *Full Moon High*, with Alan Arkin and his son, Adam Arkin. This was sort of unusual casting; even though Alan is Adam's father and appeared in the movie, they felt I was more believable in the role. That's some compliment. Adam played a high school football hero I took on vacation to Transylvania and while there he got turned into a werewolf.

I've acted in several movies made for television. I worked with Gary Coleman in a wonderful remake of the baseball fantasy *The Kid from Left Field*. In the miniseries *The Star Maker*, Rock Hudson played a famed movie director who turned his beautiful conquests into movie stars. I played his manager, and Jeffrey Tambor, who created the role of Garry Shandling's sidekick, Hank Kingsley, on *The Larry Sanders Show*, played his lawyer. A lot of people don't remember that I was in the semiclassic *Great American Traffic Jam* and a movie about the Los Angeles Olympics, *The Golden Moment*, with Stephanie Zimbalist. The last movie I made was Disney's *Safety Patrol*, with Leslie Nielsen. I was offered a role in the comedy feature *PCU*, meaning Politically Correct University, but against the wishes of my agent at the time, I turned it down.

The producers offered me quite a bit of money, and my agency put great pressure on me to do it, but I just didn't see myself in that kind of movie. Actually I ended up leaving the agency because of this. There was a lot of contemporary, colorful language in the script and I was uncomfortable with that. I don't use that language in my home, so I just didn't feel comfortable using it on the screen. Besides, I was hosting *Star Search* at the time, and it didn't seem feasible to me that I could play a character using foul language, then turn right around and introduce a nine-year-old young man playing a piano concerto.

Even though I've done an incredible variety of things, I've turned down many, many more opportunities. For example, I almost left *The Tonight Show* to become the host of *Good Morning, America*. I didn't want to leave, but NBC did not want to properly compensate me for the work I was delivering. So I secretly flew to New York and met with executives from ABC. The negotiations were very serious and they went on for a long time. But I didn't like the thought of getting up every morning at four, and I wasn't sure I was ready to move back to New York. Most of all, when it came down to making the decision, I didn't want to leave Johnny Carson. As far as I was concerned, we were joined at the desk. So I turned it down.

The brilliant broadcaster Al Masini, who created *Solid Gold* and *Lifestyles of the Rich and Famous,* wanted me to host his new show, *Entertainment Tonight.* I liked the concept, I thought it might work, but my contract with NBC prohibited me from appearing on any show that might be broadcast just before, during, or after *The Tonight Show.* Because *Entertainment Tonight* was to be syndicated, meaning each station that bought it could run it whenever they wanted, Masini couldn't guarantee the time slot.

Another show created by Al Masini that I initially turned down was *Star Search.* The amateur talent contest is one of the oldest formats in broadcasting. Major Bowes and Ted Mack had been very successful at showcasing amateur talent. Arthur Godfrey's *Talent Scouts* had been a big hit on television. Even my friend Dick Clark had briefly experimented with a show called *World of Talent.* The executive producer, Bob Banner, said that they specifically wanted me to host *Star Search* because I wouldn't be in competition with the talent presented on the show.

I looked at their pilot. It wasn't bad at all; in fact, the spokesmodel on that very first show was a beautiful young woman named Sharon Stone. Talk about getting it right from the very beginning. But I turned down their offer. I just didn't want to do an amateur talent show.

They persisted. We negotiated. I knew *The Tonight Show* couldn't go on forever—after the first fifty years or so I figured Johnny might start to slow down—and I'd started thinking about my future. So when Masini and Banner offered to make me their partner I agreed to host the show.

Star Search was a one-hour syndicated show. Two performers competed for prize money in each of eight categories, including male and female vocalist, dancing, comedy, and female spokesmodel. The winners returned the following week and at the end of the season the big winners competed for the one-hundred-thousand-dollar first prize. In 1984 we managed to tape our first show at KTLA in Los Angeles in only eleven hours. Eleven hours! In that time I could have taped a week's worth of *Tonight Show*s, sold a hundred slicers, flown a mission over the Korean DMZ, broadcast a parade, and filmed several Budweiser commercials. I mean, eleven hours. That's almost half a telethon. In the time it took us to tape one show, Jerry Lewis could have raised twenty-five million dollars for muscular dystrophy. "Gentlemen," I explained to the producers, "I love this show, but I think we're going to have to find a way to speed this up."

At first it was hard for us to prove to our audience that we were serious about finding real talent. The last successful TV talent show had been *The Gong Show*, which was really a comedy show featuring people doing strange tricks. But we really were searching for potential stars. In fact, when our first major discovery, Sam Harris, heard about the show, he thought, "It sounds like *Bowling for Dollars*, only with talent." Sam appeared on our fourth show, and by the time he'd made his thirteenth appearance and won one hundred thousand dollars, he'd signed with Motown—his first album went gold—and had become known throughout the country. After Sam's success we were deluged with requests for auditions and tapes. In our first year our eight talent coordinators auditioned more than twenty thousand acts, taped six thousand of them, and eventually selected the 170 people who competed on the show. We had an open call in Hollywood and four thousand performers showed up, some of them waiting on line for more than a day. We had about seven thousand people show up for auditions at a mall in Minnesota. Of course, a few of those people claimed their talent was doing dog-barking imitations, but most of them were talented young people trying to break into show business.

With such tremendous competition just to get on the show, we were able to produce a terrific weekly variety show. I mean, so many great young performers made their first national appearance on *Star Search*. We discovered Rosie O'Donnell, Sinbad, Martin Lawrence, Drew Carey, Linda Eder, LeAnn Rimes, Tiffany, Lara Flynn Boyle; Jenny Jones was a comedienne; Dennis Miller; the country group Sawyer Brown; Richard Jeni; Allison Porter of *Curly Sue* was on the show when she was five years old; the soap opera star Scott Thompson Baker, Kevin Meany, Carrot Top . . . I mean, I was in New York and one night I went to see a revival of *Grease*. In the first act Sam Harris just stopped the show cold, dead cold, standing ovations. In the second act our 1992 winner, Billy Porter, did the same thing. And Rosie O'Donnell—this was before she even started her talk show—brought down the house. The audience loved her. And how about this? At the end of the show Rosie interrupted her curtain call and asked Sam Harris and Billy Porter to join her. Then she told the audience, "We would not be standing on this stage tonight if it was not for that man right there, Ed McMahon. Ed McMahon, would you please stand up?" That was thrilling for me. That was worth my whole life in show business.

Now, although I say "we" discovered these great performers, it wasn't really me. I had the easiest job of all. I just showed up and said, "The champion has owned the stage for a week and plans on keeping it . . . here's our next challenger . . . please welcome from Detroit, Michigan . . . and the winner is . . ." I didn't even rehearse. Sometimes I'd finish taping *The Tonight Show* and get to the *Star Search* set just in time for taping to begin. Normally our great stage manager, Kenny Stein, read my lines in the rehearsal. When it was possible, I'd watch the rehearsal on a monitor in my dressing room while putting on my tux, learn how to correctly pronounce the contestants' names and enough about them to conduct a good interview, and then go out and ad-lib my way through the show.

I had absolutely no input in selecting talent for the show. Believe me, I preferred it that way. I did attend a lot of auditions in shopping malls and comedy clubs, but I didn't participate in the selections. It seemed as though everywhere I went people were ready to audition for me. If I was on the *Star Search* bus and we stopped for a traffic light people on the sidewalk would start dancing. I remember I had the same limousine driver in Detroit for several days. When he picked me up the last day to drive me to the airport, his cousin was with him, and as we unloaded my luggage from the car, his cousin started tap dancing for me. I hated to disappoint people, but there wasn't anything I could do to help them. The system was set up to make sure of that. The best I could do was hand out a card with the phone number of the production office.

The talent coordinators had to deal with this every day. Once, the office had to be evacuated because of a bomb threat. The rumor was that the threat had been called in by a contestant who didn't get on the show. While the staff was standing outside the building waiting anxiously as the bomb squad searched the premises, one of the policemen in charge asked talent coordinator Gary Mann, "So, can I get my niece on the show?"

In one city, a singer actually bought a busboy's outfit so he could get into one of our talent coordinators' hotel rooms and audition for him.

As far as I know, only once did such an approach pay off. In Detroit one day my daughter Claudia had spent ten hours auditioning acts. The crew had seen hundred of acts and everyone was exhausted. But as they were packing up, a man who worked in the building asked Claudia, "Do you think you could audition me? I don't have any music with me, but could you please let me sing?"

Claudia didn't have the heart to refuse. The man got up on the stage and began singing a cappella. Three bars into his song Claudia broke out in goose bumps. He was so good he just blew away everyone else. His name was Keith Washington, and he eventually appeared on the show and went on to become a popular R & B singer.

Hundreds of videotapes arrived every week at the production office. Most of them were pretty rough. One singer felt the acoustics were better in his bathroom, so he submitted a tape of himself singing in the shower. I mean, as he was singing, he lathered up and shaved. When we turned him down, he pitched himself as a male spokesmodel. We got a lot of tapes from comedians and singers whose living room performances were interrupted by their mother shouting from the kitchen that dinner was ready or by the phone ringing or their friends making faces in the background. But we watched every one of those tapes and if the performer showed any promise at all we would arrange to have a more professional tape made.

For a lot of performers these auditions represented their one chance at stardom. Basically they had thirty seconds to change their lives. Talk about pressure. At one audition at a mall in Kansas City, a seven-year-old girl explained seriously, "I've been waiting my whole life to be on *Star Search*."

Listen, an appearance on *Star Search* changed a lot of

lives. Rosie O'Donnell was performing in a Long Island comedy club when Claudia discovered her. Her routine was based on her experiences in Catholic school, which wasn't right for our show, but Claudia felt she had something special. So she offered her a second audition. But before that audition she worked with her, helping her select the right outfit, the most flattering hairstyle, and her best material. For Rosie, this really was a last chance. It was just a few months before her twenty-fourth birthday and she had decided to quit show business if she wasn't successful by that day. Her second audition was much better and she was picked for the show. Ironically, the first person she competed against was the owner of the Long Island comedy club where Claudia had found her. Rosie won five weeks. The late Brandon Tartikoff, head of programming at NBC, saw her on the show and gave her a part on a sitcom, which led to her movie career, which led to her great success on television. Which was exactly the way the show was supposed to work.

Tracey Ross, who won our first spokesmodel competition, was absolutely penniless when she was discovered. She'd dropped out of college and would sneak back to the campus to eat. After appearing on our show she got a recurring role on a soap opera, and a network contract.

A lot of the young comedians who worked the comedy club circuit had problems coming up with two and a half minutes of clean material for their audition. Like Martin Lawrence. Claudia found him in a club in Washington, D.C., and recognized his talent, but until he was able to do a clean act we couldn't use him. When Claudia finally called to tell him he had been selected to be on the show, his mother answered the phone and thought it was a friend of his playing a big joke. He was a three-time winner.

Young performers knew the power of *Star Search* to launch a career. When Drew Carey heard we were doing auditions at a small comedy club in Milwaukee, for example, he drove several hundred miles and lived in his car until he had a chance to perform.

We missed a few good ones too. Tim Allen auditioned for Claudia five different times and never got on the show. She felt he was much better as a comedic actor than as a stand-up comedian. Finally he asked her, "What's the problem, why aren't I getting on?"

"Your material is too male-oriented," she told him. "Car jokes and home tool jokes just don't make me laugh." Years later, after his great success on *Home Improvement,* she saw him in a restaurant and sent him a note reading "Well, at least I was right about your ability as a comic actor."

The hardest part of my job was standing on that stage and telling one of the contestants that they'd lost. Oh boy, that was tough. For a lot of people losing represented the end of their dreams, they thought it was the end of their career. A lot of tears were shed backstage. After the show, I tried to spend a little time with the people who hadn't won. I reminded them that by just appearing on the show they'd gotten great national exposure. I told them I knew exactly how they felt, that when I was trying to get started in radio I'd lost an audition for an on-air job to Ray Goulding. "That's proof," I said, "that you don't have to come in first to have a nice career in show business."

If telling adults they'd lost was difficult, imagine what it was like telling a five-year-old that they'd lost. I remember the first year we had kids competing for the one-hundred-thousand-dollar first prize. The two finalists were a twelve-year-old and the five-year-old Allison Porter. I had absolutely no prior knowledge of the judges' decision. "This is just awful," I told the producers. "How am I gonna do this? You've got to get me something to give to the five-year-old if she doesn't win. Get me a big stuffed animal or something."

When I was handed the judge's decision I took a deep breath and said proudly, "And the winner is . . . Mary Johnson. Mary gets the one hundred thousand dollars!" And then I immediately turned to Allison Porter and said quickly, "But Allison, look what we have for you!" They brought out a huge stuffed panda, it was almost as big as she was, and she was thrilled. Believe me, not as thrilled as I was, but very happy.

Several years later Allison was on *The Tonight Show*, and I saw her in the office before the show. "Everybody gets excited when they come into my room," she told me, "because I've got my giant panda bear sitting on the shelf. They all ask me where I got it and I tell them, 'Ed McMahon gave it to me when I was on *Star Search*. And you know what his name is? Big Ed!'"

The worst moments of all came when a performer froze onstage. The pressure on these people was incredible, and sometimes they would forget the lyrics, or miss a step in their routine, or as happened with several comics, their minds just went blank. Watching a young performer struggling and not being able to help was just awful. We had a woman comic come out and start her routine and suddenly she just stopped. She couldn't remember a joke. The clock was in front of her, ticking away her career. I mean, can you imagine doing jokes while watching the clock? What I wanted to do, what I have done in other situations, was go over to her, put my arm around her, and tell her, "You know, the same thing happened to me one night in Toledo. It's the worst feeling in the world. I just looked for a hole to drop into. You know what I did, I took a couple of deep breaths. I just calmed down and all of a sudden the joke came back to me. Now what was the idea of the joke you were about to tell?" But I couldn't do that, this was a competition. It seemed like the longest 150 seconds of my own life.

There wasn't anything anyone could do about it except

watch her suffer. Center stage can be a very cruel place. At times, if we had a technical problem, we would stop the tape and start again. But this wasn't a technical problem. And maybe on three or four occasions when an act had fallen apart during the actual taping, we retaped their performance after the show for broadcast. There was nothing wrong with that. It didn't affect the judging—the performer had already lost. But it saved them from potential embarrassment and it gave them the opportunity to be seen at their best by producers and agents.

Over the years the show changed. We dropped the male and female actor categories, we tried to include more contemporary music, we added a male spokesmodel category; *Star Search* had always been conceived as a variety show and we changed to make the show as entertaining as possible. But one category that never changed was female spokesmodel. Viewers always enjoyed looking at pretty women. And so did the host. With the media's celebration of the supermodel, we felt the category had its place. We were always trying to find the next Christie Brinkley. Who isn't?

Most of our spokesmodel competitors were actresses or models. They usually were submitted to us by their managers or agencies. In later years we added a question-and-answer segment to the competition, but in our early days of production it was just show and tell. Mostly show. The requirements were that contestants possess "poise, beauty, and the ability to speak effectively in a variety of situations." Basically, an attractive woman who could talk. One of our champions later won the Miss U.S.A. pageant, and several others ended up with roles on soaps or sitcoms, but it was our first spokesmodel, Sharon Stone, who enjoyed the greatest success.

Maybe my most embarrassing moment on the show occurred one night as I stood between two buxom young women waiting for the judges' decision. "This is it, ladies and gentlemen," I said. "You've seen them and you've heard them. Will our champion Tiffany come back next week, or will Stephanie be our new champion?" Then I paused and said, "I've never stood between two more beautiful treats in my life."

Star Search was a wonderful show. I loved doing it. My greatest value to the show, besides serving as host, was to get out on the road and promote it. For several years, in fact, I packed up and went on long publicity tours to promote the show. The first year Pam and I traveled by plane to thirteen cities to plug the show. We'd visit the local TV station that broadcast the show, every radio station, and newspapers, anybody who would help promote *Star Search*. It was so successful that the next year we decided to tour the country by bus. We visited twenty-eight cities. This was the ultimate promotion tour, just about everything we did was sponsored. We traveled on a magnificent (Prevost) bus, a luxurious bus with a shower, Jacuzzi, queen-size bed, big kitchen, copy machines, fax machines, several phones. The Hilton Hotel chain provided beautiful rooms at night. Snapple not only helped finance the tour, they even sent Wendy the Snapple Lady with us. There was great flooding throughout the Midwest that year, so we enlisted the American Red Cross as our official charity. Wherever we stopped, we passed buckets around; we literally raised buckets of money. I can't even estimate how many interviews I did on that tour. Hundreds. I did just about every local show in twenty-eight cities, I even did *The Today Show* four times from cities on the tour. As we left one city at five in the morning, I'd be on the phone with radio stations in the next city telling them that we were on our way.

The arrival of the *Star Search* bus was a big event in many cities. They welcomed our caravan with parades and dinners and special events, and wherever possible we held auditions in malls and at comedy clubs.

That tour was so successful that the following year we went to thirty-eight cities in twenty-five days. The show was being taped in Orlando, Florida—we were a major attraction at Disney World—and we had a big sign on the bus announcing WE'RE ON OUR WAY TO DISNEY WORLD. Our charity that year was the Starlight Foundation, which grants wishes to children with difficult medical problems. In every city, we stopped at another one of our sponsors, Boston Market, where we held a drawing for a trip to Disney World and received two thousand dollars for the Starlight Foundation—all the while promoting the show. In Washington, D.C., the bus stopped at the White House, where one of the little boys from the foundation met Hillary Clinton. The *Star Search* tour was a promoter's dream; every sponsor got tremendous publicity out of it—I mentioned each of them in every one of the hundreds of interviews I did—and in Orlando I was able to give a check for fifty thousand dollars to the Starlight Foundation.

All the work done by so many people paid off; *Star Search* was one of the most successful syndicated shows on television. Almost two hundred stations broadcast the station to just about the entire country. In some cities we were on five days a week. The move to Disney World had been so successful that on my dressing room door I insisted they put two mouse ears over the *o* in my name. I mean, the show had been on the air thirteen years and there was every reason to believe it could continue forever, even without me.

But Al Masini had sold his company to a corporation that really wasn't interested in syndicated television. In cities like Chicago and Miami we were still doing extremely well, but in New York and Los Angeles our ratings had declined—mostly because we'd been moved out of a time slot accessible to the younger audience we attracted. And the syndicated market had changed. Hour-long shows were no longer desirable. Talk shows and reality-based shows like

COPS, which were much less expensive to produce, and tabloid shows like *Hard Copy* had become very popular. So we were just eased out of existence. I pleaded with the producers, but they just decided to end it. They did the same thing to *Lifestyles of the Rich and Famous,* which also could have gone on for a long time. As far as I'm concerned, *Star Search* was not ended with any sense of style or class. I just felt a show that had introduced so many talented performers deserved a little more respect. We should have ended with a celebration of our success, rather than just disappearing. When *The Tonight Show* ended, Johnny, Doc, and I walked away feeling as though we had done it about as well as it could have been done. There was a feeling of completeness. Not so with *Star Search.*

But I took so many great memories away from that show—in addition to my red Mickey Mouse suspenders. For example, I'll never forget the adagio team who appeared on an international version of *Star Search.* I don't know what happened between this dance team before we went on the air, but in the middle of their act he tossed her high into the air—and then missed her completely as she landed on the stage. Then, without a word, he turned around and walked away. They did not win the competition.

Nor will I forget the night comedian Bob Zaney won for the third time. As he walked toward me for the traditional interview—congratulations, very funny, see you next week—his feet suddenly went out from under him and he fell flat on his face. I didn't know what to do. But before I could help him, he looked up at me with a big smile on his face and said, "I've got news for you. My lawyer's in the audience. No matter what happens, I'm gonna walk away with that hundred grand."

Hosting *Star Search* required very little rehearsal and a lifetime of preparation. It was similar, in that way, to my job as cohost with Dick Clark on *Bloopers and Practical Jokes.*

We had this great staff of producers, writers, and technicians who actually put the show together. I showed up on time wearing a clean shirt.

Dick Clark is my oldest friend in the television industry, yet somehow he still doesn't look much over 1950. Dick Clark and I were a match made in Philadelphia. I think the most surprising thing was that with all of the different programs and commercials that we've both done, it was still almost forty years before we finally worked together.

Since our days as neighbors in Philadelphia, Dick Clark has become one of the most successful producers in television history. Dick's like me; while he's busy working on two shows, he gets anxious if he has only three more shows in development. So trying to get the two of us together was sort of like trying to find a convenient time for a meeting of Workaholics Anonymous. When *Bloopers and Practical Jokes* was created I was busy doing *The Tonight Show* and *Star Search* while he was producing shows on all three networks as well as for syndication. Naturally both of us loved the idea of working together on another show.

Carson Productions had created a program called *Practical Jokes*, while Dick created and hosted *TV's Uncensored Bloopers*. Both shows did very well in the ratings and NBC put them together. We were on for several seasons and then did a series of specials. The show was a combination of mistakes, miscues, technical errors, and very elaborately planned practical jokes. I mean, I've made my share of bloopers. I am the person who introduced "President Agnew" to a large audience. Gaffes happen, and when they do, there is really nothing you can do about them except just keep going and hope nobody noticed—and then let Clark and McMahon show them to millions of viewers. The bloopers ranged from outtakes from popular TV shows to tapes of news broadcasts, although we never used anything that was humiliating or would hurt someone's career. For example, while rehearsing a *Golden Girls* episode in which one of the girls was dating a younger man, Bea Arthur said seriously, "Why are you getting upset? You see older women with younger women all . . ." At that same rehearsal Bea walked all the way across the living room to answer the doorbell—which rang for the first time just as she opened the door. One news reporter covering a hurricane had just finished explaining that the winds were dying down—when he was blown right out of the picture. And a very serious and perhaps nervous newsman said somberly, "The stock market took a big dump . . . uh, dive . . ."

The practical jokes were often elaborate and expensive to set up. I mean, for a single bit we would build a fifty-thousand-dollar set. Once, for example, we invited the football star Deacon Jones to what he thought was a costume party, for which he was beautifully dressed as a ballerina. So you can imagine his surprise when he walked into what appeared to be an ordinary restaurant wearing a tutu. The restaurant was actually an elaborate set and every person there was an actor.

We convinced heavyweight champion Evander Holyfield that we had developed a cologne for him—and it was just about the worst thing you've ever smelled. I mean, it was just awful. He tried so hard to pretend he liked it, even offering suggestions about how with just a few little changes it would be even better.

When Vanna White was launching her clothing line, we arranged a very special fashion show for her. As she described to "buyers" the dresses she'd designed, one of her models came out wearing her dress backward. Vanna kept going, calling it "very classy." The next model came out with a bizarre food-and-flower attachment sewed to the back of the dress. Vanna just kept smiling, even when Merv Griffin, trying to help a model out of a jacket, accidentally pulled off the entire dress.

Not everybody immediately got the joke. A few days

after Ernest Borgnine and his wife, Tova, had returned from a trip to a Third World country, she helped us get him out of the house. While he was gone we covered the entire house—and this was a big Hollywood home—with a canvas tent. When he came home he was stunned to find people wearing sealed space suits walking in and out of the house and very scientific-looking instruments all over the lawn. It looked as if he'd been invaded. Our "biological expert" told him that a strain of mysterious ants never before seen in North America had been found in the golf bag he'd brought back with him from the trip, and that the house had to be quarantined and fumigated. The setup looked completely authentic, and he was not happy. But when we finally told him the whole thing was a big joke— well, it took him a little while but we all breathed a sigh of relief when he laughed.

For Mickey Mantle we arranged an autograph session— and just imagine how surprised he was when absolutely nobody showed up. He relaxed when a large group of people walked in yelling, "Mickey! Mickey!"—until they went right past him into the back room where Mickey Rooney was signing autographs. Now, I'm a marine, and I've spent a fair amount of time in the great saloons, but when Mantle found out he'd been fooled, he started laughing and strung together words in combinations I've never heard. We edited out the words but kept the laughter.

Working with Dick Clark was about as easy as anything I've ever done on television. We taped two or three shows at a time. We'd show up at the studio on time wearing clean shirts and there would be a stack of cue cards five feet high ready to go. The director rolled the tape and we'd read our cards, ad-lib, and have fun, and finish within, oh, half a second of the allotted time—but only if we were being careless. When we needed to, we hit the time right on the nose. There was no pressure, no strain, just two old friends enjoying each other's company.

Now, I enjoyed watching these practical jokes being played on other people. In fact, the best thing about practical jokes is that they are never played on you. I knew that I was just a little too savvy, a little too sophisticated to ever be tricked. They couldn't fool me. Not me. Couldn't happen.

So I thought. There's a sign at the gate on the NBC lot informing drivers as they leave that their cars are subject to inspection. Now, the last time anyone was searched they had to look under the saddlebags. But one night as I left the NBC lot my limousine was stopped by a guard. I was in the back-seat watching a World Series game, when my driver, Patrick Marwick, said, "Boss, they want you to get out of the car."

"What?" I hadn't been paying any attention. Patrick had been working for me for sixteen years. He was my friend as well as my driver. I relied on him for many things. I trusted him completely.

"Would you mind stepping out for a moment?" he asked. "I don't know how to handle this."

I was tired, I didn't know what was going on, and admittedly I was a little irritated. But I got out of the car. Patrick and two NBC security guards were staring into the open trunk. When I looked into the trunk myself I was stunned. The trunk was crammed with NBC equipment and supplies. It looked like an NBC store. A guard asked me if I had a pass for all of that stuff. I mean, Patrick and I had been together sixteen years, I couldn't believe he was stealing from the network. "What the hell is all this, Patrick?" I asked.

Patrick, my friend, my driver, immediately bailed out on me. "Don't look at me, boss," he said. "It's got to belong to you."

One of the security guards started listing the items in the trunk. "There's a typewriter here, this is NBC stationery, bathroom tissues, paper towels, cups . . ."

I didn't know what to think. Naturally, I tried to protect Patrick. "He's had the car all day," I immediately told the guard. "He dropped me off this afternoon."

" . . . another typewriter, there's a pay phone in here . . ."

A pay phone! "I have no idea how it got there," I said. "I don't know anything about it."

" . . . an adding machine, some more stationery, pencils . . ."

"That's not mine," I insisted. Patrick wasn't saying a word. I was stunned. I thought I knew him so well. I couldn't imagine him stealing. "You know anything about this, Patrick?"

"Don't look at me, boss," Patrick repeated.

The guard asked me, "You know anything about this at all?"

"I know nothing about this," I said firmly.

Just then a lieutenant approached us and asked what was going on. He was hidden in shadows and his cap was pulled down partially covering his face. "He has no requisition pass," the guard explained. "He has no idea how this stuff got in here."

"This your equipment?" the lieutenant asked me. He shook his head in disbelief. "This is incredible."

Something about the lieutenant looked vaguely familiar. And as they started reading me my constitutional rights, I thought I recognized him. "Wha . . . ?" I asked, confused.

"And welcome to our practical joke special," Lieutenant Johnny Carson said.

I had been fooled completely. Tricked and caught on camera. I mean, naturally my first instinct was to protect Patrick. Or, as Carson acknowledged later, "You certainly stood up for him. He was on his way to the slammer, thanks to you."

Eventually the practical jokes became too expensive and time-consuming to set up, so I dropped out and Dick Clark continued with the blooper specials. But when I look back on that show, I can't help but think of the Australian broadcaster who said at the end of his show, "Remember what I always say at the end of a show . . ." He paused and stared into the camera. "I always say the same thing . . . but I forget what it is."

10

When I was creating my own radio programs in Katie's parlor, I would insert a commercial between each song. At ten years old I knew that an important part of every radio announcer's job was to make the sponsor's product sound so good that every listener would immediately want to run out and buy it. So even at that young age I not only knew which side the bread was buttered on, I wanted to be the spokesperson for the dairy that sold the butter.

Of all the things I am, most of all I'm a salesman. I've always said with great pride, if I can hold it up or point to it, I can sell it. In my career I've done more than sixty thousand television and radio commercials for products ranging from pants stretchers to coin collection equipment, from carpet manufacturers to banks. I've done beer commercials with Sinatra and Wayne, a gasoline commercial with Barbara Walters; I did the very first spot for *People* magazine, and I've fed Alpo to more than four thousand different dogs. In fact, when NBC decided to honor the best commercials, I was selected to host several specials titled *Television's Greatest Commercials*.

Advertising has always fascinated me. The first ad I ever paid attention to was a calendar my grandfather had nailed to the wall in the office of his plumbing company. Some calendars have pinups; this one was a nailup. It was from a tool company that made "the tools you swear by—but never at!" Isn't that a great line? I'm sure I used it in my parlor shows.

I've always loved selling. From my first day hawking the *Saturday Evening Post*, it came easily to me. Although in the other areas of my life I was shy, I was never even slightly reticent when I had something worth selling. Working as a pitchman on the Atlantic City boardwalk and selling pots and pans door-to-door were as much a part of my formal education as the years I spent at Boston College and Catholic University. I gained experience and confidence, I learned the business of selling. I believe I can sell almost anything—but I don't. Before I agree to do a commercial I either use the product myself or investigate it thoroughly to make sure it is absolutely legitimate. I've turned down many, many offers. Not necessarily because there was anything wrong with those products, but just because I didn't feel comfortable selling them. Among the products I've turned down were a spray that supposedly covered a bald spot, a roach trap, rose bushes guaranteed to bloom in six weeks, even the Playboy Channel.

In my early days of television in Philadelphia I not only produced my shows, I also did my own commercials. On those shows we didn't even pause or cut away to a commercial. There were no commercial breaks. I'd finish my interview or my song or whatever I was doing and just hold up the product and do the commercial. The transition wasn't always very smooth. I mean, seconds after I'd finished singing a beautiful love song, I'd have to pick up a rubber duck, a baby toy that would quack like a duck when squeezed—and sell it. I didn't mind at all, I was on television. I knew that without that duck and the pants stretcher and the pineapple juice and Mrs. Paul's frozen foods and everything else we sold, I would have been singing a very different song.

Even newscasters had to interrupt their broadcast to read commercials. "North Korean troops are preparing for war . . . but if you're having trouble washing away dirt, maybe you should try new improved Babbo . . ."

I think the first commercial I ever filmed was for McCafferty Ford, a local car dealership. It was a two-minute spot that took us ten hours to film. We were learning how to make commercials as we made them. The expert was the person who'd made one a week earlier. Fortunately, there were no union problems to worry about because there wasn't a union; we just did whatever we had to do. Wardrobe was whatever I was wearing, I did my own makeup, and when I needed children to model, I used Claudia and Michael.

By the time I got back from Korea everything had changed. Television commercials had become a sophisticated and very profitable business. And although local commercials were still being filmed in Philadelphia, New York City had become the center of the television advertising industry. That's where all the national commercials—the commercials that paid the best—were cast and filmed. Much like the introduction of talking movies had ended the careers of silent movie actors with high voices, many well-known radio announcers couldn't make it on TV because their appearance didn't match their voice. That created a lot of opportunity for people like me.

I was still doing very well in Philadelphia, I had my late-night show and I was getting a lot of the local commercials, but I wanted to be in New York. So I began commuting to New York every day to make the rounds of the advertising agencies and audition for commercials.

The fare was four dollars round trip, eight dollars if you wanted a reserved seat in the parlor car. I paid the four dollars, but the porters got to know me, so they'd let me take my coffee and donuts and sit in the front car with all the wealthy guys from the garment district. If I sat in the back, people would recognize me and want to talk about my show the night before or what's it like to be on television and I'd get nothing done. The front car would be filled with cigar smoke, which I didn't care for because I didn't smoke, but I'd tolerate it because nobody would talk to me. On the way to New York I'd read my three newspapers and plan my day.

My office was my briefcase. I carried a stack of index cards on which I'd made notes about every audition I'd had and everybody I'd met, and five dollars in dimes. When I got to New York I'd settle into a comfortable telephone booth—the booths in the Pennsylvania Hotel, across Seventh Avenue from Penn Station, were the most comfortable—and begin calling the advertising agencies to try to get auditions. I learned all the little tricks: I knew how to get an operator to place calls for me to make it sound as if I had a secretary, and I was on a first-name basis with all the secretaries at the ad agencies.

But there were days when I couldn't get anything going. On the trains in those days the backs of the seats could be moved from one side of the seat to the other so passengers could face forward no matter which direction the train was traveling. I'll never forget the day I got off the train and made at least two dozen calls from the lower level of Penn Station and couldn't get a single appointment. No one wanted to see me, no one had any auditions, nothing was happening. So I got right back on the same train—although they'd changed the direction of the seats—and went back to Philadelphia. I never even made it to the upper level of Penn Station.

Normally though, I'd get at least one appointment with an account exec or a casting director, or an audition, sometimes several. After spending the day in New York—this was when I started hanging out in Michael's Pub or wandering the floors at Abercrombie and Fitch—I'd catch the afternoon Congressional back to Philadelphia at four-thirty. The problem with that train was that it had a great club car. The trip to Philly, I learned, was about three martinis long, which made it rough for me to do my show that night. So instead of going into the bar car I'd find the person most unlikely to want to talk to me—a rabbi was a real find—and sit next to him. About that time I discovered something called the Five-Foot Shelf of Books, a collection of all the classics of literature, and I started reading them on the trip home. After spending the entire day trying to get an audition for a detergent commercial, I'd relax by reading a chapter of *War and Peace*. By the time I met Johnny Carson, I was almost four feet smarter. I commuted between Philadelphia and New York five days a week for eight years. I guess it was the contemporary version of a tale of two cities.

Five-minute auditions usually lasted about a minute. Sometimes as many as two hundred men would be auditioned for a spot, and that almost always included the regulars who hung out at Michael's Pub. We never knew what the agency was looking for, so there was no way to prepare for an audition. The competition was really intense; one good account could pay the bills for a year. Everybody was good, there were only minor differences between us—so no one knew why certain people got jobs and others didn't. On my way to the train in Philadelphia I used to stop at church for morning Mass. Hey, I wanted all the help I could get.

We went in, read the lines, and waited for a phone call. Sometimes all they wanted was the right sound. They wanted the proper "Ho, ho, ho," or a candy company wanted a perfect "Mmmmmm . . ." Believe me, there is no definition of a perfect "Mmmmmm." I have to admit, my "Ho!" was better than my "Mmmmmm." My friend Bob Delaney got the "Ho, ho, ho" job and remembers spending much of the day in a studio while agency executives sat in the control room debating whether his "Ho" was too happy.

The first national commercial I ever got was for New Blue Cheer. One of the premier announcers of early television was the great Jay Jackson. He was the announcer for *Philco Playhouse* as well as many commercials. But rather than seeing me as a threat, he helped me. He told me, "Ed, you're good and New York needs you." New York needed me? That was a pretty startling thing for me to hear. New York needs Ed McMahon! Boy, New York had a strange way of showing it. Jay Jackson introduced me to Michael's Pub and all the top people in the business. And he got me the audition for New Blue Cheer.

Now, this story may be apocryphal, but this is the way I heard it: at that time Procter and Gamble made Tide, the number-one-selling washing detergent. One of the major components of soap is nitroglycerin, which is also used to make munitions. During World War II Procter and Gamble had purchased huge supplies of nitroglycerin, and when the war ended they had to find something to do with it. So they created Cheer soap. The ad agency, Young & Rubicam, wanted a spokesman with a "casual, believable, warm and fuzzy" voice. One hundred fifty people auditioned, they weeded it down to twenty, then to eight, then finally to me and Fred Collins. Fred and I went out for a cup of coffee while waiting for the decision. As we sat in a coffee shop on Madison and Thirty-ninth, he said to me, "I want this, but since you're just starting out, I hope you get it." Now, that is a nice human being. The account exec called us at the coffee shop and said I'd gotten the job.

I felt like I'd just won the Olympics. All of the Olympics. In Philadelphia I'd been the king, I'd won almost every audition, but to win a major audition in New York on one of my very first attempts was a very big deal. Maybe Jay Jackson had been right, maybe New York did need me. I became the spokesman for "New Blue Cheer, for whiter whites and brighter colors." The thing I remember most about it was that my father was so proud of me. The agency would give me a typed schedule of when the commercial would be aired and my father would watch it every time. If it was on at two in the morning, he would set his alarm clock to see my commercial. For my father, television shows were just long pauses between his son's Cheer commercials.

New Blue Cheer financed my trips to New York for several months. After winning that account I figured I'd get them all. Instead, I won exactly none of them. I'd make it to the final selection, but I wouldn't get the jobs. One day, a day I will never forget, several appointments in a row were canceled, an audition went badly, and I learned that I hadn't gotten some big national account. Now, I don't get discouraged easily, but boy, after not getting a single job in several months, that was a lot of bad news. All my confidence was gone. I sat down by the fountain in front of the Plaza Hotel and had the only migraine headache of my life. I began to wonder if I'd picked the wrong business. I thought, maybe I'm not good enough for this business, maybe I should think about doing something else. There was an architectural school near the Lambs Club, so I walked down there and picked up an application. I read it on the train back to Philly. Even the application was too complicated for me. To become an architect I'd have to go back to school for at least four more years. With three children to support, that wasn't possible. I left the application on the train.

For almost a year I paid my dues. Then, slowly, my career began to pick up. I got on-camera jobs for *Redbook* magazine and White Owl cigars. I got the General Motors corporate account for radio. I auditioned for several cigarette accounts, which were very desirable, and I came within a few blocks of becoming the spokesperson for Old Gold. The fact that I didn't smoke and had never smoked did not deter me; I didn't do laundry either but that hadn't stopped me from doing commercials for New Blue Cheer. When I heard Old Gold was looking for a new spokesman, I began practicing my smoking technique on the train. I tried to look suave and manly. The fact is that people who don't smoke just don't look comfortable smoking. But after several auditions it looked as though I was going to win the Old Gold account. All that was left was meeting the president of the company to get his approval. As I was being driven to the meeting, the agency account executive, a lovely woman, noticed my technique and asked, "How long have you been smoking, Ed?"

What was I going to tell her, two weeks? Well, yes. "I gotta confess something to you," I said. "I'm not really a smoker. I've just been practicing."

She appreciated my honesty. "Turn the car around," she told the driver. She continued, "Ed, I think you're great, but you really have to be a smoker to get this account."

When I got *The Tonight Show*, the first sponsor to sign me to do their commercials was Alpo. The second sponsor who approached me was L&M cigarettes. I told them from the first day that I didn't smoke, but they didn't care. They wanted me to be their spokesman and they were going to pay me about fifty thousand dollars a year. It was a great deal, I didn't even have to smoke, all I had to do was hold up the pack. But before we signed a contract, an executive from Liggett and Myers got very nervous; he was afraid that one of the major newspaper columnists would find out I didn't smoke and reveal that the spokesman for L&M didn't even smoke them. I lost that account.

I was only upset about that for, oh, maybe twenty years. Then all the information about the effects of tobacco began coming out. Believe me, I am very happy I never did a cigarette commercial. As far as I know, there has never been any scientific evidence that Cheer was bad for anyone. And it did make whites whiter!

My briefcase was my office, but Michael's Pub was my headquarters. Everybody in the business hung out there between auditions. That's where we learned what was going on, who had gotten which jobs, what products were being cast, and what was happening at the various advertising agencies. Most of us used the same answering service, Radio Registry, and when we received an important message, their operators knew that if we weren't at Michael's Pub, somebody there would know where to find us. That was where we celebrated our victories and drowned our defeats.

One of the people who hung out there was Jonathan Winters, the most brilliant ad-libber I've ever known. He could do twelve minutes of brilliant comedy on a lamp. There were some smart, talented men in that group, but Jonathan Winters would hold court there for hours. That's where we became good friends.

Most people don't know this, but I was one of the founders of the Liberty Bowl, which has become one of the premier college football bowl games. It's now played in Memphis, but for the first two years it was played in Philadelphia. In retrospect, the concept of playing a college football game in Philadelphia in midwinter may not seem too intelligent, but at the time it seemed like a very good idea. And that time was probably very late at night. I produced a great show for our sponsors and special guests. Among the stars of that show were Johnny Carson and Winters. By that time I knew Winters well enough to know that if I wanted to be sure he would show up, I'd have to bring him there myself. So I drove to New York to pick him up, turned around, and drove right back to Philly. The whole drive back I said three words, "How you doing?" He spent the rest of the trip telling me.

He entertained me for the whole day and late into the night. About four o'clock in the morning, after the bowl game and the show, a group of us were in my suite at the hotel. We ordered sandwiches from room service. A half hour later, waiters wheeled in three large carts containing mounds of sandwiches covered completely by white tablecloths. As the waiters pushed the carts into the room, Winters took one look and said fiercely, "Oh my God, we're going to be busy in surgery tonight!"

I was such a regular at Michael's Pub that Gil Weiss, the owner, put the McMahon salad on the menu. It consisted of the heart of a romaine lettuce, carefully diced up, covered with blue cheese dressing and bacon bits. But the McMahon salad was not the only thing I did for that place. For years Gil Weiss resisted any change, he liked his saloon just the way it was. It was a big event when he finally allowed us to bring in a television set to watch the World Series. I wanted more, I wanted music to drink by. In fact, there was a girl singer performing at the Waldorf who I thought was terrific, and after a lot of pleading, Gil finally allowed her to perform there. She was a big hit; she drew a crowd. After she finished her run, Gil started booking jazz groups, and Michael's Pub became known as one of the few really good jazz clubs in New York.

When *The Tonight Show* moved to California my friends threw a surprise going-away party for me there. Purely coincidentally, during my party Woody Allen stopped by to see if it might be the right place for him to sit in with a jazz group. I left, Woody Allen came in. Seeing Woody Allen playing clarinet at Michael's Pub on Monday nights became a New York tradition for which I was indirectly responsible.

Probably my greatest skill in reading my lines in commercials was . . . the pause. I had learned from experience the value of the . . . pause in attracting attention. The longer you can sustain a . . . pause, the more . . . attention you get. When you need to emphasize something, just precede it with a . . . pause. I remember, in the Broadway show *Top Banana*, Phil Silvers has to figure out how to decorate a room. He can't figure out how to do it, until a buxom blond walks right in front of him. He just watches her chest go by without saying a word. Of course, everybody knows what he's looking at. Finally, after a long, long pause, he says, "I got it . . . We'll use balloons!"

The pause is like a . . . string. If you pause in the middle of . . . a sentence, the listener will focus on what you're saying. For example, just think about this for one split second . . . you may have already won . . . ten million dollars. The pause is effective even when I write it.

But I had a great big . . . pause. It made my delivery of my lines distinctive and effective. And it had one tremendously important effect: it helped me win a lot of accounts. Once I proved my ability, I started winning them. When City Service decided to change its name to Citgo and its color scheme from green and white to bright red and blue, Barbara Walters and I were hired to be their spokespeople. We did several commercials together.

One of the commercials Barbara and I did was filmed in the ski resort of Stratton Mountain, Vermont. We flew to Vermont and took a limousine to the lodge. I remember it was a long trip and our driver didn't seem to know where he was going. Every so often he stopped for directions. Barbara and I were in the backseat and she stretched out, put her head on my . . . leg and went to sleep. But I noticed that every time the driver stopped for directions he was having a quick drink. He was getting drunk. Pretty soon the car was weaving back and forth. Finally I told him to stop the car; I got in front and drove the limo. So I can always say I was a limo driver for Barbara Walters. I can, but I don't. But I remember the looks on the faces of the ad agency execs when our limo pulled up to the lodge, the driver's door opened, and I got out.

When it was announced that I was going to be Johnny Carson's announcer on *The Tonight Show*, the third phone call I got was from a man named Jack Macheca of the

D'Arcy McManus advertising agency. I had dinner with him and D'Arcy chairman Harry Chesley at the great restaurant 21, and they asked me if I was interested in doing commercials for Budweiser beer. I told them that I hadn't gotten the L&M cigarette account because I didn't smoke, then added, "However, gentlemen, I'm pleased to be able to tell you that will not be a problem in this case. I've spent years researching your product."

The agency and the brewery were both very pleased with the first few commercials we did. We filmed the second set of commercials at the Anheuser-Busch brewery in St. Louis. It was there I met the great Gussie Busch for the first time. Gussie was one of the most unusual men I've ever known. At lunch the day we met, he shouted across the room to me in this deep, gruff voice, "Hey Ed, when are you gonna finish these damn commercials?"

Bob Johnson, the director, told me we'd be done late that afternoon.

"All right then," Gussie continued. "I'm gonna take you coaching."

"Great," I agreed, having absolutely no idea what coaching was.

When we finished shooting that day, they drove me out to Mr. Busch's home, 280 spectacular acres known as Grant's Farm, because it was once owned and farmed by Ulysses S. Grant. In addition to the cabin that Grant built by hand, Gussie Busch kept every animal indigenous to North America. Deer, raccoons, foxes—they all ran free on the property. One night he had a cocktail party and I turned around and an entire herd of buffalo was standing a few feet away from the house. In an enclosed area he kept very exotic animals. It was quite a place. And he took me coaching to show it to me.

Coaching means going for a ride in a carriage pulled by eight horses. Each horse is individually controlled by a thin rein attached to one finger. Mr. Busch played them like a harp; he controlled them with a slight tug of his finger. So off we went. We started slowly, but picked up speed rapidly, and just raced over the property. At one point he said casually, "Duck down, Ed," and as I did, a thick branch went right over my head. If I had hesitated or stopped to question him, that branch would have hit me in the head. Maybe that ride was some sort of test for me.

The house itself was extraordinary. I used to describe it to people by explaining, "The living room has two grand pianos, but you don't notice them right away."

"Okay, Ed," he said when we settled down in front of one of the fireplaces. "I think we earned a little drink."

"I think that's right, Mr. Busch," I agreed.

"Call me Gussie," he told me, and for the next thirty years it was Gussie. "What are you drinking?"

I had a split second to make a decision. Did I want to suck up to the boss and tell him, I'll have a good, cold Budweiser? I decided I wasn't going to do that. "I'd like some Canadian whiskey," I said.

"How do you want it?"

"Just the way it comes out of the bottle."

He smiled at me and said, "You're gonna be with us for a long time."

On the drive back to the airport Macheca and Chesley told me I had passed the big test. What I had not known was that a well-known actor had been hired to be the spokesman for Budweiser before me. His image was that of a sophisticated man of the world, perfect for an upscale beer. But before he made his first commercial, *Confidential* magazine printed an article claiming that this actor and his wife would pick up men in bars and bring them home for sex. Well, that was not exactly the image that the agency wanted for Budweiser. Chesley flew to St. Louis in a panic to meet with Gussie Busch to figure out what to do. He wanted to buy out the actor's contract.

Gussie disagreed. "There's nothing as dead as yesterday's news," he said. "Let's stick with him. By Thursday they'll be wrapping fish in this." Then he threw the magazine on the floor.

I loved that, by Thursday they'll be wrapping fish with this. Years later when I started having problems with the tabloids I tried to keep that in mind. But the problem was getting to Thursday.

But Gussie invited the actor to the farm, just as I had been invited. And, just as he had asked me, Gussie asked him, "What are you drinking?"

Faced with that difficult decision, just how much do you please the boss, the actor said firmly, "I don't drink."

Later that day Gussie told Harry Chesley, "Unload the SOB. He doesn't drink and he's proud of it." The next day they bought out his contract.

So Gussie Busch and I got along from that very first day. My association with Anheuser-Busch lasted thirty years. Over the years I did more than a thousand commercials for them, I marched in parades, I hosted events, I attended all the wholesaler and distributor meetings. In corporate surveys it turned out that many people thought I was at least equal in importance to the image of the brewery as the Clydesdales!

I spent many evenings with Gussie at Grant's Farm. One year, I remember, they held the exclusive Hunt Ball in a barn on the property. Before the ball started, we were in the house and Gussie looked at me and said, "Ed, we're going to martinis."

I said, "I'm with you, Gussie."

Gussie loved his martinis. In a restaurant he insisted that there be a silver bowl filled with cold Bud on the table for everybody to see, but he was also drinking his martinis.

Gussie loved his martinis. At his home martinis were served in silver shakers and poured into old-fashioned glasses. So before going to the ball we each had a couple of martinis. Then we got into his car and started driving over to the barn, but about halfway there we stopped at one of the many houses on the property. We went inside and there was a bartender waiting for us with martinis. Gussie loved his martinis.

I think I realized how closely I had become identified with Budweiser the year I served as grand marshal of the Indianapolis 500. When I rode around the track in the pace car, somebody threw me a Bud. So as we rode past the crowd of five hundred thousand people I held it up, as if to toast them. In response, everyone held up their own beer— and if they weren't drinking Bud, they covered the label with their hand.

Of all the commercials I did for Budweiser, my favorite one was a spot I did with the Clydesdale horses. These beautiful animals lived in complete luxury, they traveled in air-conditioned vans, they were washed every day, a magnificent crystal chandelier hung in their immaculate quarters at the St. Louis brewery. Gussie Busch believed that if you treated the animals as if they were special, they would act that way. I rode behind them in many parades. Years ago the town of Lowell honored me with a day. In the parade, Massachusetts governor Frank Sargeant and I rode on the Budweiser wagon pulled by eight Clydesdales. And as these horses clomped down the avenue, Governor Sargeant said to me, "You know, Ed, I feel right at home here. I've been in politics all my life, and here I am again, riding behind eight horses' asses."

The horses responded to their names. If they jumped out of line, the teamster would order, "Patrick!" and Patrick would jump back in place. Because I worked with them so often, I got to know them pretty well and I think they might have recognized me. In one of the commercials I was standing right next to Captain, I mean right next to him. These horses weigh more than a ton; if Captain had moved two inches and stepped on my foot I would have been crippled. In this commercial I was holding a microphone in one hand and a paper cup filled with Bud in my other hand. As I finished the commercial I was supposed to say, "That's why Budweiser is the largest-selling beer in the world. Right, Captain?" and he was trained to look as if he was nodding in agreement. But while we were filming, when I looked at him and said, "Right, Captain?" he not only nodded, he stuck his snout in my cup and took a sip of the beer. The horse drank the beer!

Well, on camera it was gorgeous. Just perfect. When the director cut the commercial, he finished with a close-up of Captain drinking the beer. Everybody loved it, everybody except the ASPCA. They complained so loudly that we had to stop using it.

Besides working with the Clydesdales, I also did several commercials with both Frank Sinatra and John Wayne. In addition to commercials, Frank Sinatra did five television shows for Budweiser. He didn't have to pass the same test I did to get his deal. He had dinner at Chasen's with Jack Macheca, Harry Chesley, and Gussie Busch. After the terms of the deal had been agreed upon, Frank turned to Gussie and said, "What can I do for you?"

Gussie told him, "Just sing 'The Girl from Ipanema.'" That clinched the deal.

Sinatra and I had a terrific time doing the commercials together. A man named Johnny Delgadio would stand in for him during rehearsals and then Frank would arrive and do the actual shooting in one take. He hated doing retakes, and fortunately they weren't usually necessary. But once, I remember, we were doing a spot in which we were dressed as cavalrymen. Supposedly we had been captured by Indians and tied to a wagon wheel. There were arrows stuck in the wagon. My line was, "What do you think made those Indians so upset?" and then Frank was supposed to respond, "Telling all those Indians the gold they found was unredeemable quartz." Then the commercial ended with Frank saying, "Don't worry, we're going to be okay. Yonder lies Custer's last stand." At which point the camera cut to a big wagon with a sign reading CUSTER'S BUDWEISER STAND.

That day he just couldn't get his lines right. We did it three times, four times, this wasn't like him at all, five times. He couldn't remember the word "unredeemable." Each time he blew the line he got just a little angrier. Everybody on the set was absolutely still. No one said a word. Talk about tension. So just as we were about to do it a sixth time, I reached my arm around and pretended to look at a watch and said, "You know, Frank, I haven't got all day."

He laughed so hard he had to leave the set. In another commercial we were in a bar and he was supposed to slide a bottle of Bud the entire length of the bar. I was supposed to stop it, pick it up, and pour a glass of beer with a perfect head. We had to get it just right. Just as we were about to start shooting, I looked over at him and said seriously, "You know, Frank, I'm only going to do this once." The only time Frank Sinatra wanted to do retakes was when there was a problem with the music. On one show he sang the beautiful song "It Was a Very Good Year" with Nelson Riddle's full thirty-five-piece orchestra. After he finished the song, he asked Riddle, "Didn't I hear the violins come in early?" Riddle nodded, explaining he'd brought them in a few bars early. Imagine that, a thirty-five-piece orchestra and he hears the violins coming in early?

I did help Anheuser-Busch convince John Wayne to do a television special for them. Until that time John Wayne had turned down every offer to do TV. Tony Amendola was meeting him at the Polo Lounge and asked me to join them. We sat down and started drinking scotch. When John Wayne realized he couldn't drink us under that table, he started ordering doubles. That started a long evening and a longer friendship. When we were introduced, I said, "It's an honor to meet you, Mr. Wayne."

"You call me Duke," he said.

"Okay, Mr. Wayne," I told him, " . . . uh, Duke."

At that meeting he agreed to do the show. "Give me a million dollars," he said, "and I'll do the show for you. I won't guarantee who'll be on it. I won't tell you I'm going to have all these people, but you can take my word for it that they'll be there." Anheuser-Busch gave him a million dollars and he produced and starred in a ninety-minute variety show celebrating the history of America titled *Swing out Sweet Land.* As he promised, stars like Dean Martin, Bob Hope, the cast from *Bonanza,* and the Smothers Brothers appeared on the show. It was the most expensive TV show ever produced—but it was the highest-rated variety special in history.

The afternoon before we were to begin taping the special we met with the director in the Polo Lounge. When the meeting was finished, Duke suggested that we have dinner that night. "I'd love to," I said. "The problem is that I'm entertaining a whole bunch of people at Sneaky Pete's tonight."

"Well, what the hell is a Sneaky Pete's?"

It was a great restaurant, I explained, good food, good people, good music. After doing *The Tonight Show* that evening, I met my friends there. Several hours later a hush suddenly came over the entire restaurant. I looked up and there was John Wayne standing in the doorway. He always looked bigger in person than on the movie screen. And on the screen he was about fifty feet tall. I like to tell people he was wearing Sneaky Pete's. And with perfect timing, he roared, "Where is that goddamn McMahon?"

"Over here, Mr. Wayne . . . Duke," I said. We closed the place that night. The last thing I remembered was putting him in his car about four o'clock in the morning.

We were filming a commercial for the special the next morning. I was playing a bartender in an old western town. I had to be there at eight to rehearse; Duke didn't have to be there for several hours. But at eight-thirty, once again, I heard that unmistakable voice booming from behind the set. "Where is that goddamn McMahon? He kept me out till five goddamn o'clock in the morning . . ."

I grabbed two cans of cold Budweiser and popped them open. When he came around the side of the set, I handed one of them to him. He took it and said, "Well, that's the best goddamn idea you've ever had, McMahon."

We became great friends. When *The Tonight Show* was still in New York, I hosted the NBC weekly radio program *Monitor*. It was a general-interest show and I loved doing it. When we moved to California I wanted to continue doing it, but NBC wanted it based in New York. So instead of hosting it, I became a contributor. I finally convinced Duke to do an interview with me for that show. We did it at his house in Newport. He opened the door and said, "The beer is waiting for you, pilgrim." He wasn't wearing his hairpiece and he asked me if they were going to take any pictures.

"They'd like to take some stills for publicity," I said.

He sighed deeply—and no one sighed more deeply than Duke Wayne. "All right," he said. "I'll go put on my god-damn hair." It wasn't that he was vain, he didn't care, but he knew what people expected from him. So when he appeared in public he always wore his toupee. He used to make fun of it, he used to say, "Goddamn right, this is real hair. It's just that it belongs to somebody else!"

When we finished recording the interview and posing for photographs, his face lit up and he said happily, "Now, shall we hit that tap?" And he began pouring cold Budweisers for everyone.

For thirty years I traveled across the nation for Budweiser. We filmed commercials in the snows of New Hampshire and in the swamps of Louisiana. We did them in the air, in cars, in hot-air balloons, and in carriages. My association with the Busch family and the people at the brewery and at D'Arcy Advertising was one of the nicest things that has happened to me in my life. But as much as I liked these people, that didn't mean I wanted to die for Budweiser.

Who knew doing commercials could be so dangerous? Once, I remember, we were on a plane going to a meeting and the pilot wasn't sure the wheels were down and locked. We circled for an hour—while all of us in the back were reassuring each other the wheels were down—until he was convinced they were down and landed without incident.

Somehow I let them convince me to fly in Budweiser's hot-air balloon. Going up was fine, it was coming down that was the problem. Until that day I never knew hot-air balloons could bounce so high.

The most dangerous commercial I ever did for Budweiser was shot in Crowley, Louisiana. One of the many things that made Budweiser taste so good—and remember, I'm not on the payroll anymore, I don't have to say this—was that it was beechwood-aged. The bottom of the copper tanks in which the beer ferments are filled with beechwood chips. I flew to Louisiana on a private plane to serve as king of the Rice Festival parade as well as shoot a commercial. During the trip I started talking flying with the pilot and we hit it off, so I invited him to come watch the commercial being filmed.

We had to go pretty deep into the woods to find beechwood trees. It was a terrible day, about 120 degrees, 100 percent humidity, and no chance of rain. The sweat was just pouring off our bodies. In the commercial I was supposed to walk through the forest to a beechwood tree and explain that this was where Anheuser-Busch got the beechwood chips that gave Budweiser the unique taste that made it the biggest-selling beer in the world. But just as we were ready to start filming, I spotted a black snake about six feet away—and maybe it was my imagination, but he seemed to be staring at me.

In addition to all the people from the agency, we had two forest rangers with us. I said, "I don't want to alarm anybody, but there's a big snake right over there and he looks hungry."

One of the rangers laughed. "Oh, don't worry about him," he said confidently. "That's just a tree snake. It won't hurt you."

I wasn't so sure about that. "Does the snake know that?" I asked. "I mean, he's a snake, right? I don't want to take any chances, I'm sorry."

The pilot, who had tagged along because he had nothing else to do, whispered in my ear, "Don't go near that snake, Ed. That's no tree snake." With that, he broke a branch off a tree and got the snake's attention. The snake snapped at the branch. That was the first time I had ever smelled snake venom. It smells like death. Only worse. That "tree snake" turned out to be a cottonmouth, one of the most deadly of all snakes. If it had bitten me, I would not have survived long enough to get to the hospital. The ranger killed it.

By now the temperature had gone up a few more degrees, we had two very embarrassed rangers, we had the pilot who just might have saved my life, and we had got one other thing—somewhere in the area there was another cotton-mouth snake. As the ranger informed me, they live in pairs, and apparently we had killed the female. That meant the male, the big snake, was still around. And he wasn't happy. There is such a thing as dying for your art, but I'd never heard of anybody dying for their sponsor. Being the first was not something that appealed to me.

We shot that commercial in one take. One very, very fast take. It was one of the finest acting jobs of my career. I had to act calm. Eventually we finished the commercial—and found the second snake.

A phrase I often used in Anheuser-Busch commercials was "Someone still cares about quality." In the thirty years I spent working for Gussie and the brewery, that was always the truth. And in all that time there wasn't a single day when I had difficulty using that product. In fact, only once in my career have I lost a sales job because I didn't use the product. And it was not Alpo—my dogs asked for Alpo by name! At least that's what it sounded like to me. The sponsor I lost because I failed to use the product was Jenny Craig's diet meals.

I was overweight. I needed to go on a diet but I needed some kind of incentive. My assistant at that the time, the wonderful Madeline Kelly, provided the incentive. She negotiated an agreement with the Jenny Craig people that paid me quite a bit of money to become their spokesperson—but only if I lost a certain amount of weight by following a Jenny Craig diet plan. If I kept the weight off an additional six months, the deal was automatically renewed.

I faithfully followed their diet plan. I ate their frozen dinners. And I lost thirty-two pounds. Now, what could be better than being paid to lose weight? The commercials were very successful. I was very happy with their products and I think the Jenny Craig people were very happy with our relationship. All I had to do was keep the weight off for six months.

Unfortunately, it was just after I lost all that weight that my marriage to Victoria broke up. I was very unhappy and when I'm unhappy I eat. Of course, I also eat when I'm happy, which is why I needed to diet in the first place. But this was a difficult time for me and I regained most of the weight I'd lost. Now, this was completely my fault; the meals did exactly what they were supposed to do. I believed if I could just get through a couple of bad months I'd go back on the diet and lose the weight again. So we told the Jenny Craig people that I wasn't gaining weight, I was just wearing bigger suits. We blamed my weight on my suits. Was I over the weight stipulated in my contract?

Weigh-oooo!

Eventually I had to admit to the Jenny Craig people that I had regained the weight, and they did not pick up my option.

Now, what, you ask, what could possibly be better than being paid to lose weight? Being paid to give away somebody else's money. Talk about an offer I couldn't refuse. Years ago American Family Publishers, the fine company that uses a national sweepstakes to attract attention to its magazine subscriptions, wanted me to be their spokesperson.

Before I accepted their offer I had to make sure they really had the money to give away. I did some research and discovered the company was partly owned by Time Inc. Okay, I figured, they got the money. And that's how I came to be the guy who says, "You may have already won ten million dollars."

When I started working on this campaign I had no idea how much a part of American pop culture it would become. American Family Publishers sends out about two hundred million pieces of mail every year. Just about every household in the country has received an entry form and stickers to order magazine subscriptions. *The Tom Snyder Show* got one addressed "Dear Mr. Show . . ." When my daughter Katherine Mary was only six months old she received a letter informing her, "Katherine Mary McMahon, you may have already won two million dollars and Ed McMahon will award this giant prize to you on *The Tonight Show* . . ." And when then senator Bob Dole received his entry form, he wrote back to me, explaining, "As I am seriously considering running for President, I am prohibited by federal law from accepting contributions which exceed $1,000 per person. . . . However, Ed, I might suggest that you and your wife each contribute $1,000 and, to make up the additional $9,998,000, ask 9,998 of your friends . . ."

The prospect that Ed McMahon might unexpectedly show up at your front door with a big check has become the subject of numerous cartoons and greeting cards, even the punch line of jokes. Hallmark did a greeting card with a forlorn figure on the front, and inside it asked, "If Ed McMahon has time to write me, how come you don't?" Even a small rug-cleaning company sent around a flyer listing ten reasons people should have their carpets cleaned. The tenth reason: when Ed McMahon rings your doorbell, you don't want to be embarrassed.

"You may have already won ten million dollars" has become one of the best-known lines in the history of advertising. Once, when I walked down a street, people would greet me with either "Hi-oooo!" or "Heceeere's Ed!" No more. Now it's always, "Hey Ed, where's my ten million dollars?"

"I was over at your house this morning," I sometimes reply, "and you weren't home. So I gave it to your neighbor." Or, "I've been looking all over for you. What time are you going to be home tonight?" Dick Clark responds to that question by telling people, "Ed's home counting it out in singles. He's going to be at your house in ten minutes. What are you doing here?"

I have become so well known as the man who gives away tens of millions of dollars in prizes that when I make a phone call I often begin by saying, "Hi, this is Ed McMahon. You didn't win yet, but . . ."

Now, how could I possibly go wrong by giving away money? I thought, if there is one sure thing in life, it's that people are going to love me for doing this. And generally that has been true. But in 1998 American Family Publishers, as well as myself and Dick Clark, received a great deal of publicity after American Family Publishers signed an agreement with thirty-two state attorneys general around the country. As part of the agreement, American Family Publishers agreed to make certain changes in its mailings to make it even more clear that the mailings were entry forms, not notifications that the recipient had won. In much of the publicity, the point that was often lost was that American Family, along with Dick Clark and myself, had over the years helped to give away more than seventy-seven million dollars.

This sweepstakes has changed lives. It's sort of like *Star Search*—without the talent portion of the show. I called one winner to inform him that he had won two million dollars on the day the bank was going to repossess his house. Literally. They had already taken his car and by the end of that day he was going to be homeless. Talk about good luck. When Dick Clark handed a check for ten million dollars to a struggling musician, he asked, "What are you going to do with the money?"

"Go out and buy a new set of drums," the musician told him.

The only people ineligible for the prize money were employees of American Family Publishers—which includes me—and their relatives. I guess I didn't realize the impact of that restriction until Pam professed her love for me by pointing out, "Look what I gave up to marry you."

When the giant Colonial Penn Insurance Company wanted to market a whole-life insurance product, they asked me to be their spokesperson. The difficulty Colonial Penn had in selling this insurance was that it seemed too good to be true. This is a life insurance policy aimed at buyers more than fifty years old, the people who need the insurance most and often can't afford it or pass the physical. The point that

Colonial Penn wanted me to emphasize was that there was no physical examination required, everybody qualifies, no one who wanted to buy this insurance could be turned down. Yes, ladies and gentlemen, it is hard to believe, but you cannot be turned down for this insurance. Let me repeat that sentence, you cannot be turned down for this insurance.

Now, these are not large policies. The benefits are not substantial. They are usually supplemental policies or replacements for life insurance policies that were lost at retirement. They generally pay in the twenty-thousand-dollar range, enough to cover the expenses involved with death and burial; the idea is that your family should not have to go into debt. The benefits are restricted for the first two years, but after that period these policies pay the full amount.

Admittedly, life insurance isn't as much fun to sell as beer or as exciting as the sweepstakes; I mean, when friends drop over to the house I don't get to offer them a life insurance policy, and I won't be coming to your house to surprise you with the benefits. But believe me, many people have come up to me and told me how vitally important this money was to them at a time when it was really needed.

My contract with *The Tonight Show* made it difficult for me to work for companies that might compete with our national advertisers. But that didn't stop me from representing local businesses. My business manager and I realized that local businesses could benefit by being represented by someone with national recognition. Banks, for example. There are no national banks, so I could represent as many noncompeting local banks as wanted to hire me. And I was perfect for the job. Who could possibly be a better representative for financial institutions than a person known for giving away money?

Eventually I ended up becoming the spokesperson for thirty-eight banks and financial institutions in eighteen states. Basically, I was selling a sense of confidence. I was telling viewers that I was willing to put my name and reputation behind these banks. Imagine that, banks needed me to tell people they were honest. That's a long way from selling slicers on the boardwalk. And before I agreed to represent a bank, we did do a lot of research to make sure the bank had a good reputation in the community and was financially in good condition.

It was a good program for the banks. For only slightly more than they would have paid to produce local commercials, they got network-quality commercials and me as their spokesperson. So when a viewer in Oklahoma City was watching me with Johnny Carson, he was, I hope, reminded about the Liberty National Bank. One Chicago bank told me that they'd decided to hire me after doing extensive research "to determine who would be the least offensive spokesman and carry our message the strongest." It turned out I was considered to be one of the least offensive people in Chicago! How about that!

The concept was a very good one and for several years this was a very successful program for both me and the banks. Several of the banks I represented became the leading financial institutions in their local market. For a while I thought that this was going to be something I would be doing for a long, long time, like Alpo. Banks didn't go out of business, banks put other people . . . But then there was this thing that happened called the savings-and-loan scandal.

Kay-ooooooooooo . . .

At least dogs always have to eat.

I've been in television fifty years now, and in that time I've seen numerous innovations once thought impossible.

I've seen that tiny little box showing grainy black-and-white pictures broadcast only locally grow into giant screens on the sides of buildings broadcasting in sharp color from anywhere in the world. I've seen two-hundred-pound cameras reduced to cameras light enough to be carried easily by one person. I've seen historic events as they happened. I've seen pictures broadcast live from the moon. I've even seen Tiny Tim get married. But maybe more than anything else, I've seen the creation of one thing I never dreamed possible: the cable shopping networks. All selling all the time. A channel that exists only to sell. A channel on which all the performers are pitchmen. The channel I've been waiting for my entire career!

Selling on cable television is very similar to standing up on the block and selling on the boardwalk; you have a limited amount of time to capture the attention of your audience, pitch your product, and finally close the sale. The difference is that you have a much bigger audience—we call them "eyes," as in "there are a lot of eyes out there." Instead of selling inexpensive items, we can sell very expensive merchandise, and although on the boardwalk a rainy day is terrible, bad weather is the best possible thing for selling on television.

And I found the perfect product to sell to home shoppers. Something every household needs. A unique product. Le Dome cookware. Cookware made by the largest French manufacturer. Cookware made especially to ensure that nothing, absolutely nothing, will stick to the bottom. Cookware with the handles on the corners making it easier to balance and thus safer to carry. It's the kind of cookware that no household should be without. Now, I know a lady in Bayonne, New Jersey, who bought a set of this cookware and . . .

My first day on the channel I sold almost two hundred

thousand dollars' worth of this wonderful product. And, I didn't even have to throw in the juicer.

After fifty years in the business, after becoming one of the most recognized personalities on television, after hosting or cohosting tens of thousands of hours of television programs, I was right back where I started: selling pots and pans.

I loved it, I absolutely loved it.

——— 11 ———

W hen *Star Search* went off the air I found myself without a television show for the first time in my professional career. From the day I'd begun at WCAU in Philadelphia, September 12, 1949—except for the time I'd spent in Korea—I'd always been under contract to a network or a show. I had assumed *Star Search* would continue indefinitely. We'd become a major attraction at Disney World, and what could be more permanent than that? So being without a show was very strange for me. And I didn't like the feeling at all. As much as I tried to dismiss the thought, I couldn't help but wonder if my career was over.

Maybe the most difficult thing for me to deal with was free time. For me, time had always been just like money—I spent just a little more of it than I had. I was always busy, always going from one appointment to the next. But with the end of *Star Search* I actually had time to do whatever I wanted to do—unfortunately, what I really wanted to do was have every minute of my day filled.

Johnny Carson's retirement allowed him to fulfill his passionate love of tennis; he had time to play the game and follow the professional tour around the world. My passion—besides my wife, Pam, and my children—was broadcasting. Same as it had been when I was a child. And one thing you can't do when you retire is work.

I've never had a real hobby. Tennis, for example, Johnny's passion, never really interested me. I've tried golf because I wanted to play with friends like Newhart and Dick Martin. I bought a set of clubs, joined the Bel Air Country Club, and took lessons. I always hit the ball a long way, unfortunately even when I was putting. I'm not good at not being good at something. I get frustrated. After one particularly bad day, I emptied my locker, resigned from the club, and gave my beautiful clubs, gloves, shoes, and golf balls to Patrick Marwick, who loved golf, telling him, "From now on, you're my designated golfer."

I don't think I realized how bad I was until I lost a putting contest to a . . . blind golfer. Please note the judicious use of the pause right there. This contest took place at my golf tournament. I may well be the only nongolfer to have had his own celebrity golf tournament. The Quad Cities Open, played in the cities of Bettendorf and Davenport, Iowa, and Moline and Rock Island, Illinois, was having difficulty surviving because it was played annually on the same weekend as the British Open. The local Jaycees hoped they could draw attention to the tournament by attracting celebrities. Now, they realized that my greatest strength as a golfer was that I made a great host. I was great after we finished the first eighteen holes. So I became the host of the Ed McMahon Quad Cities Open. And the plan worked: among the celebrities who came to play in my tournament were Bob Hope, Telly Savalas, Buddy Greco, and Tommy Sullivan. Tommy Sullivan is a wonderful singer, and although blind, he is a good golfer and played in the Ed McMahon Open every year.

My third year as host, Tony Amendola, Tommy Sullivan,

and I were having dinner with our drinks, and Tony suggested that a putting contest between Tommy and me would attract a lot of publicity. At the time, that seemed like a great idea. It was only when I woke up the next morning that I realized I was in a terrible situation; if I won, I'd beaten a blind man. If I lost, I'd lost to a blind man. How could I explain either result?

Part of me wanted to play for fun, to make it obvious to everyone that I wasn't really trying to win. But I realized that wasn't fair to Tommy. So I played it straight—it's just that my putts didn't go straight. We played eighteen holes on a large putting green. He beat me on the last hole.

I hosted the tournament for five years. I stopped when NBC hired me to go to Russia as a feature reporter during the Moscow Olympics. I was going to do Ivan-on-the-street interviews. That was the year that we boycotted the Olympics in response to the Russian invasion of Afghanistan. If I'd gone, just imagine what might have happened to my career! But that was the end of my association with my golf tournament.

With one exception. When I was in Florida with Michael, Jeff, Lex, and my son-in-law Peter, we had our own tournament. I had trophies made for Very Best Golfer, Could Have Been the Best Golfer, Might Have Been the Best Golfer, Possibly Could Have Been the Best Golfer, and Tried Very Hard. I got the trophy for trying.

I was a much better fisherman than golfer. In fact, I was a member of a very exclusive fishing club known as the Skipjacks. When I had my summer house in Avalon, once each year six of us would charter a deep-sea fishing boat with a captain and mate for a day. It cost us about five hundred dollars, which was a lot of money in the late 1960s. We'd start the day with Budweiser for breakfast and when we finished several cases of beer we'd ease into the vodka. For years we didn't catch a single fish. But one day, one incredible day, I was strapped into the deep-sea fishing chair and I got a bite. Everybody got excited, they were all screaming instructions: give him line, yank him in, fight 'im, tire him out. I fought that fish as best as I could. And finally I won, I reeled him in. This was a great moment. We finally caught a fish.

When I got him close to the boat, the mate said, "Oh, it's a goddamn skipjack."

A skipjack is a small fish, it's a cousin of the bonita. I don't swear often, but when I heard the mate say that, I turned to my friends and said, "Five hundred dollars a day, four cases of Bud, six bottles of vodka, and it's a goddamn skipjack?" We unhooked the fish and threw it back in the water. I suspect that fish was embarrassed enough having been caught by me.

That day we decided to form a club called the Skipjacks and vowed that we would never go deep-sea fishing again. More than that, I designed an emblem for the Skipjacks: a big marlin hook, almost life-size, with a marlin leaping through it and looking back in disdain that he hadn't been caught. Underneath it was our motto: *pisces non florent,* which is Latin for "We saw no fish." I had red, white, and blue jackets made for everyone with our emblem emblazoned on the pocket.

But the real reason I stopped fishing was the relationship I formed with my koi. The house that Carson Wright designed for me on Crescent Drive had a pond that ran under the deck, and I stocked that pond with small Japanese koi. Koi can be extremely valuable, with their price based on their markings. A few years ago a white koi with a red circle on its head—the colors of the Japanese flag—sold for more than one hundred thousand dollars. As a gift, someone gave me a baby koi that when grown was worth about five thousand dollars. Koi are really smart fish. They were like pets. They would eat pellets right out of my hand and I got to know them. When I walked on the deck, they would come rushing toward me from wherever they were, but if anyone else walked out they would ignore them.

Well, after that I couldn't go fishing anymore. I mean, I could still eat fish, I just didn't want to catch them myself.

I've also tried skiing and scuba diving. In fact, one night on *The Tonight Show* we showed a little home movie of me scuba diving. In this film I was swimming peacefully until I spotted something strange and beautiful and started digging in the soft sand. Finally, I reached down and pulled out . . . a six-pack of Budweiser. As I've stated, my only real hobby is working.

Probably the only positive thing about not having any show at all was that I could devote more time to my charities. I get hundreds of requests every year to participate in charitable events. It's a very nice feeling to be in a position to help others and I try to participate as much as my schedule allows. I'm constantly sending signed ties for auctions and my favorite recipe for inclusion in books and pamphlets. The recipe I send is for my very special turkey stuffing. I've developed it over many Thanksgivings and Christmases, each year adding a new ingredient. Currently it consists of country sausage, mushroom, pineapple wedges, applesauce, marmalade, walnuts, pecans, sage, and parsley flakes bathed in half a bottle of Courvoisier. The Courvoisier gives it a woody taste. I've tried to convince Pam that during cooking the alcohol burns off, but she doesn't believe that.

In addition to being an active fund-raiser for St. Jude's Ranch for Children and the Horatio Alger Association, I've worked for many, many charities, including the Bedside Network, City of Hope, the National Multiple Sclerosis Society, various animal shelter organizations, and several college scholarship funds. I'm very proud of the fact that I served two terms as president of the Catholic University

Alumni Association. At the time I ran for office a major battle was being fought between conservatives and liberals about the philosophical path the university would follow. Because Catholic University is where many members of the clergy were educated, this wasn't just an intellectual exercise; it really would have an impact on the future of the Catholic Church in America. The liberal faction asked me to run and I won a very close and hard-fought election. During my two terms I think we were able to make important contributions to the modernization of the university.

One of the things I tried to do while serving as alumni president was convince the university to build a modern communications center, complete with studios and radio and TV facilities. It would be a place where priests would learn how to communicate. I mean, the dullest thing in the world is going to Mass and listening to a priest who doesn't know how to connect with his audience.

To initiate the building fund I turned the closing of New York City's historic Capitol Theatre into a benefit for Catholic University's Center for Communication Arts. The Capitol Theatre, at Fifty-first and Broadway, had been built in 1919 as one of the first great movie palaces. It was also where some of the first television cameras recorded the New York City premiere of *Gone with the Wind* for broadcast on an experimental station. It was fitting that I would produce the closing show, because the first theater manager had been Major Edward Bowes, who later created the amateur talent show on radio that eventually led to *Star Search*.

It was an incredible event. Bob Hope, who played the Capitol when it was a vaudeville theater, was my entertainment chairman. Jerry Lewis sang a song that had flopped the night the theater opened, "Swanee." Among the other people who appeared were Mr. Carson, Alan King, Florence Henderson, Leon Bibb, Jan Peerce, Billy Eckstine, the entire cast of the Broadway show *George M!*, Doc and the

NBC Orchestra, and the new Miss America, whom I had crowned two weeks earlier in Atlantic City.

After the show the performers rode to a champagne dinner at the Americana Hotel on Anheuser-Busch wagons drawn by the Clydesdales while the audience walked there on a red carpet that had been laid down on Broadway. We sold out and raised almost one hundred thousand dollars to begin the building fund.

Eventually we raised several million dollars, but instead of building the communications center, the university built the beautiful Hartke Theatre. It's a terrific place, and honors an extraordinary human being. There is one room in the building devoted to teaching mass communications and there is an Ed McMahon Scholarship given to a student who intends to go into broadcasting, but I still wish they had built the planned communications center.

Years later I did get my communications center built—but not at Catholic University. My daughter Linda is a very talented musician. She plays the flute, piano, and guitar. Now, believe me, this story does result in a mass communications center. She wanted to go to a college where she could study jazz. I spoke to the brilliant trumpet player in the *Tonight Show* band, Clark Terry, and he introduced me to Quinnipiac College in Hamden, Connecticut. We drove up there one night in a rainstorm and I spoke at a dinner. I liked the place immediately, I could see they were trying to do innovative things there. Linda eventually attended Quinnipiac, and the more I got to know about the school, the more impressed I became.

In the late 1980s the impressive young president of the university, John Lahey, flew down to meet me in Florida and told me Quinnipiac wanted to build a state-of-the-art communications center—and they wanted to name it the Ed McMahon Mass Communications Center. He didn't expect me to donate a huge amount of money—although he wasn't going to turn it down if I wanted to donate it, either—but he hoped that my name would attract the attention of both contributors and students.

Now that was pretty flattering. Lowell, Massachusetts, once dedicated a park bench in my name, so an entire communications center was very impressive. (Actually Lowell did offer to name the whole park after me, but I was quite pleased with just my bench and I flew in for the dedication.) The communications center was to occupy a wing of a large business education center named after Quinnipiac graduate Murray Lender. Murray Lender had made his fortune in the bagel business, so I guess they felt it was appropriate to combine the bagel king with a big ham. The Ed McMahon Mass Communications Center, which is part of the Lender School of Business, contains state-of-the-art classrooms, television and radio broadcast studios, film and videotape editing equipment, and print journalism resources. I'm very, very proud of the McMahon Center. At its dedication Claudia told me the equipment was better than what she was then using at ABC News.

I've gotten involved in several charities because my friends asked for my help. For example, at Frank Sinatra's request I served as master of ceremonies at a fund-raiser for the Italian-American Civil Rights League held at the Felt Forum in Madison Square Garden. The Italian-American Civil Rights League had been organized to help dispel the notion that most Italians belonged to the Mafia. Unfortunately, it had been organized by Joseph Colombo, who ran a Mafia crime family. On the bill that night were Italians like myself, Vic Damone, Connie Francis, Jerry Vale, and black comedian Godfrey Cambridge. "I got a strange invitation to this thing," Godfrey Cambridge told the audience. "A rock came through my window."

I didn't really know what it was all about. Frank Sinatra asked me to be there and that was all I needed to know. I flew in from California on the red-eye the night before. That afternoon I'd gone over to the Felt Forum with my manager at the time, Bob Coe, to find out where I was supposed to stand and which microphone I was supposed to use. While I was there, a polite young man named Joseph Colombo Jr. came up to me and said, "Mr. McMahon, I'd like to speak to you privately for a moment."

"It's all right," I told him. "This is my manager, he's in on everything I do."

"I'd prefer to speak to you alone," he insisted. We sat down in the audience and he told me, "My father wanted me to extend his greetings. He'll be here tonight, but he wanted you to know how appreciative he is that you flew all night to be here today. You're not Italian, you have no reason to be here, but it's an important night for my people. My father told me to tell you this: if you ever need anything . . . ," and he grabbed my arm with both hands to emphasize his point, "and I mean, anything, you just have to call and it's done."

"Okay," I said. "I'll remember that." Now, like just about everyone in show business, I'd heard all the stories about Mafia involvement, but until that moment I'd never had any involvement with them. I immediately got in touch with my friend Jimmy Breslin, who knew about all this stuff, and asked him, "Did I make a mistake agreeing to do this? Am I involved in something I really don't want to be involved in?"

"I'll find out," he said. Several hours later I saw Jimmy again. He had spoken to several FBI agents and apparently they told him to tell me that it was okay that one night. I will never forget my opening line that night: "Good evening, fellow Italians."

My involvement with the Muscular Dystrophy Association began when my friend Jerry Lewis asked me to appear on his Labor Day telethon in 1967. At that time I don't even think the telethon was broadcast nationally; it certainly wasn't the spectacular event it was to become. I wasn't working with Jerry, I was just a guest. I was going to make a brief appearance, explain why viewers should pledge money to help Jerry's kids, and leave. But almost as soon as I got there, Jerry told me, "I have to go to the bathroom." Now, in those days we never said "bathroom" on television. We couldn't even use the word "pregnant"; the expression we were instructed to use was "in a family way." There was no alternate expression for "bathroom." The reason for that was simple: nobody on television ever went to the bathroom. As far as anybody knew, for example, Ozzie and Harriet Nelson's house didn't even have any bathrooms.

So without any explanation, Jerry disappeared, leaving me standing there onstage. Being a professional, I introduced the next performer at the proper time. "Ladies and gentlemen, here they are, let's give a big round of applause, aren't they great, the Flying . . ." As I finished I looked into the wings and saw Jerry standing there, arms folded, watching me. "Go ahead," he told me, "you're doing a great job." That first year I hosted for about ten minutes.

The following year I did eight hours. "Oh, Ed," Jerry said, "you were terrific. I really leaned on you. I wish you could do the whole show with me."

He needed me for the whole show? We could raise millions of dollars for kids? One billion five hundred million dollars later, I'm still doing the Labor Day telethon with Jerry. I don't think anybody realizes how much of his life he has devoted to helping kids with this terrible disease. It's a year-round cause with him, not just something he does on Labor Day weekend.

My job on the telethon is to be his support system, to provide some sort of structure to what is basically a pretty loose program. Jerry is the entertainer, the showman; his job is to push all the emotional buttons. I'm the broadcaster; my function is to make sure we hit the cues on time, that peo-

FOR LAUGHING OUT LOUD

ple get the proper credits, that the telethon moves along smoothly. I'm the anchor. Jerry is free to do whatever he wants to do, knowing that I'm always there to bring him back to center stage.

Nothing I've ever done is like the telethon. Twenty-one and a half hours on the air. The only way to prepare for that is to stay up that long in a rehearsal, which would be like running a marathon to get to the marathon starting line. For more than twenty years I did the whole show; I never left the studio, I never got out of my tuxedo. Every few hours I'd go into my dressing room and touch up my makeup, have a cup or two or three of coffee, and then go right back out there again. But I found that taking short breaks, getting away from the stage for a while, enabled me to be strong at the end when Jerry started to get tired.

Jerry's stamina is amazing, although there have been times when he's collapsed backstage from exhaustion and I had to take over the show. On occasion he's been so tired that he's allowed his frustration or anger at the pace of contributions to show and I've had to calm him down. Like Johnny, Jerry trusts me. This is his telethon, these are Jerry's kids, and I've always been careful not to get in his way, but many years ago he told me, "Ed, you interrupt me any time you want. Just come right in when you think it's necessary."

And sometimes when it's not quite so necessary. The hours do take a toll. Twenty-one hours and thirty minutes. It's like doing twenty consecutive *Tonight Shows*. It's more television in one weekend than the cast of a sitcom does for an entire season. And sometimes we do get a little giddy. One year, for example, when we were doing the telethon at the Aquarius Theatre on Sunset Boulevard, I surprised him by walking out from the wings dressed in my pajamas and carrying a big teddy bear. "Could you hold it down a little?" I asked him. "I'm trying to get some rest." Then I turned around and left.

Even after the first twenty or thirty cups of coffee everybody starts to wear down. There are certain times when fatigue comes over everyone like a wave. There are times, like at three o'clock in the morning, when the phones aren't ringing quite as much, you really wonder who's out there watching. But then the sun comes up, and with it the phones start ringing again and bring a renewed energy.

The Muscular Dystrophy telethon is unlike any other show ever done. Filling that much time requires an extraordinary range of talent. And we've had it all, the singers and dancers, the comedians, rock groups and jazz groups, marching bands and choirs, plate spinners, the entire cast of Broadway shows, jugglers, magicians, impressionists, actors and athletes, even the animal acts. We've had just about everybody from Frank Sinatra to Bobby Berosini and his Orangutans. Every year we put on a great vaudeville show for an audience estimated at seventy-five million people.

After doing the show for three decades and at least a thousand acts, the shows run together in my memory. But one of the things I'll never forget is the reunion between Dean Martin and Jerry Lewis. I helped make it happen. Martin and Lewis had been one of the most successful teams in show business, but after breaking up they hadn't spoken in decades. The reunion was actually Frank Sinatra's idea. I was with him one night several weeks before the show and he said, "You know what I'd like to do? I want to come on the telethon and bring Dean Martin with me. How do I do that?"

Jilly Rizzo and I worked out the details. While Jerry was onstage we snuck Dean into my dressing area and had him wait there. Jerry was completely surprised when he saw Dean walking toward him. Almost without a pause he said, "So, what have you been doing?"

I'm an unpaid volunteer on the telethon. For me, the

payoff has been the progress we're making toward eliminating this disease and the assistance we're able to provide for those people who suffer from it. When I started working with Jerry, not only wasn't there a light at the end of the tunnel, they hadn't even started building the tunnel. It was a hopeless situation. Each year they would introduce me to the Muscular Dystrophy poster child, I'd spend a little time talking to this child, but I didn't want to get to know these kids too well because I'd be devastated a few years later when they were no longer with us. For a long, long time, progress in fighting this thing was very slow. Every few years there would be some sort of scientific breakthrough, just enough to keep hope alive. No one ever dared use the word "cure."

But the situation has changed drastically and rapidly. They've isolated a few of the genes believed to cause this disease. Now scientists use words like "gene replacement." In 1995 for the first time I heard one of our researchers say flatly that we will have a cure. We're still in the tunnel, but now at least we can see sunlight at the other end.

The billion and a half dollars that you gave has made that reality. Using money raised by the telethon we have been able to fund research centers around the world. There are now approximately four hundred research centers connected by computer, enabling scientists at UCLA to confer instantly with researchers in Sweden. Now, when I meet these poster children, I know they've at least got a chance at a full life.

The money we've raised has also been used to improve the quality of life for people afflicted with the disease. Since we've started, I've seen the development of things like motorized wheelchairs and lifts that make vans and buses accessible to the handicapped. I got to know firsthand how the money we raised actually helped people when Claudia spent a year working for the Muscular Dystrophy Association. "I've never seen anything like it," she told me. "I've never had to say no to a patient's request. Whatever they need—an electric wheelchair, a ramp built onto their home—the organization provides it for them without any red tape. It's the most incredible thing."

Sometimes, when I started to get tired after sixteen straight hours, I remembered that. It was a lot better than coffee.

Of all the jobs I've done on the telethon, I've taken only one donation. But it was a big one. I was in my dressing room one evening and the great Bob Ross, the executive in charge of everything at the telethon, came and asked, "Would you recognize Frank Sinatra's voice on the phone?" A man claiming to be Sinatra was pledging twenty-five thousand dollars and they wanted to verify that it was really him.

"I think so," I said. "We've got a little code that I can use to tell if it's really him." When I got on the phone, I said, "Is this Mr. Sinatra?"

"Ed," he said, "how are you?"

Now, Frank Sinatra and I long shared a little private toast. Whenever we had a drink, he'd raise his glass and proclaim, "To the festival," to which I would raise my glass and respond, "To the incredible festival of life." So I asked the person on the phone, "To the what?"

"The festival," he said.

I turned to Bob Ross and told him, "Take his money."

How do I feel when I've completed a telethon? Well, each year I join with friends to celebrate Harry Crane's birthday. My responsibility at this party is to supply the cake, which I have specially made. One cake I had made was called "The First Joke." On it a little caveman in a loincloth, Harry Crane, was sitting in front of a cave scribing into stone tablets. Next to him were tablets he'd tossed away, and into them were carved bits and pieces of the jokes he'd rejected, "that was no cavelady . . . ," " . . . two nuns get off a wheel . . . ," ". . . a man walked into a bar with a pterodactyl on his head . . . " But the tablet he was finishing was the world's first joke, which read, "I spent a week in Phoenicia one night . . . "

That's what it feels like to complete a telethon. I spent a week on television one day. Believe me, entire careers haven't lasted as long as a single telethon. It's not just the broadcast, it's trying to prepare for the broadcast several days before and recovering from it for several days afterward. That's why nobody does two telethons a year. Well, almost nobody.

When Anheuser-Busch was looking for a spokesperson to reach the black community, I recommended Lou Rawls. He'd done *The Tonight Show* several times, and besides being a terrific person, he was a great talent. After the brewery hired him he conceived the idea of a telethon to benefit the United Negro College Fund. Anheuser-Busch, who sponsored the telethon, asked me to be his cohost. They offered to pay me the same amount as I was getting to do the Muscular Dystrophy telethon! Now, how could I turn down an offer like that?

In fact, I was very pleased. The United Negro College Fund was an organization I'd strongly supported for a long time—there are forty-six excellent colleges connected to the fund, and the money we raised on the telethon was to provide an education for deserving kids who would not otherwise be able to go to college—so I gladly accepted.

I did it for fourteen years. The telethon was twelve hours long for several years, but eventually it was cut down to six hours because we found the pledges slowed down late at night. Believe me, it was very different from the Muscular Dystrophy telethon. One year, for example, I was introduced as LL Cool Ed, the Beverly Hills rapper. Lou Rawls started a rap song, Nancy Wilson picked up on him, and then I came out to finish it.

America's hope, America's future, that's what we're all about.
America's hope, America's future, c'mon, lemme hear you shout!
Let me hear you shout. I said, let me hear you shout . . .
Let me hear you shout, let me hear you shout.
This is LL Cool Ed, and here's what I said,
If we're gonna reach ya, we gotta teach ya!

Now, I couldn't dance at Lowell High School, and I certainly didn't get better as I got older. But they taught me all the moves and gestures and, actually, I looked just like . . . like Ed McMahon doing a rap number.

This was not a job for my tuxedo. I dressed properly, including a baseball cap worn backward. It was my favorite cap, it was bright red with the gold letters USMC, and above those letters were gold wings exactly like those I'd earned in the Marine Corps. When I finished the number, I turned the cap around to reveal the letters and wings. After we'd finished the song, I went backstage and someone asked if they could have the hat. "No," I said. "Not this one. I'll get you another one just like it."

"Tell you what," he said. "I'll pledge a thousand dollars if you give me that hat."

I took it off my head and handed it to him. We got the pledge, he got my cap. The problem is that I haven't been able to find another one just like it. And I really liked that hat. So if anyone knows where I might get another cap just like that one . . .

If my show business career was winding down, there were always charities who needed my help, but I knew that wouldn't be enough to keep me busy. One area I knew I would not be going into was politics. Not that I couldn't have. How does this sound . . . Senator Edward McMahon. It almost happened. The only two elective offices I've ever held were president of the freshman class at Boston College and president of the Catholic University Alumni Association. However, I have met several presidents of the United States; Lyndon Johnson and I once drank Canadian whiskey out of Slurpee cups on his ranch in Texas, as he proudly showed me the carpentry work he had done personally in a new bathroom. I remember thinking, this is the man whose finger is on the button to blow up the world, and what he's most concerned with is how well the corners were mitered.

I had a shot and a beer with John Kennedy when he was running for president. He was campaigning at the country club I managed outside of Philadelphia, and the Secret Service had him wait in my office for a brief time. I had the opportunity to tell him that we were cousins, I told him all about Katie Fitzgerald McMahon and how maybe because of his brother, Joe Kennedy, I had become a marine aviator. He was polite and seemed interested, but I suspect he didn't go home that night and write in his journal that he'd met cousin Eddie.

I advised Richard Nixon how to make the best possible impression on *The Tonight Show* and produced an inaugural gala for him. I met George Bush at a luncheon for Catholic University in Washington. I'd just ordered a vodka martini when the then vice president came in and sat next to me. "That looks good," he said, "I'll have one, too." Somehow he knew I'd been a fellow navy aviator and we spent part of the afternoon talking about flying.

I first met Ronald Reagan when he was governor of California. When he was reelected president in 1984 I hosted a closed-circuit inaugural celebration that was broadcast to embassies around the world. But it was Nancy Reagan who invited me to be the secret Santa for the press corps Christmas party. I was brought into the White House through the back door and hidden upstairs in the presidential quarters. Eventually I went downstairs dressed as Santa and the press corps tried to guess my identity. I disguised my voice, I probably have the most recognizable "Ho ho ho" in America. After they guessed who I was, Sam Donaldson ended up sitting on my lap, and I warned him, "You'd better stop being so mean to the president or you're going to have a very stingy Christmas this year."

Bill Clinton appeared on *The Tonight Show* after making one of the longest nominating speeches in American political history at the 1988 Democratic Convention. As he sat down, Johnny said, "Before we start, let me just do one thing." Then he pulled out a giant hourglass and turned it upside down.

I was offered an opportunity to participate in national politics. Near the end of my second term as president of the alumni association, I mentioned casually to one of the people who had championed my cause, "You know, politics have always intrigued me. I'd love to be a United States senator." I mean, I was just fantasizing. I didn't expect anyone to take me seriously.

But he did. Several months later I was invited to a meeting with the leaders of the state Democratic party of New Jersey. The back room in which we met wasn't exactly smoke-filled, it was more martini-filled. At that meeting I was offered the Democratic nomination for the United States Senate and told that if I chose to run, "we can guarantee you'll win."

I owned a house in New Jersey, so legally I was qualified to run. It was tempting. Senator McMahon. I'd received honorary doctoral degrees from both Brown and Catholic Universities so I was already Dr. McMahon, but Senator . . . "I don't know," I said. "I've got contracts with NBC, Anheuser-Busch, American Family Publishers . . ."

"We've spoken to everybody," I was told. "We can get you out of those contracts."

This wasn't a joke. This was a serious offer. And I considered it very seriously. For some people, an opportunity to serve in the United States Senate would be a dream come true. But for me, my dream had already come true. I was a broadcaster, I was doing exactly what I had dreamed of doing as a child. No matter how enticing it was to be able to say, "Heeeeere's the Senate majority leader," I just couldn't give up my career. I loved what I was doing too much to give it up. I mean, no politician I'd ever heard of had given away ten million dollars. So after careful consideration, I declined that wonderful offer.

No matter what happened with my broadcasting career, there were many business opportunities available to me. I had a lot of experience as a businessman. In fact, the last time in my life I'd been involved in business it had cost me only one million four hundred thousand dollars.

In the early 1970s with some friends from Catholic University I founded Unicorn Creations, a cutting-edge design company. We started with a great board game, the Game of Love. It was sort of a combination of Monopoly and Spin the Bottle. Instead of street names, each square had an instruction: kiss your partner's elbow, take off your sweater, give your neighbor a big kiss. Players rolled the dice to move and had to follow the instructions wherever they landed. It was a bit risqué, but this was the beginning of the sexual revolution.

From the game, we expanded into a larger stationery company. We created all types of psychedelic paper products and gimmick items. We hired very bright, very clever artists, many of them right out of the Rhode Island School of Design, who created a wonderful product line. Even the great artist Peter Max designed products for us. Unfortunately, our products were a lot better than our knowledge of business.

I am reminded of an old black-and-white movie costarring Jack Oakie. In this movie he announced proudly to his partner that he had managed to get them an airplane for free. When his partner looked out the window and saw the airplane, he was overwhelmed. He couldn't believe that Jack

Oakie had actually managed to obtain an airplane for free. "How did you do it?" he asked.

It was easy, Oakie explained, all he had to do was buy a thousand planes and then he got this one for free. Well, that was the way my partner in Unicorn Creations did business. His business philosophy was that in order to wholesale a paper product for four dollars, our production cost had to be under a dollar. That made sense, that was a four-to-one ratio. The problem was that the only way to get production costs down to that price was to order a tremendous amount of the product. Believe me, we had warehouses full of psychedelic stationery. It was coming out of our ears in very bright colors. And if we had ordered twice as much, we could have saved even more on our production costs.

The biggest problem we faced was that most of our customers were small stores who often paid late or failed to pay for the products they ordered. These weren't big orders, so it would have cost us more to pursue payment than just write it off. Maybe the one good thing about this company was that when we had to write off our losses, we certainly had a lot of paper.

I think what eventually killed the company was that we tried to do too many things. If we had focused our attention on one product line, the game or the stationery, we might have been successful. Instead we ended up owing more than a million dollars. When the company failed, I could have just walked away from our obligations, but I didn't want to do that. I refused to file bankruptcy. I just couldn't walk away from the people who had loaned us money to start the business or the suppliers who had trusted us. So with the guidance of Lester Blank, I personally paid off every penny that we owed.

I've been involved in several other business ventures, but none of them has been very successful. When the franchise industry was just beginning, I had an A-to-Z Rental Center, a little company that rented business equipment. For a little while I owned a drive-through grocery store in Florida called Pick-a-Pack. The concept was that people would drive up to a window and order their groceries without getting out of their car. It seemed like a good idea to me. The fact that I rarely shopped for groceries didn't stop me from investing. The best thing about both A-to-Z and Pick-a-Pack was that they were less unsuccessful than Unicorn.

I discovered that I was a much smarter golfer than businessman. As a golfer I had been smart enough to quit. I wish I'd done that with some of my business ventures. But I was always able to convince myself that business was going to get better tomorrow. And who knows, maybe it still will.

As it turns out, Pam is the businessperson in our marriage. Pam and her partner, Greg Mills, the former senior vice president of Perry Ellis and president of Isaac Mizrahi, have created a full collection of exquisitely tailored clothes. *Women's Wear Daily* loved their first collection. And although the Pam McMahon line is now carried by major department stores and fashionable shops, the dresses have actually been carried across the country by Ed McMahon, *schmatta schlepper* extraordinaire.

I'm not a businessman. And I'm not interested in being a politician. The closest thing I have to a hobby is the work I do for charities. What I am is a broadcaster, an announcer, a host, an actor, a master of ceremonies, a second banana, a spokesperson. I'm an entertainer, a performer, a salesman. I've got a nice tuxedo and a clean shirt, I'll be there when the band starts playing, and I'll know all my lines. I can tell a joke, sing a song, play the good guy or the bad guy. So for the first time in nearly five decades, I began to look for a job.

Almost immediately people started approaching me with ideas for shows they wanted me to do. We started developing a sitcom titled *After You've Gone*, on which I played a man who'd died and gone to heaven. The only person able to see me or talk to me was my widow. It was a ghost comedy, like the classic series *Topper*.

We hired several top writers and developed the concept. We approached the great actress Rue McClanahan to play the role of my widow. We found a recording of the song "After You've Gone." Then we made our pitch to one of the most respected executives in the television industry. "It won't work," he said, shaking his head knowingly. "See, ghost shows won't work on TV anymore. The audience is too sophisticated for that."

Obviously that was before *Touched by an Angel* became one of the highest-rated shows on television. Technically, though, he was correct: an angel is not a ghost.

I nearly became the host of a new version of the old quiz show *The Liar's Club*. It's a simple game, contestants have to determine which of our panelists are lying. We were going to use some of the great young comedians on our panel, many of them from *Star Search*, the format would give them an opportunity to stretch their imaginations. We spent more than a year and a half developing it and finally found a production company that wanted to buy it and put it on the air. Hours before we were going to make our final presentation—literally hours before—and after we'd made all the changes they'd requested, the president of the company was fired and replaced with someone determined to wipe out everything he'd done. We were first to go.

Fifty years and I never knew that television was such a tough business.

Pam and I developed a concept for a syndicated radio program called *The Comedians*. This was a daily five-minute show featuring material from three living comedians and one legendary figure. We were unable to sell it.

I was working regularly. I did a television movie, I made several guest appearances. I wasn't getting desperate, but I was beginning to wonder if maybe the well had run dry.

I began getting asked to audition for sitcoms. One popular show offered me the role of a slick car salesman, but I turned it down. This was a really unpleasant character, not a role I would have enjoyed playing. Then one day my theatrical agent, Harry Gold, called and told me that he'd found the perfect part for me; the producers of a new show titled *Spin City* wanted me to read for the part of the mayor. It sounded like something I would enjoy doing; the pilot script was very funny and Michael J. Fox was the star. But just as I was about to audition, somebody with the show decided I would be too noticeable, too widely known to play that role. My audition was canceled. Coming when it did, that was very disappointing.

Several months later Harry Gold called again to tell me he'd found an even better role for me. A new show to star Tom Arnold was looking for someone to play the host of a breakfast show in St. Paul, Minnesota. Well, that was perfect for me. I'd actually hosted a breakfast show in Philadelphia in the 1950s. Supposedly the breakfast show had been on the air for forty years and the people of St. Paul wouldn't think of starting the day without having *Breakfast with Charlie*.

Now, coincidentally, Tom Arnold has been a friend of mine for several years. We share the same birthday and have started celebrating it together. I don't know how much I believe in astrology, but Tom is so much like me that he could be my son. But he had no idea I was auditioning for the role. He was on the road promoting his new movie and I didn't want to put any pressure on him at all.

Eight of us auditioned for the role. They were all about my age, all character actors, all of them recognizable. A group picture of us might have been captioned "Oh, look, there's what's his name. I remember him from . . ." This was like the old days in New York when I auditioned for commercials; everybody was very good. I read my lines with the talent coordinator, who told me, "Thank you very much, we'll call you." I wasn't particularly pleased with my reading, I didn't think I was going to get the part, but at least she didn't send somebody to my house to rip out the phone.

I made the first cut. Four of us were asked to audition again. Once again, "Thank you very much . . . ," and out I went. The next day they called again, and asked me to read again that night. What I didn't know was that Tom Arnold had been told I was auditioning for the role and wanted to read with me. After we read a scene together, he stuck out his hand and said, "Welcome aboard."

We began shooting *The Tom Show* in April 1997. Charlie was an old codger, a man set firmly in his ways, an old fuddy-duddy, which is exactly the opposite of how I am. But I do have friends like that, friends who eat at the same time and order the same foods every night. Tom Arnold played Tom, the producer of the show, a man who had worked for Charlie many years earlier, then gone to Hollywood where he had married a big star, and returned to St. Paul after the divorce to get his life started again. Where do they come up with these wild ideas?

I wasn't a bit nervous about doing the show. When we went on the air my reviews ranged from "much better than I would have dared to write myself" to "aren't there laws against writing things like that?"

The show was produced by Universal but broadcast on the WB, the new network owned by Warner Bros. The WB asked me to help promote the show around the country. Appear on TV to talk about *The Tom Show* on the WB? Do radio interviews to tell people why they should watch *The Tom Show* on the WB? Speak with magazine and newspaper writers about *The Tom Show* on the WB? Naturally, I hesitated . . . Offering me a microphone is like putting a ten-thousand-dollar pledge in front of Jerry Lewis. I toured the country telling people why they would enjoy *The Tom Show* on the WB.

Believe me, I know how difficult it is to attract attention to a new network. ABC had been a distant third network when Johnny Carson and I had started together on *Who Do You Trust?* I think we were one of the very first afternoon shows they broadcast. So at every opportunity, I told people about *The Tom Show* on the WB. And the WB was very pleased with my work.

How pleased were they?

Well, every network has a logo: CBS has its eye, NBC has the peacock, and the WB has the frog. The network's logo is a frog. But they're so pleased with my work promoting *The Tom Show* on the WB, they began to refer to me as the network's first "spokesphibian."

That's quite a compliment. I was particularly pleased by that after noticing that Budweiser now uses talking frogs on its commercials. So perhaps . . .

Besides working with Tom Arnold on *The Tom Show* on the WB, I finally found a product in which I believed strongly enough to do an infomercial. Incredibly, this was a product I actually helped create in my own kitchen. When my doctors told me that for health reasons I had to give up most fried foods, I tried to find a way I could enjoy the great taste of fried foods without being hurt by the fat and grease.

Impossible, you say. Can't be done. Fried foods need that fat and grease. Now, I know you believe that. I did too. But suppose, ladies and gentlemen, just suppose I was able to prove to you that you can now enjoy the incredible taste of fried foods—cooked in your very own kitchen—without worrying about the damaging effects of fat or grease.

That's right, forget about the twenty-eight grams of fat usually found in fried chicken. Now you can have the great taste of fried chicken containing only six grams of fat. Onion rings, which normally have twenty-three grams of fat, now have . . .

Zero. Make your own potato chips—with absolutely no

fat! How can I make this claim? The answer is . . . the all-new, unique, guaranteed Ed McMahon miracle fryer.

That's right, my friends. Developed with the great young five-star chef George Engel, the Ed McMahon miracle fryer enables you to use the thermal rays that circulate in your oven to fry low-fat and fat-free foods. This patented system consists of a mesh rack that, sitting on top of a deep-base pan, allows the hot air to circulate all around your food, locking in the taste. Delivering the great taste of fried foods without the added oil and grease . . . The fat drips away so the food doesn't sit in it while cooking . . .

French fries, pizza, sausages, even fish and hamburgers—all the foods you love—now with reduced fat or no fat . . .

And if you act right now, we will also send you your own copy of *Ed McMahon's Favorite Low-Fat Fried Foods,* featuring more than forty recipes by world-class chef George Engel . . .

And yes, there's even more. Tell you what else I'm going to do. As an added bonus, we're going to throw in . . . the miracle fryer slicer! The perfect frying companion because the adjustable blades allow you to slice potatoes for potato chips, and onions for onion rings. And even more, let me demonstrate on a red ripe tomato. Look how you can adjust the blade so low, you can slice a tomato so thin you can read a newspaper through it. I know a lady in Bayonne, New Jersey . . .

Index

INDEX

INDEX